SHOOT STRAIGHT AND STAY ALIVE

A LIFETIME OF HUNTING EXPERIENCES

SHOOT STRAIGHT AND STAY ALIVE

A LIFETIME OF HUNTING EXPERIENCES

BY
FRED BARTLETT

ROWLAND WARD PUBLICATIONS
JOHANNESBURG

ISBN 0-9584188-5-3

© Fred Bartlett 1994

Second Edition May 2000

Rowland Ward Publications
P O Box 2079, Houghton 2041
South Africa
Tel: 011 728 2542
www.rowlandward.com

Photographs by kind permission of Cecil Bartlett
Cover design by Collage Graphics
Printed & bound by Waylite Press, Johannesburg

In Memory of
RICHARD GEORGE BARTLETT

CONTENTS

ONE

THE EARLY YEARS: 1923 - 1948

I have led a very interesting life. I was born in Nairobi in 1923. This was a few years after Europeans started coming to Kenya to develop and farm her land. Even at that time, the native tribes often fought one another, but the Masai were the most powerful and ruled the greater part of the country. To escape the Masai, the Kikuyu retreated into the forest areas below Mount Kenya and the Aberdare Mountain ranges above. The Turkana, infiltrating down from Ethiopia and Lake Rudolf, engaged the Masai in battle. Some say that had the Europeans not come when they did, the Masai would have lost out to these Northern tribes.

As a Colonel in the New Zealand cavalry, my grandfather had fought in the Boer War, after which he took up farming in South Africa and brought his family from New Zealand to join him. My father was seven years old at the time. Father served in the Royal Flying Corps as a fighter pilot and went into battle in France in 1916. In 1917, at the age of 18, he was awarded the Distinguished Flying Cross. A few months later, while flying on the Italian Front, he and a fellow officer, Allan Gerrard V.C. (Victoria Cross was highest award for valour awarded to British Forces in time of war), were engaged in a dog fight over Austria. Both of them ran out of fuel and made a forced landing, where they were captured by the Germans and imprisoned behind barbed-wire. Allan and my father became great friends. They managed to escape into the mountains for three weeks but the Germans hunted them down with dogs and they were eventually recaptured and ended up once more behind barbed wire.

Back in England when the war ended in 1918, Allan Gerrard introduced my father and mother and eventually became my Godfather. In 1919 my father took up a Soldier Settler farm in the Lumbwa-Kericho area of Kenya. At that time the British government was encouraging Europeans to emigrate to the country. In 1922, Mother joined my father in Kenya where they were married and started farm life. A year later I was born. At that time most settlers grew flax and everybody lost fortunes when the market collapsed.

Father was a good athlete, as well as a sportsman, and could beat the Lumbwa in a flat race over some distances. Their esteem for a white man who could outrun them rose immensely. During this period the locals lost a lot of stock to a marauding leopard so they tracked the culprit into some thick bush and sought Father's help to shoot it. Armed with a 12 bore shotgun, he took up a likely shooting position. The warriors, armed with spears and *simis* (Masai swords), closed the circle around the leopard which eventually came out of the bush with a rush, straight for Father. It sprang at him and he shot the beast in mid air. In the throes of death, the leopard landed just behind my father, who deftly managed to dodge the body as it hurtled through the air.

My family sold the farm because of debt and various other commitments and moved to new land offered to settlers on the slopes of Mount Kenya. It was a pity they did not stay in Kericho as it later became a very successful tea-growing area. My parents put all their worldly possessions into an ox-wagon and trekked to our new home. A Kikuyu family came along. Their father, Thongoro, had two wives and many children. Later, one of his sons, Wanyahoro, became my shooting companion. Thongoro had been a soldier for John Boyes, who was known as the 'King of the Kikuyu'. John Boyes (Father often spoke of him) is best known for forming the Kikuyu into a fighting unit to take on the Masai. These Kikuyu were very successful and won their battles against the Masai before the British stepped in and took over.

As the roads in those days were very poor and were often made impassable by heavy rains, the trek to the new farm took three weeks. Lions were a problem and, when camping for the night, Father had to organise fires to keep these great cats from killing the oxen. I was a three-month old baby during this trek.

The smaller children of the Kikuyu family frequently had difficulty in keeping up and so my mother often allowed them to ride on the ox-wagon. These children had jigger fleas in their feet and this made walking painful. Jigger fleas burrow into one's toes and their favourite place is between the nail and the quick. After digging in, they lay their eggs which then forms a sac. Eventually they spread throughout the foot and if nothing is done about it, they cripple the host. Consequently our toes were continuously inspected.

When we arrived at the farm on the slopes of Mount Kenya, Father built a house using local materials. The were hundreds of cedar trees nearby which provided ample raw material. This wood was cut into building boards and gradually the house was finished. Grass was cut for the roof, the walls were plastered and later white-washed and window frames and doors were added. When supplies were needed, the ox-wagon was sent to the nearest railhead 110 miles away. It normally took three weeks to complete the round trip. On one of these excursions, the Africans in charge of the wagon outspanned near a cattle dip and the oxen fed off the surrounding green grass. The whole span died from arsenic poisoning.

The farm was at an elevation of 7,200 feet and due to the high altitude, the climate was always pleasant – warm during the day and cool at night. It was healthy and there was no malaria or any other tropical disease. The soil was very fertile and most English fruits as well as potatoes, vegetables, wheat and maize thrived.

My parents had more children and eventually I had two brothers and two sisters. We were very isolated and seldom had visitors, so we enjoyed each other's companionship and as a result became a very close family.

There were many hardships. Money was scarce, especially during the Depression years, so Father took on many different jobs. He built houses and cattle dips and surveyed irrigation canals for farmers in the district. He also took up professional hunting. His clients included British army officers serving in India and also American hunters.

Frequently, lion killed our cattle and my father's favourite method of dealing with them was to dig a pit big enough to accommodate two adults lying down. He covered it with a flat corrugated iron or timber roof, raised on one side about ten inches above the ground so that it was possible for the person or persons in the pit to look out and observe the kill which was pegged to the ground about ten or fifteen yards away. The other three sides were closed in with loose soil, and more was put over the roof. As a result it was not possible for the lion to pick up human scent. Father shot several lions using this method. On one occasion he sat up for two nights and the lion did not return. On the third night a South African Dutch family were passing through and a fourteen year old boy asked if he could sit up. As he was tired and did not think the lions would return, Father agreed. The lions put in an appearance and the young boy shot three!

The main road wound through the back of the farm where there was an outspan area set aside for people to spend the night and let their oxen water and graze. Once a family of South African Dutch settler farmers were passing through and outspanned here. Under the full moon the family slept beneath the wagon with boxes arranged in a line between the front and

3

back wheels. The mother heard a noise during the night and looked up to see a lion trying to snare one of her children through the spokes of the wagon wheel. She screamed and the lion ran away.

Another time a family passing through, outspanned in the same area. As it was very cold at night their Africans were wrapped up in blankets and slept by the fire. During the night a lion crept up, grabbed one of the forms sleeping on the ground and ran off. The beast had a mouthful of blanket and as he ran off the blanket unraveled and the African was left behind.

When I was twelve years old, I was allowed to spend the night with father in the pit but, unfortunately, the lions did not cooperate. Having stayed awake the whole night, I was deeply disappointed. Later, when serving in the Kenya Game Department, I used this method for dealing with cattle killers and had the same good results. The farm had a lot of game so my brothers and I did quite a bit of hunting of bushbuck, reedbuck and impala with .22 rifles.

One day we had visitors. The woman went to the toilet, which at that time was a pit latrine made up of a long seat with a round hole in the middle. The bathroom was fairly dark and when entering from the bright sunlight into the darkness, one was temporarily blinded. The woman stepped into the building and a moment later she came running out pulling up her knickers and screaming that she had been bitten by a snake. Mother started to laugh as she knew that there was a goose sitting on eggs by the side of the seat. The goose hissed just before she pecked and the victim genuinely thought she had been attacked by a snake.

There were quite a few characters in the farming area and various stories were told about them. Billy Beale, who tended to be on the fat side, was very cheerful and well-liked but he was inclined to indulge in alcoholic drink, especially during his wife's absence. His wife had to leave for England in a hurry as her mother was desperately ill and she asked two spinster neighbours to call in periodically and check on Billy. A day or two later the spinsters knocked at the front door. Billy staggered to answer the call, opened the door and said, "Hello, come in ladies." They took one horrified look at Billy and fled. He looked down and realised he was stark naked.

On a visit to Nairobi, he went into a bar and had quite a few beers. A couple of hours later he came out, got into his old car, reversed and hit a new car parked close by. The owner came tearing out screaming, "Look what you have done to my new car!" Billy calmly looked at the damage, took out a ten cent piece, flicked it at the irate owner and said "Here. Go and have it painted."

On another occasion when his wife was away, Billy and a friend finished all the booze in the house and wondered how to replenish the supply. Billy suggested they get some local brew. He called in the cook and said "Go and get some *tembu*." *Tembu* in Kiswahili has two different meanings – alcohol or elephant. The cook said "*Ndio Bwana*" and went off. Late that night, Billy and his friend waited patiently for the cook's return. Eventually they heard thumping and something being dragged down the passage. The door opened and the cook came in dragging an elephant tusk.

The local town, Nanyuki, was about fifteen miles away. Here young whites from the surrounding farms took to copying the cowboy styles of America. They wore Stetsons and cowboy boots, carried six-guns, and often galloped down the main street firing their guns for the amusement of the bystanders. A favourite sport was to gallop after warthog and shoot them with six-guns. The fad died when one member shot his horse through the back of the head while at full gallop.

Two people were very good to my siblings and I. One was Uncle Cecil, my mother's brother. He used to disappear periodically for months and sometimes years as he worked as a gold miner in Tanganyika (now Tanzania). Whenever he stayed on the farm, he kept us amused by drawing cartoons. He had a vivid imagination and invented all sorts of odd looking animals and gave them fictitious names. One I remember was a Porkodillo, the fiercest thing on the earth. It had a crocodile head at one end and a porcupine head at the other end. The reason it was so fierce was that it could not go to the toilet!

Uncle Cecil was a very good rifle shot and often showed us his skills. He once told the Africans to inspan our scotch-cart (a two wheeled ox-cart) and during this excursion he proceeded to shoot two waterbuck across the valley at about 600 yards, using his .318 Westley Richards, with one shot each.

Tom Salmon, another family friend, gave us our first .22 rifle, which we used to good effect. He was also a very fine rifle shot and often took us hunting on his farm which was next to ours.

In the early 1930's, a few murders were committed by young Samburu warriors, whose reservation was not far from the farm. It was custom for young Samburu to blood their spears on humans in order to prove their manhood. Great excitement was caused in our area when a herdboy was run down and speared while looking after cattle on our farm. Later on another was killed not more than a mile from the homestead. Then a Mr Powys disappeared while out riding and days later his body was found with the head missing. A few months later the police, acting on a tip, arrested three young Samburu men who admitted to having speared him. They led the police to a nearby *manyatta* (Samburu huts and cattle enclosure) where the head was hidden. The story circulated that Powys came across the young men who were out looking for a victim. He asked whether they knew where there was water and they offered to show him. He was riding his horse just ahead of the young men when they speared him through the back and cut off his head to take back and show the young girls that they had proved their manhood. The tribes in the area were very primitive. Most wore only animal skins and beads for clothing and daubed their bodies with red ochre and animal fats.

Father's first car was a Model T Ford which was not well maintained and therefore did not last long. Later he bought a Harley Davidson motor bike. One day he nearly lost control when a locust hit his forehead while he was travelling at high speed. Late one evening he was driving back on roads which were very wet and slippery after heavy rains. A mile before he reached the house, he was unable to negotiate a steep hill and abandoned the bike and walked. The next morning when he went to recover the motor bike, he found lion tracks all around it.

One of my early chores was to operate the local mill where the Africans brought their maize to be crushed. At about this time Father acquired a 4-cylinder ton-and-a-half Chevy truck. This was a good vehicle which lasted for many years and I learnt to drive in it. I also learnt quite a lot about mechanics.

Our financial position improved when Father started to grow pyrethrum (a plant that has a white daisy as a flower). The flower is picked and dried on trays, then milled, and the powder becomes a powerful insecticide. The market was good and increasingly profitable. As a result of our improved finances, all of us were sent to boarding school in Nairobi. Here I met other young pupils including Harry Selby who later became a well-known professional hunter, and Buster Percival whose father was a well-known Kenyan game warden. Buster was later lost, with many other Kenyan troops, when his ship was torpedoed while en route to the Far East to fight the Japanese. Also at school with me was Ian Henderson who in later years became well-known in the Kenya Police for fighting the Mau Mau. He wrote a book entitled "The Hunt for Kimathi", the forest leader of the Mau Mau terrorists.

In 1938, my grandfather and Uncle Billy came from South Africa to take our family back to that country. My grandfather had a farm close to Jan Smuts Airport in Johannesburg and wanted Father to manage it as he was planning a world tour, visiting relatives in New Zealand and a son in America. My parents realised that we would get a better education in South Africa and parents accepted the position.

The road trip was the first long one that we, as children, had ever enjoyed. We motored through Kenya into Tanganyika on gravel roads that were kept in pretty good condition. My grandfather purchased a new International 3-Ton truck for the excursion. We went through part of Northern Rhodesia (now Zambia) and then into Nyasaland (now Malawi), crossed the Zambezi River by ferry and entered Moçambique (now Mozambique) at Tete. The bridges in Moçambique were mainly wooden and not very well maintained by the Portuguese, and frequently the wheels of the truck went through the rotted boards of the bridge decking. We then had to jack up the truck, cut heavy branches and put them under the wheels before we could cross the remainder of the decking. At the border between Moçambique and Southern Rhodesia (now Zimbabwe), one incident occurred which could have had serious consequences. The whole way down we had slept on the ground next to the truck. One night near the border we were awakened by shouting and screaming from a nearby village. One shot from a black powder gun was fired. The next morning father was informed by the villagers that a man-eating lion had jumped on the roof of a hut, clawed through the thatch, grabbed a woman and jumped out with her.

When the Second World War broke out a year later, Father enlisted in the South African Army and went off to fight the Italians in Ethiopia and Somalia. When the Italians were defeated, he was sent to the Western Desert to fight the Germans. Here he was attached to the Eighth Army Headquarters. Three years later my brother, Albert, and I left school and joined the South African Army. After basic training, we found ourselves on a ship bound for Egypt. The trip was terrible as we were crammed below deck and seldom allowed up. At night the portholes had to be closed so that enemy submarines would not see our lights. When the weather got rough everybody was sick and the toilets smelt terrible. We eventually landed at Tufik and travelled in cattle trucks to Helwan outside Cairo. My brother and I found ourselves in the 6th South African Armoured Division in Signals and I was trained as a wireless operator. Finally, we found ourselves on a ship, this time bound for Italy, and after a few days we landed at Toranto. The green countryside was a welcome sight after the time we had spent in Egypt.

We went into action at Monte Casino where there had been some very heavy fighting and the Germans were in retreat. I remember passing many burnt out tanks belonging to ourselves and the Germans. Casino had taken heavy pounding from artillery and air bombing. Our Division had many engagements with the Germans as our troops were among the first into Florence. Then came more fighting in the mountains between Florence and Bologna. When winter arrived the fighting died down and we pulled out to the west coast for a rest. While I was there I took the opportunity to see the Leaning Tower of Pisa and spent a few days visiting Rome. In the spring the final offensive started and once more we found ourselves heading north. One bright moonlit night we were camped in an apple orchard when a German fighter bomber machine-gunned us and killed the driver of a jeep moving down the road.

Later I was sitting in the back of the wireless van, again travelling at night. We were leaving the fighting area to go to the assistance of one of our vehicles which had overturned. Our Sherman Tanks were en route to forward positions and we were passing them on a narrow road on the side of a mountain. As our vehicle came to a bend we met a tank on the inside lane. It locked tracks to turn and the rear of the tank caught our truck and pushed us off the road. We found ourselves going down the mountainside backwards. After travelling for about thirty yards, the truck came to a sudden stop against a ledge. Everything in the back of the vehicle fell on top of me, including the heavy radio batteries. I was all right except for some bruising, but I was unable to get out of the vehicle (the door was at the back) for what seemed like hours. Eventually a recovery vehicle happened to come along and winched us back onto the road. It was only then that I managed to extricate myself. Later on near the Po River we had another mishap, once again while passing a Sherman Tank. We were forced off the road and the vehicle turned over and guess who was in the back – me again! This time I broke a bone in my hand but fortunately nothing else.

We were just outside Venice when the Germans in Italy capitulated. After that our troops did garrison duties all over Northern Italy, including Lake Como and Turin. Near Milan, at the Monza Race Course, we held our Victory Parade and General Mark Clark took the salute (we were attached to the American 5th Army in the latter period of the fighting). In November 1945, I was flown from Foggia in Italy to Cairo and then by Dakota to South Africa, arriving four days later. My two brothers, who were in the same Division, returned some months later. Shortly thereafter, I met a lovely girl, Elizabeth, and a few months later we became engaged.

My father served in the Royal Flying Corp

Thongoro - father of Wanyahoro

Our first homestead constructed by my father out of local material

View of Mount Kenya from our homestead

Albert and myself in Italy during World War II

Father, Uncle Billy and myself (a few months old)

After being released from the Army, Albert and I did a short course at an agricultural college. Our intention was to return to Kenya and manage Father's farm, which had been sadly neglected during the war. In October 1946, Albert and I bought a Willys Jeep and $^3/_4$ ton trailer to drive to Kenya. Father purchased a Nash Sedan and suggested that we travel north in convoy. The trip was accomplished in ten days without a mishap. Travelling at that time was easy as most of the countries we drove through were still under British control and we only had to produce our passports on three occasions. Today all this has changed and these same countries are now independent with border controls.

We found the farm in fairly good order although a lot had been neglected during the war. The Kikuyu families had remained and taken care of things. Thongoro was now an old man and his sons Wanyahoro and Kenwa had taken charge. Throughout the war years they killed quite a few lion and leopard which were killing the stock. Wanyahoro became my right-hand man on all my hunting trips both when I served in the Game Department and later when I worked as a professional hunter in East Africa and Botswana. After establishing Albert and myself in charge, my parents returned to South Africa.

Our farm had cattle and sheep, with cattle being the main source of income. We started to grow crops while also adding to the existing pyrethrum fields. We had trouble from the buffalo which came into the pyrethrum fields and other crops, so Albert and I went out at night with a spotlight to hunt them. Ammunition was still in short supply and we did not have much in the line of firearms. We used mainly .30-06, 7mm and Italian .256 army rifles.

The first time we went out I shot a buffalo and found it very exciting. Shortly after this I shot a buffalo late in the night and wounded it. The next morning we followed the spoor and blood sign into the nearest forest. We brought all our farm dogs along in the hope that they would bay the wounded buffalo when we got close. After tracking it for a couple of miles the trail led into exceptionally thick cover. The dogs started to bark and the buffalo grunted. We did not know what to expect. I remember thinking, 'What if we get a charge? Would we be able to stop the animal?' Well, the buffalo did come charging out with the dogs at its heels. Both Albert and I fired and the buffalo went down. One of us had hit his neck.

We received a report from a cattle herder that a male lion had killed one of his oxen and badly mauled another, which subsequently died a few days later. Once again we took the dogs and started tracking the lion. I was

9

armed with a .30-06, Albert with a 7mm and Wanyahoro a .256 Italian. Albert had acquired a young cocker spaniel with long droopy ears. We followed the trail which led towards a cedar forest. After a short distance we heard a commotion ahead, the dogs started barking and the lion grunted in anger. During this tracking, the spaniel had been darting to and fro, probably looking for birds, but when he heard the other dogs barking in front he dashed forward and disappeared. Then he suddenly reappeared with ears extended and nearly knocked Albert over before disappearing behind us. All three of us were expecting the lion to be right behind him but in fact nothing appeared. There was only silence. We went forward and found where the lion had taken off, with the other dogs in pursuit. Eventually the dogs came in one by one and the hunt ended. A few weeks later we heard that the lion had been shot in the reservation by a Wanderobo tribesman. This happened about 25 miles away from where we hunted it. The lion had killed another cow and the tribesman had sat in a tree and shot a poisoned arrow at it when it came to feed on the kill.

We had trouble with leopards killing our calves and made a box trap to catch the culprits. We caught two male leopards and kept them in separate cages. In order to feed them we shot whatever we could find: impala, warthog, Grant's gazelle, bushbuck and even baboon. We found that they ate a young baboon but if we shot a big male baboon they did not touch it – it rotted where we left it. This showed that leopard are afraid of big male baboons even when they are dead.

The next year Albert and I motored to South Africa to get married and brought our new spouses back with us. The jeep went down and back without any trouble. Shortly after our return we took an old truck and all the farm dogs out on the farm to check on some steers that we were getting ready for market. We arrived at a watering hole and sent an African off to bring in the steers. While we waited for the cattle, we sat in the shade watching the dogs wander off into the bush behind. After only a few minutes, we heard a grunt and a crashing of bushes and a bull buffalo came lumbering out. I grabbed my rifle and hastily put one bullet into him. The buffalo carried on and disappeared over the next hill with the dogs in full cry. We followed as fast as we could. With the dogs was a Staffordshire bull terrier bitch, very young and untried. She had been given to us by an uncle who was the British Consul at Mega, Ethiopia. He decided against keeping this terrier as she had bitten a couple of Ethiopians and he needed to get rid of her before diplomatic relations with the locals deteriorated any further.

We struggled up the hill, following the dogs, one buffalo and a local African herdsman armed with a spear. When we reached the top, we heard the dogs baying in the valley below and increased our pace in that direction. Before we reached the scene where the buffalo was bayed up, the African came running towards us shouting "Come quickly, come quickly, the buffalo is eating the dog!" I found an irate buffalo bull with a bull terrier attached to its nose and the terrier was being swung from side to side. I promptly shot the buffalo and the dog was none the worse for its ordeal.

Another time, also out on the farm, the dogs bayed up some baboons. We hastened to the scene of action. The same bull terrier bitch was trotting at our heels when we came into a small clearing in the forest, where, sitting on the ground and surrounded by the dogs, was a big male baboon. The dogs were keeping a respectful distance but every now and again the baboon would make a dash at a dog which came too close. The bull terrier increased her pace and headed straight for the baboon which, of course, made a dash towards this new intruder. The terrier, however, was very quick and soon there was a squeal from the baboon for the dog had it by the throat. All the other dogs piled in and made short work of the baboon.

At a later stage this same bull terrier bitch had her leg broken by a kick from an eland that she tried to take on. Albert took her to the local vet who set the leg in a plaster cast and she recovered. Soon after this she was attacked while on her own by some baboons and they tore her to pieces. Albert had to put her down. We had become very fond of her and were sorry to lose such a spunky dog.

During this period a big spotted hyena started to kill our milk cows. In order to keep milk production up, we let the cows graze at night. This hyena attacked the cows from the rear and usually tore the udder out. Then it chased the cow until it was exhausted. When the cow collapsed, the hyena grabbed it by the throat and killed it. The hyena then ate as much as it wanted and left.

The hyena would not come back for several days, so we were unable to put out traps or poison. However it usually returned within a week to kill again. We always recognised its tracks because it had a club foot. At some time the hyena must have been caught in a jaw trap and chewed its way to freedom leaving part of the paw behind. This probably explained why it never returned to its kills. Albert and I tried all sorts of things to catch it with no success. Eventually we put up a set gun (an old rifle) in thick bush. The gun was in a horizontal position with the barrel protruding only slightly from the bush. In front of the gun we arranged a semicircle of cut thorn bush and left a small opening. The rifle was positioned to fire at the opening and was set at the chest height of a hyena. In the opening we laid a tennis racket-like frame on the ground. It was made out of wood with small gauge

11

wire netting stretched tightly across it. At one end, the frame was raised slightly from the ground and at the other end we attached a thin wire, which went back on pulleys to the rifle trigger. The tension was just enough so that when an animal stepped through the opening and put its foot on the racket frame, it would immediately cause the gun to fire. Then, to attract the hyena, a carcass was put in the enclosure. We left the gun set for weeks and checked it periodically, always observing from a distance so as not to leave any human scent around. During the third week, when the carcass was a crawling mass of maggots, the clubfoot beast tried to go into the trap and set it off. We never found the hyena, but at the trap there was a pool of blood and its tracks were all around. It must have run off and died, because no more cows were killed after this.

Albert and I used the box trap whenever we had leopards prowling around our calves. One day we had it set and a ratel or honey badger got inside. The next day we went to examine the trap and found it completely wrecked. The entire wooden frame had been chewed and the whole trap had collapsed. There remained only a pile of mangled wire on the ground. The honey badger made good his escape, and the trap was never rebuilt.

Soon after Albert and I started on the farm, Father bought additional land and added it to our existing block. Eventually we owned 18,000 acres of land, most of which was excellent cattle country and had a lot of valuable timber, primarily cedar, on it. The majority of the game such as eland, oryx, impala, Grant's and Thomson's gazelle, bushbuck, reedbuck and waterbuck, was conserved, as these animals had sadly been shot out during the war years. After the defeat of the Italians in Ethiopia and Somaliland, the British held thousands of Italian prisoners of war in camps situated about fifteen miles away. Prison authorities encouraged local hunters to shoot game on the surrounding farms to feed the prisoners. As our farm had no European manager, these shooters would come onto our land and hunt. I noticed the difference as soon as I returned from the war but nothing could be done about it.

On his way back to Tanganyika, Uncle Cecil had a narrow escape from death. He drove a Ford truck loaded with all his possessions, including camping gear. After he crossed the border between Kenya and Tanganyika, he stopped on the side of the road to sleep. It was hot and dry and the rains had not started so he did not put up a tent but made his bed on the ground next to the car. His African servant, afraid of the numerous lions that could be heard roaring in the vicinity, slept in the car. During the night, mosquitoes started to bite and my uncle pulled a thick blanket over his head and went back to sleep. The next thing he knew was terrific pressure and pain on his head. He managed to sit up and throw the blanket off and immediately saw a big hyena standing a few paces away. In the bright moonlight every detail of this very bold animal, which just stood there, was clearly visible. Uncle Cecil grabbed his revolver which fortunately was lying next to him and fired at the hyena. Although suddenly blinded by blood pouring into his eye, he continued to get off a few more shots, before calling to his servant for help. The servant led him down to a nearby river where he managed to wash his face and get the blood out of his eyes. He dressed the teeth wounds on both sides of his forehead and bandaged his head. Hyena have been known to kill sleeping humans and the blanket saved his life.

The next morning he looked around but found no blood so he presumed his shot had missed the hyena. Uncle Cecil then drove several miles to a local store where the Greek owner asked whether he had been in an accident. Uncle Cecil told him what happened to which the Greek replied that he had been very lucky as quite a few Africans had been killed in that district by the very same hyena.

Before we acquired the new land, my father and a friend came up from South Africa and we went on a lion hunt in the Northern Frontier District of Kenya near Isiolo. Father managed to get two rifles out of storage from the police armoury. They were a .425 Westley Richards Magnum and a .318 Westley Richards which formerly belonged to Uncle Cecil. (At this time both lion and leopard were considered vermin. They were either not on licence or if they were, there were about five lion allowed per licence.)

We camped on the Ngare Ndare River which by now had become mostly a sand river. As children we often camped on this river, and back then it was a flowing stream with enormous fig and yellow fever trees growing on its banks. The water was clear and fish could be seen swimming in it. All this changed because on the ground above the escarpment, Wanderobo tribesmen continuously overgrazed the land with cattle, sheep and goats. Vegetation and grass had been destroyed and during the rainy season floods washed topsoil down the water courses thereby choking the streams below. This is a common sight in Africa today where much harm is done through bad farming practices.

Quite a few lions inhabited the area and it was easy to find signs to track them. Albert found some tracks which he followed into thick bush growing above the sand river bank. He crawled into the bush and came face to face with a lion crouched down inside. He carefully backed out and whistled for us. We surrounded the bush. My two brothers were on one side and my father and I were on the other.

Albert then fired into the bush and with the shot a lion came bounding

13

out towards Father and me. We fired simultaneously and the lion did a somersault before landing on the bottom of the sand river. I glanced at it several times and saw no sign of life. There was still another lion in the bush so we waited. Eventually Albert and Robert shot the one in the bush. When they established that it was dead, Robert came round the bush to where we were standing and said "Let me see the lion you have shot." At the sound of his voice, the first lion suddenly came to life, and with a roar, sprang up the bank at us. Both Father and I fired at point blank range and the lion collapsed at our feet. This experience was a lesson never to be forgotten. Throughout the years I hunted, I always treated lion with caution and always checked any lion we shot to make certain that it was really dead. Experience is always the best teacher.

Many years later a professional hunter, Henry Poolman, had a similar experience and it cost him his life, although not from the wounded lion. Henry and a client shot a lion and while they were approaching, the lion suddenly sprang up and attacked the client. The lion was in the process of dying and in fact collapsed on the client. Henry had taken hold of the lion's tail to pull it off the client when he was shot from behind by a novice gun bearer and died as a result.

I found that lions frequently went into a coma after being shot and sometimes showed signs of coming back to life a few minutes afterwards. I am sure that they go into a state of shock as humans very often do under similar circumstances.

Albert and I made periodic hunting trips into the area. Once when we went miles up the Ngare Ndare River in the jeep and camped where the water ended in the sand, we had a surprise visit from George Adamson, who had seen our tracks and followed us. This he had to do through thick bush, as his two wheel drive vehicle was unable to traverse the sand in the river bed. We had just found the carcass of a big male giraffe, killed by a male lion, and nearby we also found a dead dog. We assumed the dog, attracted by the smell of the giraffe carcass, decided to have a meal. The lion came upon the dog and killed it after a short chase. We were examining the carcass when we heard a vehicle and George Adamson appeared. He introduced himself and after checking our licences, said that he had great difficulty in getting through to us as he had to cut tracks in the thick bush. We were amused because with the four wheel drive jeep it was plain sailing. In those days four wheel drive vehicles were just appearing in the country. Later on I worked with George while I was stationed on Mount Kenya, the adjacent area to the south.

14

TWO

FIRST ENCOUNTERS IN THE GAME
DEPARTMENT

In 1949, through the influence of our old family friend, Tom Salmon who was a game warden at that time, I joined the Kenya Game Department as Game Control Officer for the whole area of Mount Kenya and the Northern Aberdares range. My duties were mostly to deal with problem animals in the settled areas of both the European Farmlands and African Tribal Lands. The areas were considerable in size and I was always busy, mainly dealing with buffalo and elephant coming into the cultivated lands. At that time the only really effective method was to shoot one or two animals out of the herd so that the rest were scared away and retreated into the forests or bush. I also had to deal with lion, leopard and sometimes hyena killing the stock. The cats I shot, but I used strychnine for the hyena.

During my first leave period Albert and I took out elephant licences and headed into Wakamba country selecting the Yatta Plateau on the lower Athi River area for our hunt. J.A. Hunter, who was still serving in the Game Department and was then stationed at Makindu, had advised us to try this area.

When we arrived we picked up a Wakamba guide who turned out to be a local witch doctor with a leather bag made from the skin of a small antelope. In the bag he carried small bones, and before setting out to hunt, he threw the bones on the ground, crouched down and observed which way they pointed. He decided on the direction and we set off. After walking for a couple of hours we arrived on the far side of a plateau overlooking the Athi River where we picked up fresh bull elephant tracks, and within a short distance spotted four bulls standing in the shade of some trees. Three were together but one was standing a few yards away on his own. The lone bull was resting his tusks in the fork of a tree. His tusks were long and big – without a doubt over 100 pounds each. The other bulls' tusks were not so big

15

– around 60 to 70 pounds.

A cautious approach was required, but before we could get into shooting range of under fifty yards, the wind suddenly switched. The bulls started to walk quickly away with their trunks and tails up, which indicated they had got our scent. We ran around more or less parallel with them, keeping the wind in our favour, and eventually found ourselves on the edge of a down slope with the elephants above. There they stopped to test the wind with their trunks and then moved off again. The big one was opposite us so I told Albert to shoot which he did and the elephants took off. I could not shoot because Albert was standing in front of me. After following them for some distance it became obvious that the animal had been shot too far back. At first there was a little blood and then nothing. We lost the tracks when they intermingled with those of other elephants in the area.

The next day while we were looking for the wounded animal, I came across a 70 pound elephant and decided to shoot it to cover my licence. I regretted this, for later, on the third hunting day, while sitting on the top of a small hill, we observed a herd of about 300 cows in the process of migrating. Among them was an enormous bull which towered above the others. An Indian shot a big elephant in the same area some time later. His bull was also among a big herd of cows and its tusks weighed 172 pounds and 164 pounds. We never found Albert's wounded elephant.

Most of the area in which I worked had very thick bush or bamboo. The buffalo usually retired into this bush after rampaging through the crops and I used a pack of dogs to bay them. This was highly dangerous as I had to get very close before it was possible to see the animal in order to shoot it – sometimes only a matter of yards. Occasionally the buffalo left the dogs and charged me when I approached. Having been chased around by the dogs, the beast would be in a fine rage and I had to shoot to kill before it reached me. Most of the time it was possible to drop the buffalo with a head or neck shot. If its head was up and its nose pointed towards me, I would aim for the tip of the nose so that the solid bullet would penetrate back to the brain or vertebra. But if its head was down and ready to toss me, I would aim just behind the head for a neck shot, rather like a bull fighter aims his javelin. In this country, shooting was at very close quarters and frequently I had to jump out of the way to avoid the falling body. Most of the time the buffalo was coming at top speed and the impetus carried it forward skidding along the ground. I was very fit and nimble in those days as buffalo hunting required a lot of running up and down the sides of valleys where the dogs chased the animals. The buffalo only stood their ground for a short time before breaking away and running with the dogs in hot pursuit. Sometimes they went a considerable distance before standing at bay again. Meanwhile I would be following at a fast pace, usually accompanied by Wanyahoro. Where the visibility was poor, we proceeded with caution as straggling buffalo often lurked behind, or part of the herd would break back and we would suddenly be confronted by animals travelling at top speed in our direction.

For these buffalo and elephant hunts I usually carried a double barrelled .470 English-made rifle which fired a 500 grain bullet. I always used solid bullets to get maximum penetration as both animals are massive and heavily boned with plenty of meat and muscle. However, for the soft skinned animals such as lion or leopard, the soft nose bullet was ideal. Wanyahoro usually carried a .404 or .375 H & H Magnum. He backed me up and saved my neck on numerous occasions.

I never used a sling on my heavy rifles when big game hunting. They can be dangerous in thick bush as they are inclined to hook on branches, and this is even more dangerous when one has to move or turn quickly to shoot at close quarters. All my heavy rifles were equipped only with iron sights which had a rather large foresight bead and shallow back sight. Telescopes mounted on big bore rifles are not good for dealing with animals that are charging in thick bush at close quarters, for this is when you need to be able to shoot quickly.

Wanyahoro was an outstanding person and I was fortunate to have him working with me. No matter what happened he was always calm and collected and never panicked. This characteristic I found was rare among the Africans I worked with. Wanyahoro was light skinned, athletically built, pleasant with a good sense of humour, and completely honest and reliable. Furthermore, he never drank alcohol.

We would keep the dogs on leashes when tracking buffalo in cultivated areas as there were many other animals such as warthog, giant forest hog, bush pig, bushbuck, waterbuck, monkey and leopard to distract them. When we got close to a buffalo, the dogs were unleashed. It was very exciting to hear the heavy baying of the dogs and the angry grunts of the buffalo. The dogs often got injured, occasionally by buffalo, but more than likely they would leave off chasing the buffalo and get mixed up with pigs and baboons. The dogs had a fatal attraction to pigs and frequently came to close grips with them. Some very bad wounds were inflicted by the pigs' lower

17

tusks and I became adept at stitching up dogs.

Occasionally a dog was attacked by a leopard, especially if it was separated from the pack. Leopard would not dare to go for a dog if there was more than one, and two or three dogs could put a leopard up a tree. If the dogs were too close and the leopard could not escape, it would lie on its back and use both front and back claws to defend itself. Then the dogs usually kept a respectful distance away.

I was joined by a newcomer to the Game Department, Major Rodney Elliott. He had been sent from Nairobi by William Hale, the Chief Game Warden, to get experience at hunting buffalo with dogs as he had never done this before. Rodney was a major in the British Commandos during the war and had been badly injured by a land mine in North Africa. He recovered but was hard of hearing.

Both of us used double barrelled .470 calibre rifles. One day we decided to experiment using both soft nosed bullets and solids on buffalo. We shot quite a few buffalo, cut up the carcasses and dug out the bullets. We checked for penetration and the condition of the bullet when it entered the body, and we concluded that solids were the most suitable.

On one occasion we were called to the Aberdares to shoot a rogue buffalo bull that had killed a honey hunter and chased several others in the area. We took the dogs and a guide who knew where the buffalo was fond of lying up. The local African showed us quite a few buffalo beds in thick bush that had been used recently. This area had a lot of tall cedar and olive trees with thick clumps of creeper-like bush which had game tunnels and paths throughout. It was in these clumps that the buffalo were fond of lying up. There were also patches of *leleshwa* bush (rather like camphor) which was highly inflammable and would burn even when green. Here more buffalo beds were found.

We were shown where the buffalo caught the honey hunter, tossed him several times and eventually killed him. It was here that the rogue buffalo was finally tracked down. After a time we heard the animal move ahead of us and released the dogs which immediately dashed in and started barking. The buffalo grunted and came charging out. Rodney loaded one soft and one solid in his rifle, but I had both barrels loaded with solids as I had not been happy with the past results of softs. Rodney fired both barrels and I followed suit. The animal went down and collapsed a few paces away. We examined it and found dried blood on its horns. Rodney's soft bullet had hit the boss, making very little impression on its head. The bullet left lead on the horn and deflected. Of the other shots, one ploughed into the boss and ended somewhere in the back of the head while the other two went into the neck and the front shoulder. After this incident no more soft nosed bullets were used on buffalo.

Together we shot a good number of buffalo and had some interesting experiences in the farming areas around Mount Kenya and the Aberdares. One morning we went down below the Nanyuki Forest Station to deal with a bull which had been damaging young pine trees cultivated by the Forest Department. The week before Rodney had gone to the Nairobi dog pound and collected some likely looking hunting dogs so we decided to try out a couple of the newcomers. The buffalo tracks led out of the plantation across grassland and into a forest area with tall cedar and podo trees. Underneath the big trees were thick patches of creeper-type bush into which elephant, buffalo and rhino tunnelled when passing through. We proceeded with caution, not knowing what we might be confronted with or when. Rhino and buffalo often shared the same patch of bush and it was extremely dangerous to be in one of these tunnels and have a buffalo or rhino come charging down. Sometimes it was impossible to get out of the way as the bush hemmed one in on both sides.

We progressed a couple of miles through the area. The tracks were easy to follow as it had rained during the night and the ground was soft. Every now and again the buffalo would stop to feed on a patch of green grass or lush weed growing on the side of the track and finally it showed signs of looking for a place to lie up. He went from one buffalo bed to another but every time we thought he would bed down he just carried on. In a little while he went into a really thick patch and the dogs started to strain on the leashes and whine. We released the pack and they promptly dashed into a tunnel. Almost immediately we heard the familiar bark and grunt from the buffalo. This went on for quite a while but the buffalo would not come out. Rodney and I went around the bush looking for a likely entrance and eventually selected a path that was very narrow and tunnel-like. Rodney was in front and I followed directly behind. We had not gone far when one of our new dogs came down the path at top speed with the bull right on his heels. Rodney immediately fired two shots but the buffalo hardly altered his stride. We were now hemmed in by bush and there was no way to get off the track. I pushed my double over Rodney's shoulder and rapidly fired two more shots into the oncoming head and face. All this happened in seconds. Rodney threw himself backwards to avoid the buffalo and both of us fell on our backs just as the bull skidded to a halt, dead at our feet. We were really shaken after the experience and were lucky to get away without injury.

I had a similar experience with Wanyahoro in the same area. We tracked a bull buffalo from the same forest plantation and it went about one mile

19

before we caught up with it. The dogs bayed and the buffalo ran again for quite a while with the dogs right behind it. Eventually it stood at bay and we managed to catch up a second time. The buffalo was standing in a small clearing in the bush when we suddenly came onto both it and the dogs. As we came into view the bull immediately left the dogs and charged. I fired two shots and Wanyahoro managed one shot with his bolt action .375. Realising that the buffalo was not going down and it kept coming, Wanyahoro dived to one side. I followed and landed on top of him with the barrel of my rifle hitting him on the back of his head. The buffalo went right on over without touching us and collapsed about twenty yards away before starting its death bellow and we knew it was dying. Wanyahoro had quite a headache from the knock on the head.

I have often argued with hunters about the pros and cons of using double barrelled rifles or bolt action rifles for hunting dangerous game. Time and time again I managed to drop charging animals with my second shot, and nobody could convince me that a bolt action rifle is better than a double for getting off two shots quickly when an animal is charging at point blank range. After firing a magazine rifle, the rifle is lowered to work the bolt and precious seconds are wasted. An experienced hunter using a double would fire one shot and immediately line up for a second without taking their eyes off the animal. I also held one spare cartridge in my left hand so it was possible to break the action after firing both barrels and immediately load the spare round. Over the years I learned to perform this action quickly. At close quarters I could bring the gun up and immediately sight along the barrel without using either the foresight or backsight. The only time I aimed properly was when the animal was a little further away.

The big mistake inexperienced hunters make when using a double is to fire both barrels without lining up for the second shot. The recoil of the first shot tends to throw the barrels up, and if the second barrel is fired immediately the second shot goes high and misses even a large animal. There is no doubt my .470 double saved me on numerous occasions. Safety catches on most bolt action rifles, especially the old Mausers, require that 'precious split second' to slip off, whereas the double has a slide safety catch which one pushes forward while raising the rifle to fire and no time is wasted.

The first double issued to me by the Game Department had a single trigger with a selector which was used to select either the right or left barrel and this ensured even wear on both barrels. It was a Westley Richards best quality rifle with detachable locks. It was also the most accurate double that I ever used. I could fire it at a target 100 yards away while lying prone and place both shots right in the bull. The double rifles that I used afterwards were not as accurate. The common fault with doubles was that right and left barrels would often cross at 100 yards, or one would be either high or low and very few were synchronised accurately. Ammunition was also sensitive to heat and atmospheric conditions. All my .470 ammunition was manufactured by Kynoch of I.C.I. I found it to be consistently reliable and in over thirty years of hunting, I never had a misfire.

I used the Westley Richards .470 for six years on Game Control until the selector played up and I reluctantly decided to hand it in. I was issued with a .470 double made by John Rigby of London. This particular rifle, formerly used by Myles Turner who left the Game Department to take up professional hunting, was good but not as accurate as the Westley Richards.

For a couple of years, Rodney and I continued buffalo control work on Mount Kenya and the Northern Aberdares. We also dealt with marauding elephant and lion or leopard that killed cattle and sheep. On one occasion, we were high up on the Aberdares on a farm which bordered the bamboo belt at 8,000 feet above sea level. The farmer grew wheat, barley and oats. Above this area the bamboo was very thick and tall, about twelve or fifteen feet high, and big trees (mostly cedar and podo) grew throughout.

The Colobus monkey found in these high altitude forest areas is perhaps the most striking looking of all the monkeys with its long black and white hair, streaming white bushy tail and black face. It spends most of its life high up in the tree tops eating cedar and wild olive berries and new green shoots. It is extremely agile and can easily jump from a high branch on one tree to a lower branch on an opposite tree, sometimes thirty to forty feet away. I have never seen one fall. Their call, once heard, is never forgotten: a grunting, rasping voice that carries for a considerable distance across deep mountain valleys. On the ground they are slow, awkward and ungainly but it is not often that one sees them there. In the same area there is another type of monkey, called a Sykes, which has a short coat, and is not as impressive as the Colobus. Sykes monkeys often give warning noises indicating the presence of leopard, and once, on hearing these warning cries, I was able to approach and spot a leopard below them which I shot.

We tracked two buffalo bulls out of the oats and into the forest. The going was slow as we frequently saw tracks of other animals such as rhino, elephant and giant forest hog. On this sort of hunt one is always liable to bump into a rhino or an elephant. I found the black rhino the most aggressive and often had unprovoked charges from these cantankerous beasts and on occasion had to shoot in self-defence. We also saw tracks of bongo and bushbuck which were quite common here. The buffalo tracks led across two valleys going over ground which was wet and slippery and slopes that were steep. We came to the top of the ridge where the ground was more level and easier going, and had not gone far when a crashing sound indicated that a buffalo had just departed. It had probably got our scent or even heard us because it was difficult to walk quietly in bamboo.

We unleashed the dogs and they took off in full cry. I was soon left far behind by the others because I had sprained my ankle a couple of days before so I could not run. The barking dogs indicated that they were getting further and further away and that the buffalo was still running. One dog, a half cross bull terrier, stayed behind with me. It was one of the newcomers from the pound in Nairobi and it had not got into the swing of things. I was glad of its company and more so a little later when it was trotting just ahead and I saw it stop, face to the left and growl. Then there was a grunt and a crash of bamboo. I realised the second buffalo had stayed behind and it was coming straight towards me. I stood with my rifle ready but was unable to see anything. The buffalo came through the bamboo with its head almost at ground level. I do not remember aiming and do not think that I even brought the rifle to my shoulder because it was so close. I had an instant glimpse of head, horns and the back of its neck as it burst through and I instinctively shot into the back of the neck which dropped it on its nose and the whole body came sliding forward along the ground. The dead buffalo ended up almost at my feet.

On another buffalo hunt, this time below the Nanyuki Forest Station which was run by Peter Rundgren (brother to Eric Rundgren, the well-known professional hunter), I was with Rodney and three African game scouts. The dogs bayed a bull and we all ran towards the buffalo. Somehow we became separated and Rodney reached the buffalo first. He had two game scouts with him, one of which was a Wanderobo named Lesoli. I heard two shots, a slight pause and then a lot more shots. I heard Rodney shouting in Swahili to stop shooting. I arrived on the scene with Wanyahoro who had been with me, to find Rodney soaking wet and the buffalo dead. The circumstances surrounding this incident were then explained as follows: Rodney was in the lead, followed by the two game scouts. He was splashing through a stream when the bull charged down the slope towards him at top speed. He fired at the buffalo but nothing happened. Immediately he pulled the second trigger and both barrels went off – he had a hang fire on the first barrel. The buffalo kept coming, so Rodney threw himself sideways to avoid being hit and landed on his back in the water. The buffalo went over without touching him. Lesoli, armed with a .375 rifle, raised the gun to shoot but the buffalo knocked the end of the barrel sending Lesoli crashing to the ground. The beast stopped and turned to have a go at Lesoli when the other game scout shot it in the neck with his .303. The buffalo went down and Lesoli jumped up, grabbed his rifle, and proceeded to empty the magazine into the animal. I heard Rodney shouting at Lesoli to stop firing. Everybody was lucky not to have been injured. The man carrying the .303 rifle saved the day. (The .303 was used to finish off animals that were not quite dead to conserve the more expensive .470 ammunition.)

When we skinned and cut up the carcass, we found a soft nosed heavy calibre bullet in the flesh of the neck. The bullet had retained its shape and we thought that it came from a heavier calibre rifle than the ones we were using, probably a .500. The bullet casing around the lead was silver, whereas our .470 bullets had a bronze or copper casing. We decided a sportsman had wounded it many months previously because the wound had healed completely with no ill effects to the beast. This also accounted for its aggressive behaviour when it met Rodney and the game scouts. We found quite a few .303 rifle or small calibre bullets in buffalo that we shot on control in the forest areas. The only time we used .303 rifles on buffalo control was to finish them off.

Lesoli, the game scout, was inclined to get nervous and excitable when close to dangerous game. Soon after this hunt, around the back side of the mountain between Meru and Embu at a place called Chuka, we tracked a few elephant bulls out of African cultivations and they headed straight into the forest. After some hours of tracking we heard breaking branches just ahead. We got right up to the bulls and found ourselves on one side of a thick bush and an elephant feeding off the same bush on the opposite side. The vegetation was so thick that we could not get around to see the elephant properly, so we decided to stay put and see if he would show himself. After a while the trunk, tusks and part of the head appeared over the top of the bush as he reached for a tasty bit but the elephant had only exposed part of his head. Rodney and I were waiting for him to show more of his body when suddenly there was a shot fired from the side, so close that it made our ears ring and hurt. It is always extremely painful to the ears when a rifle is fired from behind at close quarters. The elephant fortunately collapsed with a brain shot from Lesoli, who could not stand the tension when the head of the elephant appeared suddenly over the top of the bush. Rodney turned round and reprimanded him in no uncertain terms. After this, we seldom took Lesoli along as a person with his temperament could jeopardize the safety of all the others.

There was another game scout named Kamino who, like Wanyahoro, never showed fear and was always reliable when close to dangerous game. On one hunt the dogs bayed a buffalo in very thick bamboo and we were uncertain how to deal with it. Kamino offered to shoot it. Rodney gave the go ahead and Kamino immediately disappeared into the bamboo and the next thing we knew he had shot the buffalo.

On another hunt near Nyeri, Kamino was with me and we followed a buffalo bull which had made a habit of coming into a coffee plantation, rubbing his head against the coffee bushes and breaking them. The only option was to find and shoot him. His tracks led through thick bush and then wandered down into the bottom of a valley. Tracking was difficult as this buffalo had been around for a considerable time and there were several days worth of tracks, all in the same area, but all going in different directions. After following tracks and then finding that they were not fresh and going back several times, we eventually found the right ones. Finally, we arrived at the bottom of a valley covered with thick patches of Lantana bush. Buffalo and rhino often lie up in this sort of cover, but it is extremely dangerous for the hunter as the visibility is practically zero and the buffalo can crash through with ease. We released the dogs when we realised that the buffalo was not far away. They started barking ahead of us and the buffalo grunted. We eased up as close as possible and found him in a particularly thick patch of Lantana. We could see the top of a six foot high bush being shaken by his movement, but we could not see to shoot. Kamino again offered to shoot the animal. I nodded approval and he crawled into one of the tunnels leading towards the buffalo. I then decided that he should not go alone and crawled in after him. We had not progressed far when the head of the buffalo suddenly appeared right in front of Kamino and he brained it, with the barrel of the rifle almost touching the buffalo's head. The animal collapsed right there much to my relief. Thinking about it many times afterwards, I realised the folly of exposing oneself unnecessarily to a buffalo. Should the hunter fail to drop the beast in its tracks, it could turn the tables on the hunter with disastrous results.

Two years had elapsed since I joined the Game Department and I still had no house or base from which to establish myself. The Game Department, always the poor cousin to all the other departments, was continually short of funds. All monies derived from the sale of ivory and rhino horn collected or confiscated from poachers, and all fines from poachers went to the Government Central Fund. Each year we were allocated money for expenses for twelve months ahead, but it was never enough, and we often ran out before the end of the financial year. Finally, six hundred pounds, which was not sufficient, was allocated for a house to be built near the Nanyuki Forest Station. I consulted with the Officer in Charge of the Public Works Department (PWD) as they were going to build the

My wife, Elizabeth (nicknamed Jock)

*Henry Poolman, the well-known
elephant hunter*

Major Rodney Elliott

Albert hunting buffalo in 1946

George Adamson with cubs at Isiolo, Kenya

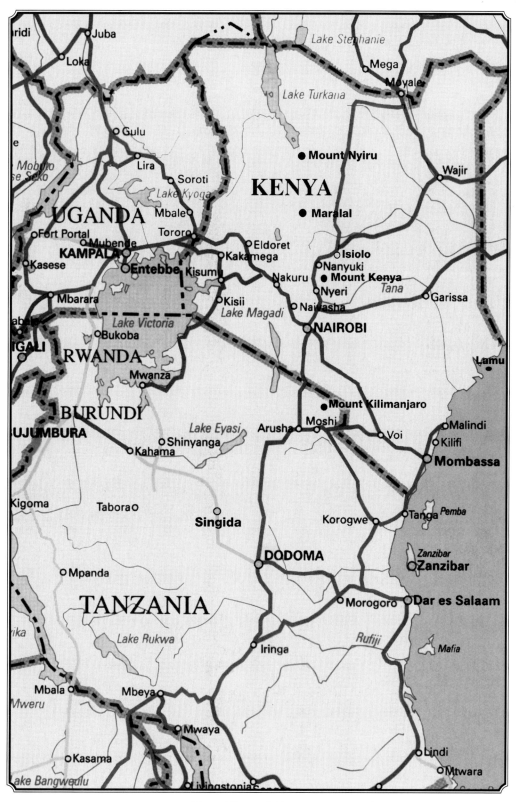

Map of Kenya & Tanzania

Jock and Rodney Elliott

Don Bousfield looking at tall bamboo on Mount Kenya

Rodney Elliott and Wanyahoro with an elephant shot on Mount Kenya

house and he came up with a fairly inexpensive plan using local materials. The PWD built a big, comfortable wooden house. The walls were built of off-cuts and the roof covered with wooden shingles, while a brick fireplace was installed to cope with the very cold nights. The house was at about 8,000 feet above sea level and at certain times of the year there was early morning frost. The rainfall was good here and we soon had a thriving vegetable garden.

Occasionally I went out in the evenings and hunted for bushbuck, which were plentiful in the area. The males were often very dark, almost black, whereas females were bright chestnut with white spots on the body. Bushbuck meat was good to eat and made a nice change of diet for us. The numerous rivers were stocked with trout, mostly the rainbow variety, and occasionally I would take off and do a little fishing. Most of the rivers and streams originated from the melting mountain snow and the water was always very cold. It was impossible to stand in it for very long as one's feet turned blue with cold.

Our house commanded an excellent view of Mount Kenya and we saw snow all year round. The Lewis Glacier was also visible from the house. On one side of the house the indigenous forest came right up to the fence. The cedar trees were enormous, but most were dead and had lichen hanging from the branches rather like Father Christmas beards. Kenya must have had a rain cycle a couple of hundred years back which brought in the forests. The Forest Station was about two miles away and from there one could look down the slopes to a magnificent view of the lower country. On clear days, we could see mountain ranges and hills one hundred miles or more in the distance.

A horse and mule track running past the house was used by mountain parties wishing to climb Mount Kenya. I once took some game scouts and set off early in the morning to walk up the track. Soon after leaving we were into the bamboo belt following along the top of a ridge. Both sides of the ridge sloped down to the valley floor and we could hear water running in the rivers below. It was especially loud where they went over small waterfalls. The going was strenuous, climbing all the way and the sounds around were strange. Bamboo rattled in the wind and occasionally cracked like a rifle shot. There were a lot of Colobus as well as Sykes monkeys in the area and we heard them calling frequently. This was the first time I ever saw the rare white Colobus monkey. Where the bamboo thinned out there was an area of big trees and bush, and we saw tufted forest guineafowl and louries with their bright red wings and blue and green plumage. The red in their wings shows up when they fly from one tree to another. We saw tracks of elephant, rhino, buffalo, bushbuck, waterbuck (Defassa) and giant forest

25

hog.

Now and again the bamboo opened up and we emerged into small grass covered glades. A lone buffalo bull appeared in one of these, and he went crashing off into the bamboo as soon as he saw us. After walking for six hours, we came onto the moorlands. The bamboo belt usually ends at 10,000 feet. On the edge of this altitude there are the lizard wood trees, which have a big leaf that sheds all year. The ground looks untidy with fallen leaves and it is covered with something resembling Kikuyu grass. It is usually kept short – I suspect by grazing animals. In many places it was quite park-like. On the moorland I often saw eland, zebra, buffalo and quite a few rhino. Even the elephant crossed the top of the moorland and to this day it is possible to see deep paths that have been used for centuries by elephant herds migrating from one area to another. Leopard and lion are also quite common. Below the highest peaks, my father once saw a leopard completely frozen in ice.

When we reached the upper levels of the forest and the bamboo, we sat and rested for a while. The view was magnificent and it was possible to see for hundreds of miles out to the Northern Frontier District (NFD) and towards Lake Rudolf. It was about 2 o'clock so we decided to head down again as we did not want to walk back in the dark. The return trip was easy and took only three hours.

THREE

MORE EXPLOITS IN THE GAME DEPARTMENT

Elephants were doing a lot of damage to the maize fields belonging to a European farmer whose farm adjoined the Nyeri Forest and the National Parks of the Aberdares and Tree Tops. Rodney and I drove over and were shown around by the farmer who pointed out evidence of damaged caused by the elephants. There were a lot of elephants in the forest, so we decided to wait for the culprits to return and deal with them when they came into the fields at night. We had a Verey light or flare with us to provide enough light to shoot by. When the bulls returned, we approached carefully in the dark, getting to within thirty yards of the nearest one. A flare was fired and the whole countryside showed up with the light. We both fired at the same bull which collapsed after running some distance.

I was to shoot so many elephants at night that I developed a shooting torch especially for this purpose. I used an old torch-head with a reflector that would give a good spot when used at night. I then soldered a length of flex to the back of the bulb and installed a press switch where it emerged from the empty torch barrel. The rest of the flex went to batteries carried on my waist. I made a clamp to go around the torch and fastened it to the barrels of the .470. Before going out I adjusted the torch so that when I put the spotlight on the body of the animal, the rifle aimed at the centre of the light. In theory I had only to put the light on the elephant's shoulder and the rifle automatically shot there. Elephants do not usually stand for light and generally stampeded as soon as it was switched on. Our approach had to be made in the dark and we had to get as close to the beast as possible before switching the light on and shooting. This was often very hazardous.

At a later stage of elephant control I had to deal with two bulls coming out of Tree Tops National Park into the banana fields in the Kikuyu Reserve. Here again I had to shoot at night to get the culprits.

This time I camped close to where the elephants were coming in and instructed the locals to call me when they heard them. The call came at about midnight. It was raining heavily at the time and there was no moon. In fact, it was so dark that I could not see at all and in spite of using my torch continuously, I proceeded with much slipping and sliding in the soft mud. This area was hilly with many steep slopes and valleys. The sides of these slopes were cultivated and there were many contour ditches with banks up to 6 feet high to stop the soil from being washed away by the rains.

When we heard the elephants breaking the banana trees, we switched off the light and groped in the dark. I had the rifle with the torch attached to it in one hand and in the other a staff which I put out ahead, rather like a blind man, to feel my way towards the noise the elephants were making. In spite of the stick, I suddenly felt the ground give way and found myself falling feet first. Fortunately, I landed safely at the bottom of one of the ditches. The rifle was all right and I checked to see that there was no mud in the action or barrels while one of my game scouts held a cape to shield the light from the elephants.

We continued to make slow progress before finding ourselves directly above the elephant but on the same slope. We sat for a while and listened, trying to make out how far off they were and also trying to determine their numbers. After a while, I decided that the nearest elephant was very close and I switched the light on. It showed up the grove of bananas and, standing broadside to me, the top half of the elephant. I tried for a side brain shot and fired before the elephant moved, but I realised that I had missed as it stumbled and immediately took off running across my front. I switched my aim to its shoulder and fired the second barrel, but the elephant kept going. A second elephant appeared below the first one and followed his companion. We followed as fast as we could down the slope and in the direction of the disappearing elephants. We slipped and slid but managed to stay on our feet, finally coming to the bottom of the slope where the ground was more level. Here, I saw the bull staggering around about to fall, and beyond it the second animal wandering slowly off. The Africans with me wanted me to shoot it as well but I declined saying that one was enough.

Early the next morning we walked to where we had left the fallen elephant. I instructed the game scout and the locals to cut up the animal and remove the tusks. The ivory would be handed into Game Department Headquarters in Nairobi and would eventually find its way to the Ivory Room in Mombasa. This was a huge shed where all the ivory was stored. Every year the Government held an auction to dispose of the ivory and rhino horns.

28

While I watched the cutting out of the ivory, two National Park scouts approached to inform me that the second elephant had been wounded and there was blood to be seen. We followed in the direction that the elephant had gone and picked up the tracks, which were easy to see as the ground was soft from the previous evening's rain. We soon saw blood, but only a drop now and again. I followed the spoor, crossing into the National Park where the elephant had broken down the wire fence demarcating the Park boundary. Here the vegetation was dense and we proceeded with caution, keeping our eyes open for rhino, which were also common. After about three miles of slow progress we found ourselves among a huge herd of cow elephants noisily breaking branches and feeding all around.

We were discussing what to do next when one elephant started screaming and immediately the others converged on the one making all the noise. We decided to move out and backed away as the elephant had got our scent. Then several more elephants trumpeted from where we had been and we continued to walk away. An elephant gave the alarm little closer and we realised they were following our scent. We broke into a trot and continued for about a mile. All this time we could hear trumpeting behind us and they seemed to be getting closer. We broke out into a big clearing and I decided to wait for the elephants to shoot the leader in order to stop them chasing us. The two National Parks game scouts, fearing repercussions for shooting elephants in the park, begged us not to shoot. I may add here that once Rodney Elliott was also dealing with a troublesome elephant herd in the Nyeri Forest. The whole herd charged and he was forced to shoot five or six before the rest turned back. For this Rodney came under a lot of criticism from the local owners of Tree Tops and from Jim Corbett who had retired from India to live in Nyeri. Jim was the well-known hunter who killed many man-eating tigers in India. Rodney and I met both Jim and his sister at the Outspan Hotel in Nyeri where they were staying. I was surprised to find a person who looked as insignificant as a school teacher and could not imagine him hunting man-eating tiger and leopard. He was a small person, probably in his late sixties, but he was highly regarded in India as a hunter and there is a tiger sanctuary named in his honour.

I was now faced with the same situation as Rodney Elliott. I decided to carry on running. We were now winded, in spite of the fact that we were really fit. A little further on we crossed a river. The whole herd of elephant cows arrived right behind us. Their numbers were considerable – we could not even count them. They milled around, putting their trunks on the ground to get our scent. At the water they lost all interest and eventually wandered back into the bush. We followed the river downstream as it was

29

our way out of the Park, and had not gone far when we were attacked by a swarm of bees and forced to run again to get away from them.

When I thought about it afterwards and tried to work out why the elephants charged and why the bees attacked, I realised that there were two local Africans in our party who had been cutting up the elephant we had shot earlier and they were covered in blood and guts and really "hummed"! The elephants and the bees strongly objected and I didn't blame them.

Around this time I bought my first short-wheel based Land Rover. I had to get a loan from the Government and repaid it with deductions from my salary. We were all poorly paid, but in those days money went a long way. For the brand new Land Rover, I paid £450. Today a similar vehicle would cost about £5,000. This shows how the value of money has eroded through the years. Someone recently referred to it as "monopoly money."

Until I acquired the Land Rover, I relied on a 3-ton Chev truck which gave me good service and was used right up to the time I left the Game Department. The Land Rover had just appeared on the market and was becoming an extremely popular four-wheel drive vehicle. For years it was the best in the field until the Toyota Land Cruiser came on the scene. I also bought a secondhand 15 cwt trailer to tow behind the Land Rover. I preferred the Land Rover for short trips because it was extremely good in the red slippery mud and mountain tracks. When the going got really difficult, I put chains on all four wheels and got up some steep slopes.

My wife and I had two children, a boy and a girl. We named the eldest Cecil after my Uncle, and our daughter, Elizabeth. Elizabeth was my wife's real name, but we all called her Jock, which was a name her parents had given her and it had stuck ever since. We later had two more children, Richard and Brian.

Rodney and I found ourselves at Marania on the slopes of Mount Kenya in the merino sheep farming area dealing with sheep-killing lion. The afternoon we arrived we went into the area above the farm where all the trouble was occurring. Beyond the fence line of the farm boundary were valleys and slopes covered in bamboo. We spotted a lioness sunning herself on the edge of the bamboo. She had not seen us and we did a short stalk, but found that we could not get close without her spotting us. Rodney decided to try a long shot. He was using a 8 x 57 Mauser rifle fitted with a scope. I had seen him use the rifle and knew he was a pretty good shot. He fired and immediately the lioness rolled over. I knew the shot had found its mark.

There was still a family of almost grown lions around, about six in number, so our work was not over. A few days later the lions killed a whole lot of merino sheep and we used the carcasses for bait. We then dug a place for ourselves in the side of a bank, covered it with logs and sheeting and left a small opening from which to observe the sheep carcasses that had been pegged down a few yards away.

Rodney and I sat up that night. It was dark with a clear sky and a little visibility from the stars. After a couple of hours the first lion appeared like a ghost all of a sudden out of the dark background and walked silently up to the bait. Shortly afterwards the others appeared and we switched on the light and fired. Much to the delight of the local farmer, we got two that night. Rodney came back later and shot one or two more.

There was one young male left on his own and he stayed in the area and killed more sheep. My brother Albert and I went out to deal with with him. We inspected the dead sheep and decided to track this lion. The tracks entered an area of thick bush with a scattering of cedar trees. We realised the lion would hear us because the vegetation was very thick so we agreed that Albert and Wanyahoro would follow the tracks while I circled ahead and positioned myself where there was a break between the thick bush and forest on the other side. I felt sure that the lion would come out of the bush where we had seen his tracks enter it and, when disturbed, would head across the short open belt towards the thicker forest.

I positioned myself where I could see him as soon as he came out of the bush and tried to cross over. I was using a 8 x 60S rifle fitted with a scope as I thought I might have to take a long shot and the .470 double would be unsuitable. A short while after I had taken up my position, the lion came into view, walking slowly towards the forest on the other side. He was quite close, about forty yards, and he stopped about thirty yards away, looking ahead but standing broadside. I took careful aim and fired. The lion fell and did not move.

We thought we had accounted for all the lion but heard later that a bigger and older lion appeared in the area and killed cattle and sheep. The local farmers tried unsuccessfully to hunt him but he had learnt from inexperienced hunters not to return to his kill. The only way to get him was to track him.

The first attempt Rodney and I made was also unsuccessful. His tracks left the carcass of a steer he had killed and headed into the area where I had previously shot the young lion. We had the assistance of a couple of farmers and game scouts who followed the tracks into the bush with some of our dogs. Rodney and I positioned ourselves where we had a good view and could see the lion if he emerged. We heard the dogs bark as they started to bay up the lion. We waited in vain for him to appear. The dogs stopped barking and eventually the farmers, game scouts and dogs reappeared. They were surprised that we had not seen the lion. They showed us the tracks which led right where we had expected the lion to go. It was evident that the lion had seen us and crawled on his belly, using the cover of a small water course to slip past us and get away. He was a smart lion.

In the hope of seeing him again, both farmers and game scouts followed in the direction of the lion. For some reason Rodney and I did not accompany them. The lion walked out right in front of one of the farmers and he had a shot but missed, and it got away.

We stayed in the area waiting for the lion to kill again. About ten days later we were called out by a cattle herder and when we arrived at the *boma* (cattle enclosure) where he kept the cattle penned up at night, he told us that the lion had roared close to the boma at 5 o'clock that morning. Rodney and I found tracks close by and followed them. After several hours the tracks took us across the hills in the direction of Isiolo, about ten miles away. That afternoon we were still following the tracks which were easy to see on the soft ground, but now and again we got to grassland where we would lose the tracks and have to find them again. This wasted precious time and by 5 o'clock we had progressed only another five miles. We had been tracking since early morning and everybody was tired. The sun had been hot that day which did not help matters and the dogs kept looking for shade, lying down and panting. When we were beginning to lose hope of getting up to the lion, the tracks suddenly led right to a steep hill. The lion was looking for a place to lie up and would most likely find a suitable place on or near the top of the hill. I continued to follow the tracks, taking some game scouts and the dogs, while Rodney went around to the back in case the lion, when disturbed, should head in that direction.

We made slow progress up the hill following the lion tracks. Near the top, in a thick patch of bush, the dogs found him. They barked a couple of times and then stopped. We ran in their direction but there was only silence. Shortly afterwards two shots were fired and I knew that Rodney had shot the lion. We proceeded with haste and found Rodney standing next to the lion. Everybody was shouting and congratulating each other when suddenly the lion showed signs of coming to and Rodney had to fire another round. This lion had hardly any mane, typical of those found in the Northern Frontier District. He also had many scars from going through barbed wire fences to get at cattle kept in enclosures.

Rodney left temporarily to stand in for a game warden who was going on leave at Kapenguria. In my area there was no let up in requests for help and I would go from area to area wherever assistance was most needed to deal with problem animals.

A coffee farmer at Nyeri was killed by a rhino while taking a stroll with his wife one evening. They had a couple of terriers with them and apparently the terriers had found the rhino in thick bush alongside the road. When the rhino charged the dogs, they headed back to their master and the elderly couple suddenly found themselves confronted by the rhino. The man had tried to save his wife and had then been attacked and killed.

I was urgently sent for by the police and arrived the next day. I looked around the bush close to the scene of the attack. The animal had obviously made the area his home because there were a lot of rhino tracks. We picked up fresh bull tracks and followed them. We had not gone very far, having proceeded cautiously, trying to make as little noise as possible as we knew the rhino's hearing was very good, when it suddenly got to its feet right in front of us and stood with its ears moving back and forth. The rhino had heard us but was unsure of our whereabouts. I felt sure that this animal was the one responsible for the farmer's death so I promptly lined up on its shoulder and fired. It went straight down and gave the peculiar pig-like squeal that rhinos normally give in their death throe. It was not necessary to fire another shot. We found a lot of dried blood on the head and horns which convinced us that we had shot the right animal.

After this I was called to the Regati Forest Station by a Mr Howarth, the Forest Officer of that area. He wanted me to deal with a herd of elephant which had been in the area for some time and were doing a lot of damage to the pine plantations. He tried to keep them out by digging ditches and covering them with brushwood. In some places this deterred the elephants but eventually they found their way over the ditches in spots where buffalo had pushed the bush aside to make a pathway.

We followed the herd out of the plantation and into the main forest. Kamino and Wanyahoro came along as game scouts and a couple of forest guards joined as well. Tracking them was not difficult because there were about fifty cows, calves and bulls in the herd. The trees here were big, mainly cedar, olive and camphor trees as well as podo and a few others that I could not identify. The ground vegetation was thick with many varieties of stinging nettles, some had stems an inch in diameter and stood about six feet high with hair-like prickles. If one brushed the leaves or stems with a bare leg or arm, one immediately felt a burning or stinging sensation rather like a bee or hornet sting and sometimes worse. So, as we proceeded on the elephant trail, we cautiously avoided these plants as much as possible. I usually wore khaki shorts and canvas ankle boots with ankle putties wrapped over socks or stockings. My bare legs were often stung by nettles, so I had partially grown used to them and after a while the stinging usually wore off. The

33

reason I wore shorts was that the mountain areas usually had a lot of rain and heavy early morning dew. Wet long trousers were heavy and uncomfortable, and made a lot of noise in the bush. I could walk more quietly when wearing shorts.

We heard the elephants making considerable noise ahead. In order to test the wind, I carried an old sock filled with fine wood ash. The ash floated down when shaken, and if there was a breeze, this indicated the direction of the air current. This time the wind was in our favour. In these mountain areas the direction of wind changed considerably, especially in depressions or small valleys. One minute the wind was in your favour and suddenly it switched and blew in a different direction. So I had to test it frequently as we approached the herd. After a while I spotted a young bull in front with a lot of cows and calves beyond him. I approached as quickly as was possible, hoping to get close before he moved on again. I waited for him to turn his body so that I could put in a good shot. Angle shots are always tricky, especially on big animals. The best position for a head, brain, neck or shoulder shot, is when the animal is standing broadside. The elephant suddenly turned his head and I decided to take a side brain shot. I could not see his shoulder which was screened by bush. With my first barrel from the .470, the animal went down but was only stunned, and immediately tried to get up. I quickly reloaded and my next shot put him down for good.

While this was happening, I heard a commotion behind me. I saw Kamino turn suddenly, put up his .375 and fire. Kamino was standing slightly to my left, about five yards away. I spun round to see a cow elephant plough the ground almost on top of me. Kamino had brained it with a head shot and fortunately saved me from the cow. She had charged out without making a sound. Luckily Kamino had seen her and taken action.

The other Africans reappeared in fits of laughter. When I asked them in Swahili what was so amusing, Wanyahoro told me that when the cow suddenly charged out of the bush behind them, the two forest guards tried to climb up onto his shoulders and they all collapsed on the ground. They darted off to one side as the elephant bore down but they did not give any warning cries to alert me or Kamino because they were too frightened to make any noise. Wanyahoro had to untangle himself after being flattened by the others.

At about this time Tom Salmon, who was stationed around the mountain at Keragoya near Embu, was called out to deal with a lioness which had killed and eaten the younger wife of a chief. This occurred just below Meru. He explained to me what had transpired. On his arrival, he was led to the remains of the human body. The whole area was covered with

34

thick elephant grass six to eight feet high. It was late in the day and in a very short time darkness would fall. Tom realised that the lioness would return shortly and the only action he could take was to put strychnine in the body. He turned to the Chief and asked permission to use his dead wife's body. The Chief agreed and said, "By all means, she is no good to me anymore!" Tom put poison in the body and the next day the lioness was found dead close by.

Tom told me another interesting story that happened when he had to deal with two elephant bulls damaging African crops. A new veterinary officer, who had just arrived in the area, asked whether he could come along and if Tom would let him shoot an elephant. He had never shot one previously. Tom agreed and they duly arrived on the scene late in the afternoon and waited for the elephants. The locals assured him that the elephants would come out of the forest as they had every day for the past few days. Sure enough the elephants appeared on the edge of the tree line and walked into a pea patch. The two animals were like combine harvesters. They moved forward picking up whole bundles of pea plants and stuffing them into their mouths.

Having agreed beforehand on what to do, Tom and the officer approached, and when they were close enough, they prepared to shoot. Tom had explained to the officer where to place his shot and they had decided that Tom was to shoot the elephant on the left and the veterinary officer would take the one on the right. Tom fired and his animal went down with a brain shot. The officer never fired a shot, and when Tom turned around and looked, he saw the officer put the rifle up and then lower it and eject the live round onto the ground. He did this several time until he emptied the magazine. Tom asked him what he was doing and he replied that there was something wrong with his rifle as it would not fire. By this time the surviving elephant was high tailing it for the forest and soon disappeared from view. Tom examined the rifle and found that it had no mechanical faults. He realised the officer's brain had frozen with excitement, resulting in him acting as he did. When Tom and the officer were having a drink together back at camp, Tom told him that he must do a little more shooting of less dangerous animals before he went after the big ones otherwise he could find himself in more trouble in the future.

I met Tom a few months later and he told me the veterinary officer had been killed by a lion near Embu. I had heard on the radio that a veterinary officer had been mauled by a lion and had later died of his wounds. Tom said the officer was on the rounds of the district near Embu. The locals complained to him that a lion had been killing their stock and they had seen

35

it lying up close by. The officer went out accompanied by his truck driver and assistant. He saw the lion and had a shot at it but only wounded it. The lion ran off and in the follow up it suddenly charged them in thick bush. The officer never even fired a shot and the lion knocked him over and started to chew him up. The truck driver, who was unarmed, ran up and started to pelt the lion with stones. It promptly left the veterinary officer and started to maul the driver. The other African also began to pelt it with stones and the lion then slunk back into the bush. The plucky African dragged both injured men back to the truck, and somehow managed to get them in. Even though the African had very little driving experience, he managed to drive the truck back to Embu and got both men to the hospital where the officer died.

Tom went to the scene and found shoes and hats strewn around. He picked up the rifle which was lying on the ground and found the bolt was still open and a live round was lying nearby. The veterinary officer had repeated what he had done on the elephant hunt. Some people react in funny ways when exposed to danger or excitement. Tom cast around with a couple of the game scouts accompanying him and found the blooded trail leading off into the bush where the lion had retreated. He found a few places where the animal had lain down and then moved on again. Tom had not gone very far when there was a low growl and he looked up to see the lion coming very fast. He fired both barrels of his heavy double and the lion collapsed at his feet. This lion almost got him too.

I moved down to a big cattle ranch on the lower Lolldaika foot hills of Mount Kenya where the farmer had a lot of game. He wanted me to shoot some buffalo and giraffe. Shooting giraffe was not to my liking because I always enjoyed seeing them and they are such harmless creatures. However the farmer felt there were too many and, as they were always breaking his fences, I had to do something. The first afternoon, after pitching camp, I decided to take a stroll and shoot a game bird for the pot. I carried my .22 rifle and headed to where I has seen guineafowl. After a while I came across the birds scratching the ground for seeds. I had to cross a small grassy water course to get to them, so I lined up a thick bush between myself and the birds. The bush acted as a screen and hid my approach. I was walking through some grass about a foot to eighteen inches high, looking ahead and not at my feet, when suddenly out of the corner of my eye I caught a movement. It was directly ahead near my feet. After that things happened quickly. I glanced down and registered in my mind the black and shiny coils of a snake. It was a huge Egyptian cobra and its head was already coming up. I reacted quickly and jumped backwards. The snake struck out at me and just missed my leg, then calmly slithered into a bush nearby.

I shot a few giraffe for the ranch owner. On the last day I had one on the ground which we still had to cut up and load onto the 3-ton Chevy truck. A strange African, a Wanderobo who lived in a reservation not far away, approached me. He asked for meat and I replied that he could have some, but he must first help us load it onto the truck. When we had it loaded, everybody climbed on board. I was about to climb into the cab and drive away when I saw some of the game scouts and the stranger sitting on the low sides of the body. I told them to sit inside, not on the low sides, and drove off. I had not gone very far and was in fact travelling on a good stretch of road, but there were a few stones on the side of the track and one of the double wheels at the back caught a stone and the back of the truck bucked a little. Then everybody shouted at me to stop. I got out of the truck and saw a body lying on the track behind. It was the stranger who had been sitting on the side, having ignored my warning, and lost his balance when the truck jolted. The back wheels had gone over his head and killed him.

We loaded the body onto the back of the truck and drove to the Police Station in Nanyuki. The police took my statement and that of some of the game scouts who were on the truck. The police officer recognised the dead person and told me that this same Wanderobo had just been released from prison after serving eighteen months for stock theft. I was even more surprised to learn that the Wanderobo had stolen an ox from our family farm at Timau and that Albert had tracked the ox and two cattle thieves for twenty miles into the Wanderobo reserve where he found it slaughtered and cut up. Someone saw my brother approaching and gave the alarm signal to all present who ran away. Albert scratched his initials on the water containers he found and then took the head of the beast and hid it. He walked back to the farm, arriving late at night. The next morning he called the police who came and searched the *manyattas* close to where the beast had been slaughtered. They found the water container that Albert had initialled. After questioning the owners, they got the names of the cattle thieves and the police were able to arrest them. One was sentenced to three years hard labour and the other to eighteen months. This was the very same man who had just been released and was on his way back home when he had the misfortune to meet up with me.

During another visit to the family farm, Albert showed me the skin of a leopard he had shot. He had been driving the jeep at the back of the farm and stopped to examine something when he heard a pig squealing. He took his rifle and proceeded in the direction of the noise that appeared to be coming from a hole. He heard grunting and then saw the tip of a leopard's tail. The leopard was having a tug-of-war with the pig and was in the process of pulling it out of the hole. The leopard had its front claws in the pig's head and every time he pulled and grunted the pig squealed. Albert stood over the hole with his rifle ready and when the leopard had exposed most of his body, Albert shot it and pulled both the leopard and the pig out. The pig was a fully grown male warthog.

Warthog, when they retreat into their holes, always turn around and back into the hole, facing out towards any pursuer. The leopard must have gone in after the pig and hooked its claws into the warthog's head to pull it out.

I went back to the Hind's ranch, where I had previously shot some giraffe, to shoot buffalo. The area the buffalo lived in was fairly open compared to what I was accustomed to. It was very easy shooting and I shot over sixty buffalo in three weeks which satisfied the owner, Douglas Hind.

Black leopard (melanistic) or dark leopard live on Mount Kenya and the Aberdare Mountain ranges. I came across them on occasion while hunting in the forest areas. Once, on the Siriman River track on Mount Kenya, my buffalo pack treed a leopard near where I was camping. I was able to approach close enough to observe it through my binoculars and see that it was a female. After a good look I called the dogs off and let the leopard go on her way. On several occasions I saw black leopard on the forest tracks in both mountain areas. A farmer at Nyeri shot one in the forest and showed me the skin. The coat was very dark but the faint lines of the rosettes could be seen. The Game Department Headquarters had one on their wall which had been shot at Meru on Mount Kenya.

Hyena (the large spotted variety) were always a problem in the settled areas, mainly because they were stock killers. We used strychnine on most of them which was very effective. However, where inexperienced people tried to poison a hyena and it survived, that animal often became wary and would not touch poison baits nor would it go near any carcasses put out with traps. I found that too much poison made the hyena vomit and in most cases it recovered so I used gelatin capsules filled with strychnine and inserted these into a lump of meat. Generally I made a drag (a carcass towed behind a vehicle) for a couple of miles in the area where the hyena tracks were seen and left marked poison baits at intervals along the drag. These I put down at dusk and picked up at first light, so as not to poison eagles or vultures.

We eventually resorted to tracking one hyena which refused all poison and avoided all of our traps. It had already killed quite a few milk cows and the farmer was getting desperate. I camped on the farm and went out every day looking for tracks and beating up likely looking bush thickets. Success eluded us until one night when there was a heavy rain. When the rain stopped the next morning, we went out and met the farmer, who reported that the hyena had killed another cow. We proceeded to the kill and found that this hyena had pulled down a big Friesland cow by ripping out its backside and udder and then, when the animal was exhausted and collapsed on the ground, the hyena had taken it by the throat and killed it.

The soft muddy ground was full of hyena tracks. This animal was a loner and, judging by the tracks, very big. After a while we found its tracks and easily followed them. The animal headed for the thick patches of riverine bush on the Ausso Nyiro River. There were ten game scouts with me, all armed with .303 rifles. I placed some of the scouts where they could see the hyena if it broke cover and the other scouts, together with some labourers, were placed in a "sweep". We tried to flush the hyena and it broke past one scout at close range. He fired but only wounded the animal so we followed the blood spoor and eventually lost the trail. The animal kept going and we gave up the chase. There were no further complaints or cattle killings in the area, so I assumed that the hyena had died of its wounds.

Game scouts with the dog pack crossing a river on Mount Kenya during a buffalo hunt.

Sirimon Track on Mount Kenya at 12,500 feet

Jacky Barrah (game warden) with my daughter, Elizabeth, and myself

Wanyahoro - head game scout and later head gun bearer and my right-hand man

In uniform for Mau Mau operations

FOUR

MAU MAU I

In October 1952 the Mau Mau uprising erupted. It had been simmering for some time and the white settlers were expecting something to happen. I was staying with my brother Albert on the farm when early one morning a neighbouring farmer, Ken McDougall Robertson, drove up. He was very upset and agitated, and the first words he uttered were, "The Mau Mau have attacked my farm and hamstrung all my animals. I need help to put down the animals to stop them from further suffering. Will you come over?" Albert and I took our rifles and went to the farm. The scene of carnage was appalling. Cattle and sheep were standing around with their back leg tendons cut, unable to move. Along with other neighbours who also arrived to help, we put the animals out of their misery.

The police from Nanyuki arrived and cast around for Mau Mau tracks which they found and followed. These led back towards Nanyuki and over the Siriman River to a neighbour's labour camp. The owner of the farm was Munro. The officer-in-charge searched the huts, looking for weapons which might have been used for the cowardly attack on the animals. In one hut the officer was attacked by an African who came at him with a knife. The officer was forced to shoot and killed him. The rest of the labourers, especially those whose clothes showed blood stains, were rounded up and likely weapons covered with blood were confiscated.

Not long after this, Mau Mau forest gangs came out and attacked remote homesteads. They killed quite a few farmers, many of whom I knew. These gangs were cowardly and extremely cruel in the way they went about their evil deeds. They spared neither women nor children. They even attacked their own kind, especially the ones who refused to go along with them, women and children included. The victims were usually hacked to death with *pangas* or *machetes*.

To start with, the Mau Mau had very few guns and relied on weapons stolen from the homesteads. Occasionally they raided police stations. Many were the servants in private homes, even in Nairobi and some of the bigger towns, who bided their time and when it was right, stole their employers' weapons. A great number had taken the Mau Mau oath, unknown to the employer, which was both a terrible ritual and binding tie. They may have worked in a particular household for years and were trusted entirely even with the children. Yet these so-called trustees turned on them with *pangas*.

When a gang appeared on a farm they were often harboured by the labourers and probably fed on numerous occasions as well. When they decided that the time was right to do away with the owners, they enlisted the help of the house servants, who led them in, usually during the evening meal. There was one such occasion when two bachelors were sitting at the table waiting for the servant to bring in the soup. The men duly appeared and threw the scalding liquid in their faces. It burnt their faces and eyes and before they recovered from the shock, the gang rushed in and hacked them to death.

A man named John owned a farm on the Aberdares. One night he and his wife heard calls outside and looked through the window of the upstairs bedroom. The grounds were floodlit and a barbed wire fence surrounded their dwelling. On the grass lawn they saw their headman with some labourers holding a prisoner who was trussed up with rope. The labourers informed John they had captured a Mau Mau who came in asking for food. John foolishly let himself out through the front door and walked across to the group, who at once set upon him with *pangas* and killed him. They then went into the house and killed his wife and young son. Then they fled into the forest to join the forest gang.

There was a story about an Italian working at a sawmill above Karatina on Mount Kenya. He reported to the police that he had seen the tracks of a gang on one of the logging roads. The labourers at the mill were aware that he contacted the police and reported it to the gang when they came in, along with the other labourers, for food. One morning the Italian went to work at the mill which was situated across a small valley from his house. While he was there he heard screams and shots coming from his home. He tried to run back to the house but was shot at and forced to flee. When the police or security forces arrived they found his wife, daughter and son, aged twelve and thirteen, dead. They had been hacked up, as was the African servant whose severed head was stuffed into the woman's stomach which had been disembowelled. The Italian became demented and was sent back to Italy.

42

Not all attacks were successful, and in some cases the tables were turned on the attackers. In one instance a couple, who farmed on the Aberdares, were attacked one night by the notorious leader of a large gang. Fortunately the couple were well prepared and proceeded to fight back. The house was built of stone and this stopped the bullets from penetrating. The gang managed to get into the house and tried to rush down the long, narrow passage. However the man was lying prone, armed with a double barrelled 12 gauge shotgun and each attempt to rush down the passage was met with a hail of buckshot which accounted for quite a few. The man had two shotguns and his wife reloaded as fast as he fired. The attackers even climbed onto the roof and tried to roll hand grenades down the chimney, but fortunately, these exploded harmlessly. At the same time this courageous couple managed to set off flares in order to alert the army post below to the attack. Assistance eventually arrived in Land Rovers and the gang fled, leaving behind quite a few dead without achieving their goal.

Two spinsters who lived in an isolated homestead near Nyeri were both security conscious and always locked their doors and kept pistols strapped to their sides. One night they were nearly caught off guard by their servants. One lady unlocked the door leading from the kitchen so that the two servants could serve their evening meal. They then went to the dining room table and sat down. The first servant arrived with the dinner dishes and one lady noticed that the servant seemed nervous and that his hands were shaking, so she said to her companion, "Watch out, be on your guard!" Her words were hardly uttered when in burst a Mau Mau gang accompanied by the other servant. Both women had their pistols out and commenced firing. One went to the aid of the other who was at grips with a couple of terrorists. She fired at them and shot both but unfortunately shot their pet dog, who was also trying to help. The rest of the gang fled when they realised they had lost the advantage of surprise and saw their fellow men go down. The two women noticed the toilet door was locked and ordered the person inside to come out. When he did not emerge, they proceeded to fire several shots through the door. They then set off an alarm to notify the security forces who duly arrived to find three or four bodies in the homestead. When they forced the bathroom door open they found blood spattered around but the window was open and the person in hiding had departed through the opening. They believed it was the other servant who they never saw again.

I was a member of the Police Reserve and from time to time was called on to do patrols in the forest looking for Mau Mau. Some of the patrols lasted for ten days. We all carried backpacks which included food and two blankets. In those days we did not have lightweight sleeping bags. It was always bitterly cold at night high up in the forest and the blankets were totally inadequate, so we also built a big fire and lay next to it. However, even that did not work very well because I got warm on one side and cold on the other. Initially when the heat was high, I slept quite a distance from the fire but as the flames died down and it got cooler, I moved closer. I never had a good night's sleep. One night Dougie, a member of our party, had most of his big beard burnt off when he got too close to the fire and it caught alight. We were all awakened in the middle of the night to hear him cursing while he tried to get hot coals out of his beard. Afterwards he had to trim his beard because it was lopsided. During another night a rhino came right up to the fire and woke us when he started puffing and snorting as he spun around and trotted off among the trees. He had walked right up to the fire with all the bodies lying around – I guess out of curiosity – and must have got a whiff of human odour which upset him.

In the early days of the emergency we did not put sentries out at night as most Mau Mau were poorly armed and ran away from the security forces whenever they were encountered. Later all this changed.

On one such jaunt I had to shoot a rhino which charged us at very close range. The rifle I carried was a .30-06 loaded with armour piercing bullets which were as good as solids for penetration. The area we patrolled had many elephant, rhino and buffalo, and we were always walking into them. I was never sure how the animals would react. Most of the time they went crashing off into the undergrowth but there was always the risk that one might charge the party.

On this occasion I was leading a group of about eight. We were going through short, thick bamboo where the visibility was only a few yards, and we were trying to move as quietly as possible which is difficult in that type of vegetation. I came to the edge of a small clearing in time to see a rhino bull stand up and face us. He obviously heard us moving through the foliage. The tick birds flew up and he stood with his big ears moving around trying to establish our exact whereabouts. A rhino's eyesight is very poor and he relies mostly on his hearing and scenting ability for protection against human enemies. Tick birds also warn him of the approach of humans.

The rest of the patrol bunched up against me in an effort to see what had caught my attention. I had slowly gone down on one knee and held the rifle ready. I realised I was hemmed in by the others and was hoping that the rhino would go the other way when suddenly he made his mind up and came straight for us. There was no option but to shoot. I fired the first shot into his chest, which turned him slightly at about five yards, and quickly

44

reloaded. As he brushed past, I fired the second shot into his side, whereupon he collapsed, dying behind us. Had I not fired he would have trampled us and there would have been quite a few injuries.

Of all the big forest animals I was the most wary of black rhino. I found that I could never be sure of how they were going to behave. I often observed them pick up our scent on a trail we had walked and follow it much as a dog would. Because of their unpredictable nature, many rhino were injured by the security forces during the Mau Mau uprising.

One such beast came out of the Nyeri Forest, attacked some cows and then went on looking for something else to accost. About this time, a retired army colonel serving in the Police Reserve was driving out of Nyeri back to his small farm. He was driving a Ford panel van with two bucket seats in front. He met two Police Reserve Asian Sikhs who were doing wireless duties. They were all going in the same direction so he offered them a lift. One got in next to him and the other sat at the back. After driving a few miles they came around a corner and found the narrow road blocked by a car which had been abandoned with both front doors open but no sign of the occupants. The irritated colonel pressed the car hooter several times, annoyed that people would be so careless as to leave a car in the middle of the road. Next he heard shouting from the nearby tree tops, "WATCH OUT FOR THE RHINO!" With that there was an almighty crash, the back door of the van crumbled inwards and the whole front of a rhino suddenly appeared breathing down their necks. Its two front feet shattered the flimsy wooden floor boards in the back of the truck and there he was stuck!

One Sikh went through the open window over the colonel without any visible effort and the other went out the second window without opening the door. The colonel managed to get the door open and got out of the van, which was rocking with the movements of the infuriated rhino. There were more shouts from the trees saying, "UP HERE!" He saw two women up a tree and proceeded to join them post-haste.

While the rhino was engaged with the car, one of the women climbed down, dashed up the road to a nearby farm house and phoned the police who sent a Land Rover. The canopy had been removed and the windscreen was folded down over the bonnet. The car bristled with guns and was loaded with police. It screeched to a stop in a cloud of dust. By then the rhino had managed to extricate itself from the back of the van and retired into the bush next to the road.

When the Land Rover stopped, the people in the trees all shouted at once, "WATCH OUT FOR THE RHINO!" With that the rhino charged out again and got his horn under the side of the Land Rover. He turned the vehicle over and dumped all the passengers on the road. A police sergeant grabbed a Bren gun and proceeded to fill the rhino with lead where it collapsed on the spot. The rhino was found to have been wounded by shrapnel splinter, most probably from mortar bombs.

One day I was visiting Albert on the farm when our neighbours, Reggie and Doris Smart, turned up. They asked me to deal with a leopard that was getting into their chicken run and killing many birds. It was late in the day with not much time before dark so I took a steel jaw trap with me to catch the leopard. I disliked using jaw traps for leopard or lion because these animals quite often managed to escape from them. I preferred instead to use an old worn out rifle and arrange a set gun which usually worked better.

We inspected the previous night's carnage, checked that the tracks were made by a leopard, then collected all the dead birds and dumped them in the place we selected as suitable for the trap. We built a thorn bush enclosure around the dead birds and left one small entrance where we placed the steel jaw trap. This we attached by a short chain to a weighty piece of wood so that the leopard would only be able to drag it with great effort. It is not a good policy to attach the chain to something firm as the animal could then pull against it and extricate itself from the jaws. Reggie and Doris had quarrelled and were occupying different houses about two hundred yards apart. They had two enormous Irish wolf hounds which Doris kept with her at night. I warned her to keep them locked up in the house and under no circumstances to let them out until I arrived the following day to unset the trap.

At first light the next morning, we heard a car speeding up with its hooter sounding. Albert and I came out in our dressing gowns to see Reggie arrive. As soon as he saw us he shouted, "COME QUICKLY! COME QUICKLY! DORIS HAS BEEN EATEN!" or words to that effect. He drove off as rapidly as he had arrived. We snatched our rifles and followed as quickly as possible. When we arrived at their place, we heard the two wolf hounds baying down by the river and proceeded in that direction to find that the dogs had the leopard up a tree. I had a 8 x 60S rifle with me and shot it.

We returned to the house to find the good people in the lounge doctoring the night watchman. They had him in an armchair and he was still dressed in an army greatcoat. They explained what had happened. The night watchman heard the leopard performing after it was caught in the trap and he went to Doris's house to tell her. As she opened the door, the two dogs pushed past her and dashed up to the chicken run. They had obviously also heard the leopard. The night watchman ran after the dogs, who by this time, had dashed straight in and attacked the leopard. The watchman arrived

46

outside the enclosure as the leopard scaled the wire mesh with the trap attached to its foot, dragging the chain and piece of wood. It landed on top of the watchman, flattening him to the ground but fortunately the greatcoat saved him from serious injury. The dogs then chased the leopard off. Meanwhile Doris was legging it across to the house where Reggie lived. She hammered on the door because he had locked it. (It was the beginning of the Mau Mau emergency.) He stumbled to the door and had just unlocked it when the leopard, having shaken off the trap, arrived with the dogs in pursuit. Doris dived into the house and slammed the door in the leopard's face. I saw where both the leopard and dogs skidded on the driveway outside the door. I never asked Reggie why he had said Doris had been eaten. They were obviously unaccustomed to such unusual excitement in their daily lives.

During 1952 and 1953 I spent more time on police duty, mainly tracking Mau Mau gangs. In addition I continued control work for the Game Department. During these tracking patrols we usually looked for signs of gang activity close to the African labour huts and on trails high up in forests above human settlement areas. The gangs received food from the local farm labourers. In the dry season, when the earth was too hard to show tracks and the ground was covered in knee-high dead grass, a man walking through it bent the grass slightly so that it was at a different angle to the surrounding grass. If you looked directly down you did not notice the difference; but if you looked ahead and moved about until you had the right angle, you could see the trail as clearly as a footpath. Very early in the morning after a heavy dew, any passage of bodies over grass would also show clearly and was easy to follow.

The gangs did not like to leave their tracks on bare ground when they moved around. If there was a pathway, they stepped to the side of it. By looking carefully we could see where they had pressed the grass flat. When we saw this evidence we knew they were Mau Mau tracks and not those of law-abiding citizens. The forest areas above were closed to everybody except the security forces, so any tracks or signs of people (other than military or police) moving around were suspect. On the forest trails Mau Mau food carriers sometimes left faint signs of maize meal which trickled onto the ground as a result of holes in their bags. On two occasions I tracked food carriers in this way.

Once we followed a trail leading away from some native huts on the farm belonging to the Munro family whom I mentioned earlier. The trail led straight up Mount Kenya to the bamboo level. We eventually found ourselves in a big camp and by the number of fires, the food and various items of equipment scattered around, we knew this was a big gang. While looking around we heard tapping noises coming from the nearby stream and made our way, as quietly as possible, towards the sound. We found three gang members working on the construction of homemade weapons. These were usually made out of water pipes and various cartridges could be fired through them. The striker mechanism was very crude: a nail propelled by rubber inner tubing to hit the primer to ignite the cartridge. These guns were effective only at point blank range and most were adapted to firing 12 gauge shotgun shells. The effect of homemade guns was more demoralising than physically damaging.

We challenged the three, who had not observed us. They got up and started to run so we opened fire. One died on the spot but the other two disappeared into the bamboo. We quickly located a blood spoor and shortly afterwards came across a second man breathing his last. Then we heard shooting in the direction from which we had come. Some of our party had stayed back while I and two members of the force had followed the blood trail. We knew that the main group of Mau Mau were doing the firing because after each volley we heard a voice shouting commands in Swahili (obviously the leader). They were also blowing whistles and a military-type bugle. We decided to approach in a circular movement and come upon the gang from the side. While we were doing this the shooting stopped. When we came out of the bamboo onto a ridge, we were met with a hail of bullets which whistled past our heads. The gang had retired to the top of the ridge and were lying low to see what we would do. We ducked behind a rock and decided to make our way back to rejoin our companions as being separated had weakened our position. The others were below us in the bamboo and we joined them shortly.

The gang, still shooting and blowing whistles and bugles, had come a little closer. We were not carrying much ammunition and were now short, having fired at the three gunsmiths. The enemy obviously had a lot, judging by the amount that they were expending, so we pulled out. Behind us was a very steep incline, almost a cliff, but we managed, with a lot of slipping and sliding, to climb out. The shooting and shouting went on for ages after we reached the top and left.

We returned with a larger force and found that the gang had fled, after retrieving their belongings. We found out later that this was the so-called General China's gang. He often fought against security forces and was eventually wounded and captured. The forest gang leaders often gave themselves fancy names such as General Kimbo, General Kargo and Brigadier Simba.

I had a call to deal with the leopard on Kane's Farm on the Aberdares mountain. The higher part of the farm bordered on the bamboo at about 8,000 feet above sea level. They had a lot of dairy cattle and from the milk and cream they produced products such as powdered milk and cheese. Leopard were killing their calves. Incidentally, leopard in this area grow to enormous sizes and many record book trophies have been taken by sportsmen. At a later date I shot one which measured eight feet three inches.

When I arrived at the homestead, I was shown where the leopard had attacked the calves and I set a gun, using one of the calves as bait. At dusk I loaded the gun and cocked the mechanism. This I did warily as I liked the gun to fire at the slightest pressure on the wire, which was pegged down between two posts. The rifle was secured high up between two posts with the barrel pointing to the ground. Should the leopard push its head through the gap between the posts, it would push against the wire and set the gun off. The wire was attached to a piece of wood. One end went through the trigger guard and exerted pressure on the trigger so that any pressure on the wire would pull on the wood and cause the rifle to fire.

Next morning, accompanied by two game scouts, I inspected the trap and found a dead leopard whose hind quarters had been eaten by another leopard. This sort of cannibalism was most unusual. The skin had been ruined and we didn't even trouble with what was left. I camped quite close by and that night another leopard came prowling around the camp. I had a few of the buffalo dog pack with me and they bayed the leopard in the bush nearby. I picked up my double barrelled .470 and a torch and, not knowing what the barking dogs were holding in the bush, approached cautiously. When I appeared, the dogs went into a frenzy and tried to get hold of the leopard, which made a dash straight towards me. It came so quickly that all I saw was something dark flash by too close for comfort and it was so fast I did not even get a shot off. It was indistinguishable from the dogs and I was afraid of shooting a dog by mistake.

Everything rushed by and the dogs put the leopard up a tree. I was close behind and shined the spotlight into the tree and saw the leopard sitting in a fork. It was a three-quarter grown black leopard. I decided against shooting it and had great difficulty in calling the dogs off. They were very reluctant to leave. I left the farm the next day and had no more complaints about leopard from them.

The same month I had to deal with a leopard that killed two Cairn terriers in the grounds of a farm house. The servants set a wire snare and caught the leopard but as the wire was not strong enough, it struggled, broke the snare and escaped. A couple of hours later it was heard trying to get into the chicken house. The next night the leopard climbed onto the roof of the house and chased a roosting peacock into the garden, where it eventually caught and ate the bird. I shot the leopard the following night and when we skinned it, we found peacock feathers in its stomach.

Meanwhile, we arrested a gang of poachers whom we had been after for months. They hunted with dog packs and had shotguns as well as spears. They even speared buffalo that the dogs had bayed and this took quite a lot of courage. It would not have been too bad if they had restricted their killings to the nuisance animals, but with them everything was fair game, even eland and bongo. They had a lion trap which we confiscated, and later on was the cause of an unfortunate happening at the Game Department headquarters in Nanyuki.

The game scouts cultivated potatoes and various vegetables next to our house. Being close to the forest, porcupine and bush pig started to come in during the night and their damage became a nuisance. Without telling me, the game scouts took the lion trap and set it up where the animals were coming in.

One evening I went out with my wife, Jock. Elizabeth, our 6 year old daughter, was with us. She had seen the staff set the trap and when we got close to the place she said, "Let me show you where the trap has been set for the porcupines." It crossed my mind that they would use wire snares. I never thought it would be a lion trap. Elizabeth ran forward and the next thing we heard a metallic clang. She put her foot into the trap and it caught her around the ankle. Jock and I ran forward and tried to release her but I had a lot of difficulty opening the jaws. Elizabeth was not making much noise. I expected her to be screaming as it must have been very painful. She even tried to tell us which lever to press to release the trap. Eventually we released her and, after giving her medical attention, rushed to Nanyuki Cottage Hospital, twelve miles away. There the local doctor gave her a tetanus injection and cleaned out the two wounds caused by the teeth of the trap. The teeth had gone into both sides of her ankle very deeply but miraculously missed damaging any nerves or big blood vessels. She recovered very quickly and was out of hospital in a few days. She has the scars to this day.

I launched a poisoning campaign near Naro Moru on Mount Kenya because the farmers were complaining about packs of hyena attacking their stock. We used strychnine in meat and baited along trails close to the forest wherever we saw their tracks. Afterwards we found about twenty bodies and this stopped the hyenas' stock killing activities.

While in the area, I received a request from Captain O'Hagen to deal with a rogue buffalo that had gored a herdsman. Wanyahoro and I took the dog pack to the area in which the buffalo had frequently been seen. After trying a few likely patches of thick bush with no luck, we eventually came to another patch which did not look promising but we nonetheless released the dogs and very soon heard them baying the buffalo. Wanyahoro and I went in and as we got close there was a grunt. Wanyahoro, who was in front of me, suddenly put his .375 up and fired at point blank range at the beast which burst out of the bushes onto him. The buffalo hit his rifle barrel and knocked him to the ground. As it brushed past me, I fired into its neck and put it down. The buffalo was very old and both horns had been broken close to its head, which made it look odd. Wanyahoro's bullet hole was near the ear with powder burn marks around the hole. The bullet penetrated backwards and missed the immediate vitals. My shot broke its neck. We also dug out what looked like a .303 bullet in its hind quarters. The old wound appeared to have been inflicted a couple of years back and had healed.

Wanyahoro and I had a similar experience with a rhino on Colonel Sutcliffe's farm near the Nyeri Forest. He asked us to shoot a rhino which had gored quite a few of his cattle and had made a habit of breaking into the cattle enclosures and stampeding the animals. We had gone a few miles with Wanyahoro in the lead doing the tracking, when he came to a thick bush and put his arm out to move a heavily foliaged branch aside. There was a loud noise and the rhino charged out puffing and snorting. Wanyahoro fired in its face and dived sideways. I was suddenly confronted by the rhino and fired both barrels of the heavy rifle whereupon I was relieved to see it go down.

51

En route to the coast I visited Tsavo National Park and saw many good tuskers.

FIVE

MAU MAU II

I was still on call to do police duties when one day I found myself, with my brother Albert and five other Europeans, tracking a Mau Mau gang that had wiped out a police post on the Ngare Ndare escarpment. This gang, we were told, had killed a police sergeant and two constables. They had looted the post and taken one constable prisoner and two women from the camp to carry all their goods. From this raid they had managed to get all the .303 rifles that were issued to the people manning the station.

Our tracking party consisted of seven Europeans and three Africans (one was a police tracker from the Turkana tribe). We all carried packs and prepared to stay out for a few days. The first day we followed the gang down the Ngare Ndare escarpment and then parallel to the Ngare Ndare River. The Mau Mau were brushing the trail, trying to hide their tracks, and occasionally splitting up and then converging further along. However the ground was sandy and we were able to follow without too much trouble.

The tracks suddenly left the river and headed up the escarpment, twenty miles from where we originally came down. Climbing up the steep trails was heavy going. The day was very hot and after leaving the river we realised that it was necessary to conserve our water. Near the top of the escarpment we found a Wanderobo *manyatta* (cattle and sheep enclosure with dome shaped huts plastered with cattle dung and mud). It was getting dark so we decided to stay there for the night. After relieving ourselves of the packs, which we put down in the thorn enclosure, we noticed a fire burning across the valley. Thinking that it might be the gang, we decided to investigate. We left one game scout and the police tracker with our kit and made our way across to the fire which could be seen quite clearly. It took about thirty minutes to cross the valley and when we arrived on the other side, we found another *manyatta* but this one was occupied by a

Wanderobo and his family. We questioned them about the Mau Mau but they had not seen anybody. In the dark, we headed back to where we would spend the night.

We were met by the two men who remained behind. They were very excited and could hardly speak. Eventually, we learnt that the entire Mau Mau gang had trooped past the *manyatta* without stopping. Fortunately, the two men remained quiet and were not seen by the gang. Against the skyline, our men saw the silhouetted heads and shoulders of the whole gang, as well as those of their prisoners.

Back along the trail the Mau Mau had turned off the path we were following and had lain up in a gully. As it was getting dark and cattle had obliterated the tracks, this escaped our attention. We decided to try to pick up the trail the following morning.

After a restless sleep on the hard ground, we quickly brewed tea and coffee, chewed some hard biscuits and took up the trail once more. The ground soon became much flatter and easy to walk on and we made good progress. It was easy to follow the gang as their passage through the high grass could be seen without much trouble. Now and then we lost the tracks. When this happened, we stationed members of the party who could not track on the spot where the last sign could be seen. The rest of the party then scouted ahead, looking for signs, and the person finding the tracks signaled the others. All this was done as quietly as possible, preferably with hand signals or a faint hiss. In thick bush this was essential in order not to warn the enemy if they happened to be close by. By mid-morning we came to a cattle enclosure owned by Will Powys and found the carcass of a steer which had been slaughtered and the meat had been removed.

The herdsman was nowhere to be seen. We found out later that he had been taken prisoner and had to carry some of the meat. At midday a police airplane flew over and we were able to communicate with it via our wireless transmitter. We suspected that the gang would lie up in a deep valley about ten miles ahead (this valley was situated on our family ranch) and requested that reinforcements be placed as a stop line close to the valley on the far side ahead of the gang. At 3 o'clock we came to the base of some low bush and tree-covered hills situated on the ranch. Beyond lay the valley in which we suspected the gang would be hiding. This was the area where, a few years back, I shot the bull buffalo with our bull terrier attached to its nose. Albert and I were both familiar with this whole area.

We came out on top of the hills overlooking the wide valley. It was likely that the gang would stop here during the daylight hours. Both sides of the slopes had thick patches of cedar trees with dense bush growing underneath. Between the patches of trees and bush was open grassland. We expected the gang to be hiding in one of these bush patches probably in a spot from which they had a commanding view of the surrounding country. When we reached a spot from which the entire valley could be seen, we glassed the area hoping to find something. Soon one of our men spotted a faint bit of smoke rising from a patch of bush below. This excited everybody as it could only be the people we were after.

This area of the ranch was not in use so there were not supposed to be any humans around. It was at the back of the property about ten miles from our homestead. We threw our packs to the ground and had a quick discussion on how to tackle the opposition. The party split into two groups: one group was to approach from the left and come in from the back while the other was to keep on the tracks and make a more or less direct approach. I was with the party making the direct approach and Albert was with the other group. We gave them time to complete their manoeuvre and then started to move forward. About two hundred yards short of our target we ran out of cover and were trying to decide what to do next when a short burst of automatic fire punctuated the silence.

With that the whole gang burst out of the patch of bush we suspected they were hiding in. Most were dressed in stolen police uniforms and blue greatcoats. They came out running away from us. Everybody fired at the running forms and I saw one man go down, then get up and carry on. I found myself running with Albert and one other member of our party who was a local farmer doing police reserve duty. We followed the direction of the flight down the slope towards the bottom of the valley. I was leading and stopped about 200 yards above the bottom of the slope to observe the bed of the valley and the opposite slope in the hopes of picking up any movement. Suddenly the gang filed out just below me. They had obviously joined up again. Most were dressed in police greatcoats and a couple even wore the bright red tarboosh that the police used on ceremonial occasions. I carefully sighted on the leader and fired. Nobody fell but they immediately scattered, spurred on no doubt by our sporadic firing. We kept it up until they were out of sight. I saw one stumble and fall. We approached the spot at which we had been firing but did not see any blood, so we headed back to the area where the gang was put to flight. Along the way we picked up various items of equipment dropped by the gang in their hasty flight. We found one body and signs of blood from another that I had seen fall and get up. Lying on the ground was a rifle with its stock smashed from the fall.

Albert narrowly escaped being shot by the leader of the gang. He and his party made better progress than our group and when they approached the patch of bush, Albert was leading and John Randall was just behind. Suddenly John saw a man put up a rifle and aim at Albert. John stepped out to one side of Albert and fired a burst with his Sten gun. The automatic fired two shots and then jammed, a common fault with this type of weapon.

The man at whom John shot went down. Everybody rushed forward into the hideout where they found some of the prisoners who were delighted to be rescued. The prisoners told our party that the dead man was the leader of the gang who had repeatedly told them that tomorrow was their last day. He had suddenly got up and told everybody to pack up. He picked up a rifle and said he was going to look around before they moved off. He walked out and saw Albert and his party only a few yards away at the edge of the bush. That was when he was shot.

The gang somehow never ran into the stop line and got away as darkness fell. The army and police combed the area and found more equipment dropped along the trail of flight. Three days later they picked up a wounded gangster who had crawled off and was hiding in a thick patch of bush. He had been shot in the leg which had to be amputated below the knee. I rather suspected that he was shot in the last action between Albert, myself and the farmer.

A couple of weeks later we heard that a gang had raided the labour line below the Mawingo Hotel (*mawingo* means cloud in Swahili). This gang shot a couple of labourers, took several prisoners with them and headed into the forest. The next day one of the prisoners showed up with an incredible story to tell. After travelling for a couple of hours, he was ordered to lie down on his back and one of the gang members jammed a pistol into his mouth and fired. He knew no more until he regained consciousness and found himself down an ant-bear hole. He managed to crawl out, stumbled down the mountain slope to the nearest settlement and later told his story to the police. The bullet miraculously missed all the vitals and the gang left him for dead.

The Army and police parties searched without success for a couple more days. To begin with, they followed tracks which clearly led up the mountain but eventually they lost all sign of the gang. One morning I received a telephone call from Operation Headquarters in Nanyuki asking me to lead a party of police reservists and the army back into the area to try to find the gang.

I took a pack containing a sleeping bag, food for three or four days, and a good supply of ammunition. I carried a Beretta sub-machine gun which fired 9 mm Parabellum ammunition. The magazine held forty rounds and I carried three or four spare magazines. Also in the pack was a light rain coat

Albert and Game Warden Jacky Barrah on Mount Kenya during the Mau Mau Emergency

Rodney Elliott and Don Bousfield during the Mau Mau - 1952

Mount Kenya

Game scouts with dogs during a buffalo hunt - Kamino is in the foreground

and a heavy wool pullover, as well as a spare change of socks. The nights got cold and there was a possibility of rain. I had with me a game scout who was a good tracker. His name was Seruni and he came from the Samburu tribe. In Nanyuki I met members of the police who were to accompany me. Several black army personnel from the King's African Rifles (K.A.R.) were back up fire in case we ran into heavy opposition.

In due course a truck transported us high up on the slopes of Mount Kenya. We used the Sirimon Track which had been built by the army engineers at the start of the emergency. It went all the way up the mountain, through the forest and bamboo and onto the moorlands to a height of about 13,000 feet. I started our search from a point beyond and above where the police lost the tracks of the gang. This placed us well up in the bamboo which started at 7,600 feet.

We left the truck and, with the packs on our backs and carrying our weapons, took off into the forest and bamboo. I led with a couple of trackers and the police and army followed in single file. The contour line we were following crossed the mountain and eventually led well above the area the army and police had been searching.

Progress was slow as we had to cross several deep valleys and rivers which coursed down the mountain. Most of the time we were in thick bamboo, trying to follow the elephant and game trails traversing the slopes. Over many centuries the elephant had made well-worn paths as they followed the easier gradients across the valleys. Sometimes these paths were unusable and we slipped and slid through the bamboo down some steep slopes. We encountered elephant, buffalo, rhino and giant forest hog several times, but usually they got our scent or heard us and made off in the opposite direction.

Night fell and we found a suitable clearing in which to camp. After eating a meal of tinned foods and drinking tea brewed over a small fire, we bedded down. Two of the party were detailed to stand watch at intervals and during the night the watch was changed.

Next morning, after another quick meal and a brew of tea or coffee, we again pushed our way through the bamboo, continuing in the same direction as the previous day. Whenever we came to any likely places, we looked carefully for tracks. We paid particular attention to the game tracks which went along the top of ridges.

At about 2 o'clock we came up a slope to the top of a ridge and started to look for tracks. Suddenly Seruni gave a low whistle and indicated that he had seen something. I walked over and he pointed to a track barely visible on the hard ground. We looked around and came across more signs which we followed up the ridge to higher ground. After going a couple of hundred yards, we realised we were onto the gang. We went another mile, still high up the mountain slope in the bamboo area and came out into a clearing with tall cedar trees and low growing bush or weed-like plants between them. These plants produced a purple flower which later went to seed and if one happened to knock a branch when they were dry, very fine hair-like particles fell to the ground. In earlier hunting days I dislodged these hairs and was unlucky to get some in my eye. This became irritating and for a couple of days I had trouble sleeping because my eye felt as if there was sand under the lid. Luckily it cleared up after a while. Dispersed throughout the clearing were huge dead cedar trees which had fallen onto the ground with creepers and bush growing around them.

Not more than fifty yards through this clearing, Seruni, who was a few yards ahead of me, waved his arm and pointed ahead. I could see that he was excited and looked to see what had attracted his attention. One of the Askaris (army soldiers) at the back suddenly shouted, "*Faru*" which meant rhino. The Askari had mistaken a fallen tree which was the same colour as a rhino. His shout alerted the gang, who jumped up from where they had been lying down in front of us. I became aware that a man was aiming a gun at me and immediately ducked into a squatting position, which was fortunate, for he fired and hit the tree behind me. His shot went over my head and I was showered with bits of bark. After firing, he spun around and started to run away but before he disappeared into the bamboo, I managed to fire back. I continued firing for a few seconds and then, followed by the rest of our party, ran after the gang.

It was easy to follow the terrorists as they ran down the side of the slope through the low weeds which they flattened as if they were a herd of buffalo. A policeman ran with me and we came to a small stream at the bottom of the slope. I had a funny feeling or premonition that if we continued on the tracks, the man who had fired at me would have another go. So I stopped and quietly told my companion of my feelings, suggesting that we cut off to one side of the tracks and take a course parallel to the direction of the gang. We crossed the stream, left the tracks on our right, and proceeded up a slope covered in thick bamboo. We reached the top of the ridge and came to another clearing in which a woman was bending over a body. Seruni, who had caught up with us, ran forward and took the woman by the arm and held her. Women often formed part of the forest gangs to cook and carry food. The person on the ground was another woman who shortly breathed her last. The dead woman had caught one of the bullets meant for the terrorist who had fired at me. Suddenly, from behind and slightly to the right a shot rang out, followed a few moments later by another and then a third.

We turned back to rejoin our group and found them standing around an Askari, who was staggering around with blood spurting from his arm. The white policeman, experienced in first aid, ran forward, got hold of the Askari and made him lie down while he called for assistance. Two of us held the wounded man while the policeman quickly cut away the sleeve and put a tourniquet above the wound to stop the bleeding. The bone in his arm was completely shattered from the bullet which went right through it.

After dressing the wound and giving the man an injection of morphine, we found out what happened. The rest of the party behind us followed the tracks where we left off and had only gone a short distance through the bamboo when the leading white police reservist heard a bullet whistle past his ear. He fell to the ground and from the prone position looked up to see if he could see the person firing. Another bullet whistled past his head and he ducked. With that an Askari ran past him towards the terrorist. The third shot was fired at the Askari and the bullet cut a groove across the wood of his .303 rifle stock and ploughed into his arm.

We radioed Police Headquarters and asked that a truck be sent on a certain track to the forest edge where we would await the pick up and return to Nanyuki. We made a rough stretcher and carried the Askari down the mountain track to where we met the truck. The woman gang member made a statement to the police confirming this was the same gang that had raided the Ngare Ndare police post.

A few days later a routine police patrol led by Peter Rundgren, who was a police reservist and forest officer at Nanyuki Forest Station, was fired on at close range with an automatic weapon while they were following a wooded stream bed close to Nanyuki in the farming area. Nobody was hit. The area on both sides of the stream basin was open country so Peter left half his patrol behind to stop any gang members from fleeing. He then ran with the rest of the patrol across the open plain and re-entered the stream bed lower down, where he left the men with him to prevent the gang escaping downstream. He checked for tracks to make sure that the gang had not gone through but did not see any, so was satisfied that he had them trapped. As luck would have it, a police spotter plane happened to fly overhead and Peter managed to contact the pilot and request reinforcements. These duly arrived and proceeded to sweep through the stream bed area. Seven gang members were shot and two Lancaster sub-machine guns (which had been stolen in an earlier raid by terrorists on the Navaisha Police Station) were recovered along with one .303 rifle stolen from the Ngare Ndare Police Post.

The woman we captured earlier confirmed that one of the men who had been killed was carrying the .303 rifle and it was he who had fired at me in the skirmish.

A month or two later a gang raided a homestead on Sega Bastard's farm. Sega and his family were away at the time. The gang also attacked the house where the Seychelles' farm manager and his family were living, setting the house alight and firing on the occupants when they tried to get out. The whole family were burnt alive. The gang went into Sega Bastard's house and looted it. In due course, the Police arrived and at first light tracked the terrorists towards the forested slopes of Mount Kenya and, after several miles, crossed the railway line and main Naro Moru Nanyuki road.

I was asked to lead a group of police reservists and take over the tracking when the patrol reached the forest edge. This area was my old stamping ground and I knew it backwards. We had no great difficulty following the tracks even though the gang was using every ruse to hide them. They were stepping on tufts of grass, avoiding bare ground and brushing away their footprints, but this made it obvious and we knew what they were up to.

After several miles, we entered a thicker bush area broken up by *dongas* (dry water courses) with numerous high banks. Unfortunately for us, the gang had a sentry on lookout and he started to run. Our leading tracker spotted him and also started to run forward. We all followed and suddenly came on the gang's resting place. There was a lot of gear lying around, obviously abandoned in a hasty flight. Carrying on through the gang's camp, we followed the direction in which the terrorists seemed to be heading, eventually breaking out into more open country where clumps of bush dotted the ground. When part of our group spotted two gang members running across open ground, they opened fire and dropped both. I ran up and found the patrol standing around looking at one dead gang member. He was extremely ugly, with a broad face, light skin, thick lips, a flat nose and long braided hair hanging down in true Mau Mau style. He looked brutal and I knew that he would have shown no mercy towards anybody.

I often wondered whether he had the say in the murder of the Seychelles family and could not help thinking he got his just deserts. His clothes looked ridiculous: long black tails (looted from Sega Bastard's house) and several layers underneath, such as two shirts and two pairs of long trousers. Forest gangs often wore several layers of clothing, one on top of the other, to keep out the cold. Quite often they did not carry blankets and relied on their clothing for warmth. For fear of alerting the security forces in the area, the gangs did not often make fires at night. Smoke could be detected

60

for considerable distances in these high altitudes. The security forces often used light spotter planes at night to fly over the forest areas and look for fires. Early on in the emergency, Lincoln bombers dropped heavy bombs in areas where fires had been spotted but this achieved minimal results. More damage was done to game than to terrorists and eventually the practice was discontinued.

After a few years of living like animals in the forest, these gangs developed extraordinary senses. They never washed and to us stank to high heaven. However they could smell, from a considerable distance, the toilet soap used by the security force members and also cigarette smoke. They seemed immune to the cold and wet, and became exceptionally tough. The chaps who had spotted the terrorist running across the veld said that he looked quite ridiculous with the tails flapping behind him like a scarecrow. He managed to fire the rifle over his shoulder at the patrol while still running. The gang members' eyesight improved enabling them to follow a human track through the forest in daylight at a running pace. They were also used to carrying heavy loads even at high altitudes.

One gang member we had been after for a long time lived in a cave on the moorlands of Mount Kenya at 12,000 feet above sea level. Periodically he ventured down to the farms below and stole a merino sheep, which I am sure weighed between 120 and 150 pounds. He carried it across his shoulder right up to his hideaway in the moorlands. At high altitudes I was always short of breath and had great difficulty in keeping up any pace without a load on my shoulders! At that time I was young and very fit from all my many excursions on the mountain.

I was interviewed by a magazine correspondent and the following is quoted from his article:

"Another farmer game warden, Fred Bartlett, described a tracking case he'd been called on recently. An Italian resident in Kenya had been killed together with his wife and family. For the first fourteen miles, the trail of the gang was easy to follow. It was the dry season, the earth was too hard to show tracks, but the ground was covered with knee-high dead grass. When a man walks through this grass, he bends it at a slightly different angle than the grass around it. If you look directly down you do not notice the difference, but by looking ahead and moving about until you get the right angle, you can see the trail as clearly as a footpath.

After the raiders had crossed the open bush country and reached the forest, the tracking was harder, but we could still follow them by lifting bushes and finding tracks under the branches. The branches spring back after a man has gone through and don't leave any sign, but often you can

61

find tracks on the soft earth under them. We camped that night in the brush and went on at dawn. One hour in the early morning is worth four at any other time of the day, for we could see where they'd knocked dew off the bushes and grass.

At two o'clock that afternoon, our tracker pointed to the tracks with his chin – natives don't use their fingers to point. Bent blades of grass were still oozing juice. Then we came on a bit of saliva where a man had spat. It was still damp and, although strong breezes were blowing, no dust had settled on it. The raiders were just ahead.

We caught up with them in some thick stuff. One man was still wearing the dead Italian's coat. We started shooting and the MMs bolted. We got two but the rest escaped. Today we know more about the business and wouldn't have been so keen to rush it – we'd have spread out and surrounded them."

Six

Return to the Game Department

In October 1953, I was transferred to the Coast Province and took over from Don Bousfield. The area I controlled extended from the Somali border along the coast all the way to the Tanganyika border. Don took me up the north coast to the Tana River to familiarise me with the area. I was introduced to the District Commissioner at Kipini. As my wife was in a hospital in Nairobi, I had brought my eldest son Cecil, then six, and my daughter Elizabeth, aged five, with me. Richard, who was three years old, had been left behind in Malindi in the care of friends. While we were talking to the District Commissioner, a shot rang out and I dashed to the Land Rover to discover that Cecil had been fooling with my rifle which was in a gun rack at the back of the car. He had worked the bolt, pushed a round into the barrel and pressed the trigger, sending a bullet through the canvas roof of the Land Rover.

We then drove through Witu, left the Land Rover and trailer on the mainland and caught the boat to Lamu Island where we spent the night at the Lamu Island Hotel. The streets of Lamu were so narrow that a fully loaded donkey barely managed to pass through. The buildings were all Arab style as the area had been under Arab influence for centuries. The hotel was a double story structure, with sleeping accommodation upstairs in rooms divided only by mats, giving no real privacy. The toilet was a seat over a chute which ran down the side of the building past the kitchen to a hole below. Whenever anybody used the toilet, the sounds were magnified so that everybody else around knew what was going on. It was quite hilarious! The dining room, lounge and kitchen were on the ground floor.

The next day we ferried back to the mainland, picked up the Land Rover and proceeded inland on the road to Garissa. The first half of our journey was through the Boni Forest, noted as the 'home of big tusked elephant'. It stretches from the Tana River to the Somali border. Prior to my arrival, Don's game scouts had brought in two tusks, weighing 137 and 132 pounds, from an elephant that died of old age at Jari waterhole. In later years when I had turned to professional hunting, I saw an elephant bull with only one tusk which would have weighed 120 pounds. We were not hunting elephant at that time and so I had the pleasure of watching it drink at the waterhole.

We reached Jari waterhole in the evening after stopping en route to bag some Vulturine guineafowl for the pot. These birds have very bright blue and white feathers around the neck and are streaked with black and blue and white on the chest. The head is bare and looks like a vulture's head – hence its name.

After cooking a meal, we put out our stretchers and bedding with our heads against a low thorn bush. It was quite warm and as there was no sign of rain we did not put up a tent, preferring to sleep under the bright and starry sky. During the night we were awakened by a hyena galloping around the camp and giving off blood curdling whoops and cries. The night was so still that the animal sounded like a horse stampeding on the hard ground.

We discovered that the ground was swarming with red safari ants and moved our beds away in a hurry. When we went to move Elizabeth, we saw that her bed was covered with these vicious ants. They were even in her thick curly hair and we had great difficulty removing them. Throughout all this Elizabeth slept, which probably saved her from being bitten. Usually, as soon as one moves, the ants bite in unison as if given a signal.

We then found that a couple of guineafowl which we had placed on top of the thorn bush at the head of our beds was missing. The hyena had crawled between Don's bed and mine to steal them. We also found that the greedy animal had eaten the guts cast down on the ground nearby, ready to be buried next morning. The smell of the offal and blood obviously attracted both the ants and the hyena. The hyena swallowed both guts and ants together, which must then have attacked his insides, and the resultant pain had him galloping around and protesting loudly for all and sundry to hear.

At midday we arrived at Garissa, an administrative centre for the entire North East area (all the way to the Somali border). The Tana River was close by and water was pumped to the town from the river. The administration buildings were painted white and had flat roofs with a gauzed square-framed room roofed with thatch or *makuti* reed (local palms) for coolness. Gauze kept out the mosquitoes which, with the river nearby, were plentiful. For much of the year the heat was excessive and the officers and their families slept on the roof areas in order to benefit from the night-time breezes. The area is less than 2,000 feet above sea level and on the Equator. It has been said that Garissa was a punishment centre to which officers were posted if they misbehaved. This I could understand as I certainly would not live there by choice.

Don introduced me to the various administrative officers in town and we discussed game problems in the area. That night we camped on the river bank under a huge tree and it was quite pleasant. We saw a few crocodiles when we took a walk along the river bank. Early the following morning found us on the road leading to the coast. This road runs parallel with the Tana River until it meets the coastal road, which goes north and south, at Garsen.

We had not gone many miles when we noticed big banks of black cloud coming inland from the sea. This was the start of the rainy season and it was obvious we were soon going to get some heavy rain. Fifty miles further on we met the rain in squalls but we kept going. All along the road herd after herd of elephant were hurrying away from the riverine area to the inland bush. During the very dry season, many elephant herds including the bulls congregate along the Tana riverine bush. Other animal species also like this area and I have on various occasions seen lesser kudu, buffalo, lion, leopard, rhino, fringe-eared oryx, waterbuck and dik-dik when walking through it.

Further along the road we hit heavier rain and the water came streaming down the road like a river. The Land Rover and trailer managed to make steady progress and eventually we reached Malindi. It was evening, and we had driven through rain the whole way.

Don handed over all the stores, rifles and ammunition to me and then departed for Nairobi. The Game Department did not have a warden's house at the coast, so I looked around for a place to rent, eventually selecting a house at Kilifi, about forty miles down the coast towards Mombasa.

The work here was completely different to what I had experienced inland. A lot of elephant control was needed, mainly due to their raiding native crops. Local Arabs and Indians were heavily involved in illegal ivory and rhino horn smuggling and they were buying both ivory and rhino horns from African poachers who operated all along the coast and further inland as well.

The main hunting tribes in this area were the Wasanya or Waliangulu, Wakamba, Giriama, WaDigo and WaBoni tribes. The Waliangulu were noted elephant hunters. These tribes existed for centuries solely by hunting and were expert at their craft. They used a very powerful bow, which they practiced pulling from a young age and thereby developed powerful arms and shoulders. The pull on their bows required considerable strength, especially in getting the arrow back to maximum before releasing it at a target. European men tried to use these powerful bows and were unable to pull them back as far as the Waliangulu could. They also used very long arrows with four vanes and the head was usually a six inch nail hammered flat and pointed. The edges were sharpened with a flat stone or file. Behind the arrow head, poison was smeared along the shaft for about four inches and a leather thong was bound round the shaft over the poison. This kept the air out and preserved the life of the poison. The hunter removed this thong before firing the arrow into an elephant. The arrow flights were usually made from vulture feathers and the sinews used for binding were from giraffe. Poison was procured from the acokanthera tree which grew in the coastal area of the Giriama tribe. They were experts at making the poison and sold it to the other inland hunting tribes, mainly the Waliangulu and Wakamba. Branches and roots were cut from certain favoured trees, believed to be more potent than others. These were chopped up and boiled in water for several hours until eventually a substance like tar was left at the bottom of the pot. This was the poison used on the arrows. To get enough poison, this process was repeated many times and sometimes other ingredients were added to make the poison more potent. The Wakamba used a bow that was much lighter than the Waliangulu and their arrows had only three vanes.

These poachers stalked close to an elephant usually when it was feeding and aimed the arrow just behind the rib cage. If the arrow reached the spleen or liver, and if the poison was strong, the elephant usually only stumbled for a few hundred yards before collapsing. However, if the arrow was badly placed, the elephant went for many miles. The arrow was placed behind the rib cage otherwise the rib bones prevented the arrow from penetrating. The poachers usually cut the tusks up into pieces using a hacksaw, thus making transportation easier. The smaller pieces of ivory could also be hidden which made detection more difficult, especially when they were put in a bag with charcoal or even placed under bags of charcoal loaded on lorries for transporting to the coast. The making of charcoal by the various inland tribes had become big business and it brought in a steady income with the ivory dealings as a sideline. The poor African did not get much from the traders for his bag of charcoal or for the ivory. Most of them were paid 1 $\frac{1}{2}$ shillings for a bag of charcoal and 2 shillings a pound for ivory. The middle man received many times more for the ivory than the poacher did. Most of the charcoal was shipped by Arab dhows to the Persian Gulf because firewood was practically non-existent in those countries. These same dhows often transported illegal ivory out of the country.

I soon became aware that not all the game scouts working with me could be trusted. After taking up residence at the coast, my son Cecil came in early one morning to report that the ivory store had been broken into and one of the big tusks was missing. Among the confiscated ivory and the ivory shot on control was the beautiful pair of tusks from Jari waterhole (weighing 137 pounds and 132 pounds) that Don had handed over to me.

I sent for the police inspector and while awaiting the arrival of the police, Wanyahoro, who moved with me as Head Scout, was looking around and picked up tracks in the sand. He followed them for about one mile and found the big tusk, as well as smaller pieces of ivory, hidden in the thicket and covered with leaves.

When the inspector arrived, we questioned the game scouts as both of us suspected the theft was an inside job. The game scouts were lined up for us to examine their footwear because the thief had worn a pair of tennis shoes with a distinct pattern on the sole. One scout was from Nyasaland (now Malawi) and Don often took him along when he went spear fishing as he was a good swimmer. The pattern on the soles of his shoes matched the ones that Wanyahoro had been following. The inspector singled him out for interrogation. At first he denied everything, but after about an hour of skillful questioning, he admitted to having taken the ivory and to having made arrangements to sell it to a local Arab.

The Arab was to bring a truck to an assigned place where the scout would meet him and hand over the ivory. However the Arab thought it might be a trap and did not keep his rendezvous. After hiding the ivory, the game scout went to the dealer's shop and accosted him. The Arab gave a lame excuse that the lorry had broken down and he was unable to keep his appointment. The game scout was given a twelve month sentence with hard labour.

Not long after I arrived at the coast, I was called out to deal with elephant bulls raiding plantations south of Mombasa. When I arrived in the area I could see that the elephants had been in during the night and the tracks revealed that four bulls were involved. The sun was already well up and it was beginning to get pretty warm. I carried a .600 double which fired a 900 grain bullet and was keen to use the rifle as Don had said that it was the ideal calibre for elephant control. This rifle was Game Department property issued for the use in elephant control. It weighed sixteen pounds and was much heavier than the .470 I was accustomed to which weighed only ten pounds. It was not until 3 o'clock that we caught up with the elephants. They were high up in the Shimba hills close to the Kwale Game Reserve, the only place where sable are seen in Kenya.

By the time we reached the elephants, having walked through the hottest part of the day, I was feeling the weight of the .600 double on my shoulder. I preferred not to drink water out of the bottle I carried but instead sucked the juice from a couple of oranges which I kept in my pocket. We heard the elephants breaking branches ahead and approached cautiously. After a while we saw the branches of a large bush or a small tree being shaken by a feeding elephant on the opposite side to us. When we were about twenty yards from the elephant, we stopped and tested the wind with a sock filled with fine ash. It was in our favour but the bush was thick enough to hide the elephant from our sight and we decided to wait a little while to see what direction it would take. A few minutes later an elephant suddenly stepped out towards us and came into full view. I put the .600 up and tried for a frontal brain shot but found that I could not hold the heavy rifle steady because of its weight. I pulled the trigger as the foresight bead came onto the forehead of the elephant. Both barrels went off and I was propelled backwards for about three or four feet, but stayed on my feet. The elephant went down on its knees and immediately got up and started towards us. Using his .375, Wanyahoro dropped it with a brain shot.

Immediately another elephant appeared behind the fallen one and it also came towards us. I was having trouble extracting the empty cases from my .600. It was not fitted with ejectors and the cases had to be pulled out manually. My .470 doubles all had ejectors which ejected the fired cases as soon as the action was open. The second elephant saw us and started to turn away but by this time I had slipped a live round into the right hand barrel, lined up on the running elephant's shoulder and fired. It carried on and we followed as fast as we could, keeping an eye out for the other two elephants, but we did not see them. I found the elephant dead about fifty yards from where I shot at it. We went back to the first elephant to examine it and I found a bullet hole in the forehead that was too high. The other bullet missed completely and must also have gone high.

When I used the .470 double, I always pulled the front trigger first and if I needed to fire again, automatically shifted my finger to the back trigger. Don forgot to tell me that with this .600 double it was advisable to pull the back trigger first to avoid both barrels going off at the same time. I never used the .600 again. It was too cumbersome to hold steady enough for an accurate brain shot, especially at close range.

Among the other rifles left in my care for elephant control was a .475 No. 2 double which fired a 480 grain bullet with eighty grains of cordite. The .470 fired a 500 grain bullet with seventy-five grains which was a little slower with less penetration than the .475 bullet. I often used the .475

double on elephant hunts and found it performed better than the .470 on brain shots as it had excellent penetration. However, when aiming for a side brain shot, I had to be careful that there was not a second elephant standing behind the first because the bullet could go clear through it and wound the second animal. Unfortunately, ammunition for the .475 was not very plentiful. I.C.I./Kynoch had stopped manufacturing that calibre, so I used it sparingly.

The bone in a bull elephant's head is very hard, almost like iron wood. For some brain shots the bullet has to pass through quite a lot of bone in order to penetrate the brain, so there are two important requirements. Firstly, the bullet used must be a solid otherwise it will not hold together on impact. Secondly, good penetration is required. While the .475 No. 2 had these requirements, the .470 lacked that little extra 'oomph'.

I always advised novices to aim for the shoulder or close to the shoulder, depending on the angle of the elephant, in order to hit the heart. It is a much safer shot and a bigger target. While the bullet might miss the heart, it will usually hit the lungs or major blood vessels to the heart and the elephant will run a bit before falling down. There is also less danger of losing an elephant shot in the shoulder.

I was often confronted with a herd consisting of three, four or more bulls together. I found with a shoulder shot, the animal took off in a hurry with his companions following him. However with a brain shot, the animal collapsed on the spot, and his companions stood around for a while, confused, not knowing what had happened. I have had them suddenly make up their minds and stampede towards me. When they did this, they nearly always bunched up together and rushed through, flattening all bush in their paths. If there was a solid tree close by, I got behind it to avoid being knocked over. If there was no tree available, I then tried to get to any nearby open space and stood my ground. The elephants might turn away when they saw you, but if they kept bunched up, there was no alternative but to drop the leader with a frontal brain shot. I made it my policy never to turn my back on any dangerous charging animal.

I explained earlier that brain shots can be tricky for the novice and should only be taken after the shooter has examined the skull of a dead elephant to determine where the brain is situated. This shot must be made if the elephant is in fairly open country which gives the hunter plenty of time to fire a second or third shot before the elephant can get into thick cover should the brain shot fail. If this shot fails, the hunter should switch to shoulder or kidney shots.

You can usually tell if you hit the brain, as the animal's head jerks up, the hindquarters collapse and the animal goes straight down. To make sure, it is best to quickly go round to the back of the head if the elephant is on its side and put a bullet through the back into the brain or the vertebra. If it falls straight down with its legs folded underneath, then a side brain shot or heart shot is advisable.

Frontal brain shots are difficult unless one has had a lot of experience. The shot has to pass between the upper sockets of the tusks to reach the brain and the angle depends on how the elephant is holding its head while looking at the shooter or just standing normally. The gap between the tusks is about eight inches and if the bullet goes either side, it will hit the bottom of the tusk. Approximately twenty-two inches of tusk is in the head. If the bullet goes to either side of the gap, it will merely hit a tusk and crack it.

A bullet that misses the brain will usually cause the elephant to react differently depending on how close the bullet passes to the brain. If it is very close, the elephant will go down head first and the hindquarters will collapse afterwards. The animal might lie on the ground as if dead and then slowly regain consciousness and stagger onto its feet and take off. An animal shot this way will recover. Sometimes the animal will only stumble, regain its feet and take off in a hurry. Many elephant have been lost this way.

The closer one gets to the animal before shooting, the better. Twenty or thirty yards is about average. It is never good policy to take long shots when attempting the brain shot. The hunter should do a postmortem on a dead elephant to determine where the organs lie. Even after years of experience, I only attempt the kidney shot as a final resort when the animal has not dropped to my other shot or shots and is running away. I then aim high up on the back just to the side of the visible backbone and fire. If the kidney is hit, the animal will collapse.

Elephants, especially big tuskers that have been hunted, are known to be highly intelligent. They rely on their keen senses of smell and hearing. Their eyesight is only good at close quarters, perhaps under forty yards. At the perimeter of their field of vision they can only pick up movement or light clothing. Elephant that have been hunted a lot will take off if they pick up a reflection from a rifle barrel and I have even had them stampede on a bright moonlit night when I tried to approach. This happened when I was on control for the Game Department. The elephant caught the reflection from the moon onto the rifle barrel and immediately stampeded.

Somehow they can tell the difference between noise made by their companions and the noise made by approaching humans. Should one step on and break a dead stick, the elephant will immediately stop feeding and remain motionless and attentive. Should they not be satisfied they will move off quietly. One second you see them standing in the bush in front of you and in the next moment they have vanished. I have watched them move away slowly as if they were tiptoeing and, when a safe distance away, break into a run. For its size, an elephant can move amazing quietly.

Wakamba hunters have a strange belief regarding the stingless bee or small black insect that is attracted to human perspiration. These insects make a nuisance of themselves by crawling in your nose, eyes and ears to get the salt from your sweat. The Wakamba maintain that if you are standing close to an elephant and the flies leave the humans, fly to the elephant and get up the nostrils of its trunk, the elephant will pick up the human scent and take off. I have never been able to prove this theory but I have often had elephant take off for no explainable reason. There might be something to it.

I have noticed in areas where elephant are hunted a lot that walking around during the first day in a new area, there will be plenty of elephant signs. However, after a few days one will encounter fewer and fewer signs because the elephant move out of the area once they have detected human scent.

I made numerous trips inland behind Kilifi where there were a lot of elephants. I noticed the herds moved in and out of the Tsavo East Park according to the rain pattern. It rained in patches and if there was rain outside the park, the elephants went to the areas where rain had fallen and fed on bushes with new growth. Bull herds, with some big tuskers among them, mingled with cow herds. Poachers took advantage of this influx and many elephants were shot.

Licensed hunters also took the opportunity to look for big tuskers. Once I came across a well-known professional hunter who had shot at and lost a big bull. Unfortunately his brain shot did not hit its mark and the elephant ran off and mingled with others in the area. When I met the hunter, he had been looking for his trophy for a couple of days, but was experiencing difficulty due to the great number of animals in the area. Not long after I left, he offered a reward to the local Waliangulu for the wounded bull. A local came rushing into his camp to say he had seen the elephant so the man went out and picked up the tracks where the African had last seen it. Eventually they found the elephant standing by a waterhole and shot it. The tusks weighed over 100 pounds each. They found that the first shot had gone a little too high.

I acted on some tips and collected a couple of caches of ivory buried by poachers. The informers were paid for this information. In this same area I came across a small herd of sable antelope but did not think they would survive for long as poaching was rough. I also found an antelope, red in

71

colour and small like a suni, which I could not identify. There were many other animals such as lesser kudu, oryx, eland, rhino, hartebeest and buffalo in the area.

I received a cable from the District Commissioner at Kipini (on the mouth of the Tana River) indicating that he needed me to deal with elephants which were raiding African cultivations. I set off by Land Rover to deal with the problem. Albert, who was visiting me at the time, came along for company.

We arrived at Kipini and found the Commissioner about to depart in his launch to tour the up-river stations. As the elephants were raiding the cultivations in the area the launch would be passing through, I asked him to transport our party, leave us to deal with the problem, and pick us up on his way back. We duly found ourselves going upstream in the launch. We saw ducks and geese, the occasional crocodile basking in the sun on the sand banks, and many hippo.

About twenty miles upstream we were left on the river bank with all our gear which included camp-beds, bedding, food, change of clothing and, of course, the weapons needed to deal with the elephants. These elephants had been coming into rice paddy fields and although we stayed up for three nights, they did not return. We then had a call from an area lower down the river where elephants were raiding, so we used dugout canoes and went to find the area. A herd of cows had been into a banana plantation, done quite a lot of damage and then left the river. A few miles away we saw two or three herds of topi antelope and the tracks of lion. Ten miles from the banana plantations, we caught up with the elephants and shot two with no great difficulty. We left the local Pokomo tribe to cut out the tusks and bring them in.

Mosquitoes were a problem here. Once the sun set they appeared in swarms or should I say clouds and there was no option but to get under a mosquito net. All night long we heard the continuous humming outside the net as they tried to get at us. Occasionally, an arm might lie against the net when we moved in our sleep. The mosquitoes then bit through the net. Malaria was very bad in the coastal area and I always took preventive medicine.

The Africans in the area lived in cone-shaped, windowless grass huts thatched to ground level. The single door was a framework of saplings with thatching grass or palm leaves laid over it and tied firmly onto the framework so that nothing could pass through. It fitted snugly into its frame. In the evening the inhabitants crowded into the hut and pulled the door closed so that the mosquitoes could not get in. A fire was lit inside as a

Arab dhow - Kenya coast

The house we rented at the coast whilst in the Game Department

Big tusker in Kenya

Big tuskers in the Tsavo National Park

deterrent. I have often walked passed these dwellings in the early mornings, observed smoke coming through the thatch and wondered why they were not overcome with smoke or carbon monoxide. I was told by medical authorities that there was a high rate of tuberculosis in the area which was not difficult to believe considering the living conditions.

After darkness fell on the evening of the elephant hunt, Albert, the game scouts and I were lying in our camp beds under mosquito nets when a lion started roaring nearby. He kept it up at intervals for a long time and he must have been aware of our presence. We slept uneasily, often getting up and stoking the camp fire during the night. The male coastal lion usually has no mane, only occasionally a short ridge along the neck. This makes it difficult to tell the difference between the sexes.

The next day the District Commissioner came by and I asked him to take us a little lower down the river to where I had to deal with more 'elephant' complaints. I asked if he would send the launch back for us in a couple of days. He refused, explaining that the launch had to go back to Mombasa for a refit and we would have to find our own way back.

I rented dugout canoes from the locals and moved along the river to another place where elephants were causing crop damage. We tracked a small herd from the river but never caught up with them. Late in the afternoon we gave up and made our way wearily back to the river. Earlier in the day we had come across quite a lot of game such as topi and zebra. The mosquitoes were active even in the daytime and whenever we sat in the shade of a bush for a rest we were immediately attacked by these pests. That night I was attacked by red or safari ants, which swarmed over my net and through it to bite me. I quickly got out of bed and moved away from the ant column. Immediately the mosquitoes attacked. It took quite a while to pick the ants out of the net before I could get back into bed. Meanwhile the mosquitoes had a ball.

In the morning I made preparations for the journey back to Kipini. I hired two dugouts and fastened two poles across the gunwales front and back so that we had a sort of catamaran. We loaded all our gear into the two canoes, climbed in and made our way downstream. The current was slow but with a couple of paddlers we made fair progress over the seventeen to eighteen miles back to Kipini. A couple of times we were threatened by bull hippos. One came very close to our dugouts and we pulled in against the bank as a precaution. I stood with my double rifle ready to shoot if it attacked the boats but, much to our relief, it turned back only a few feet from us and rejoined the herd. The locals told me they were often attacked by hippo along the river. Many dugouts were wrecked and occasionally the occupants killed, particularly if they were slow in getting to the bank. Bull hippos resent boats coming near the cow herds or into their territory. Cow hippos with small calves have also been known to attack boats which come too near.

At approximately 4 o'clock we reached the mouth of the river where we encountered a gale blowing in from the sea. The paddlers made slow progress against the wind and the waves and we could not land on the north side of the bank at Kipini. We got out of the dugouts and shouted and waved our shirts hoping that somebody would bring a launch and ferry us to Kipini. After a while a launch did arrive.

In Kipini, we noticed the District Commissioner's boat still moored at the jetty. We felt more than a little peeved as the Commissioner could have saved us a very uncomfortable river journey had he been more considerate. There and then I decided not to be in too much of a hurry to render any assistance to that gentleman in the future.

Near Kipini there are some very old buildings, built a few hundred years earlier from coral rock blocks. Nobody knew who had built them. At Gedi, south of Malindi, there is another old settlement, deserted now for a few hundred years, and an interesting museum with various artifacts collected during excavations.

For hundreds of years the East African coast was active with trade from the Persian Gulf, the Far East and even from China. To this day, Arab dhows trade as they did in the past, but now mainly with the Persian Gulf countries. There are big trees growing among the ruins at Gedi and the vegetation and local forest is very thick, so it is obvious that the settlement has been deserted for several hundred years. All sorts of explanations have been put forward as to why the town was abandoned, the most popular being disease or plague or even attacks from hostile tribes.

Shortly before I was due to go on long leave overseas, I received a telephone call concerning an honourary game warden named Commander Blunt, who lived about twenty miles north of Mombasa at Mtwapa Creek. He had been badly injured by a buffalo and was in a hospital at Mombasa. He wanted me to go to the place where he had been attacked to find the wounded buffalo and retrieve his rifle.

Early the next morning I went to the area and was directed to the place where the Commander had been attacked. We found his rifle, a .416 Rigby, lying on the ground as well as his hat and spectacles. The buffalo had died during the night and was lying in the vicinity. It had two rifle wounds in its side and shotgun pellet wounds in its hindquarters.

I asked an African who had been present what had happened. He replied that Indian hunters from Mombasa came out at the request of a local Indian farmer to shoot buffalo in the area. They used a rifle and a shotgun to shoot a couple of buffalo and in the process wounded some more. The next day two Africans were walking through the area when a buffalo charged out of the bush and chased them. They were separated and one African, after running a considerable distance, waited for his friend who did not appear. After a while the man went to the local police station and reported that he feared his friend had been killed by a buffalo. The police then phoned Commander Blunt.

After we found the rifle, hat and spectacles, we searched for the missing African and found him dead about 300 yards away. The buffalo had knocked him to the ground and hooked him in the body a couple of times. The horns had gone into the side of the man's body and penetrated his stomach, lungs and heart, killing him instantly. The buffalo then proceeded to bulldoze him along the ground so that there was hardly a patch of skin that was not damaged or grazed. The body was a mess.

After loading the corpse onto a truck to take to the Police Station, we returned to the buffalo. I wanted to dig out the bullets, hoping both to establish the calibre used by the Indian hunters and to prosecute them for illegal hunting and not reporting the wounding of a dangerous animal.

The coastal buffalo is generally smaller than his inland cousin. The shape of the head is similar but with a smaller boss and the horns are slender with long sharp tips, which gives it a deadly weapon to use against its enemies. The animal becomes extremely aggressive when wounded. This fact is borne out in my story.

I instructed my game scouts to dig out the bullets in the buffalo and bring them to me for use in the case I intended to bring against the Indian hunters. I went into Mombasa where I found the Asian who had wounded the buffalo and asked for his rifle. He produced a 9 mm rifle. We had picked up some empty cartridge cases at the place where the Indian had shot at the buffalo, and these were of the same calibre as the rifle used by the Asian.

I went back to Mtwapa and met the game scouts who handed me two bullets - one was a .416 calibre (Commander Blunt's), and the other was a 9 mm (obviously from the Indian's rifle). The Indian's rifle, cartridge cases and bullet were sent to police ballistic experts in Nairobi to determine whether the bullet dug out of the buffalo was in fact fired from the Indian's rifle.

I visited Commander Blunt in the hospital and found him in better form than I expected. He was in considerable pain and I was appaled at the terrible wounds to his leg. The buffalo horns had torn out the flesh in his thigh and exposed the bone and muscles, but fortunately missed the main arteries in the leg. He told me this story. He received a call from the police asking him to go to the area where the African was reported missing. He went along with Mrs. Blunt. They arrived to find a crowd of Africans and some Indians standing and looking towards the bush. He got out of the car, took his .416 rifle and walked up to them. They pointed to a buffalo lying just inside a patch of bush with only its hindquarters showing.

The Commander walked up to the buffalo and decided to get around to where he could see its head and shoot it. This was a grave error as he should not have gone too close before ascertaining whether or not it was dead. He had two possibilities, and I would have taken both of these two consecutive actions. Firstly, to shoot it up the root of its tail using a solid bullet with the .416. This would have penetrated to the chest cavity. Secondly to throw a stone or heavy piece of wood at the buffalo to see if there was any reaction.

The Commander's actions gave him no room to manoeuvre. To see its head he had to walk around its side, and as he stepped alongside it, the animal suddenly jumped up and whipped around. He only had time to fire one shot into its stomach before the buffalo tossed him into the air and worked him over with its head.

When the Commander was tossed into the air, the crowd ran away. Mrs. Blunt realised what had happened, jumped out of the car and ran towards the scene. As she passed the Indian who was running away, Mrs. Blunt snatched the shotgun from him and ran up to the buffalo. When she got close she saw that it was on its knees working the Commander over with its head. She fired both barrels of the shotgun into the buffalo's backside and it immediately left her husband and rushed off into the bush. She grabbed the Commander, dragged him away, then fetched the car and drove him to the hospital. He was extremely lucky that his plucky wife had been along and that she had bravely dashed in and saved him from being killed.

The police duly certified that the bullet dug out of the buffalo had indeed been fired from the rifle I had confiscated from the Indian. The court case had not come up by the time I went on long leave. Afterwards I heard that the Indian got off because he was defended by a clever lawyer. The case hinged on the bullet we had dug out of the buffalo. The defence argued that the bullet had been handled by too many people, namely the African who had found it in the buffalo, and the game scout who had taken it over and then handed it to me. The defence argued that the bullet could have been switched. I was most disappointed at the outcome and realised how easy it was for a criminal to get off on a minor loophole.

SEVEN

MAU MAU III

My long leave overseas came up. Jock and I packed our possessions and returned to our home behind the Nanyuki Forest Station. We then took a flight from Nairobi to London, which was plagued with engine trouble, first at Entebbe in Uganda and next at Khartoum in the Sudan, where we were forced to spend the night. The heat was so oppressive that we lay on the cement floors with our three children. The rooms had big ceiling fans but they offered very little relief as the air blown onto us was also hot. The next afternoon, assured that the faults had been rectified, we boarded the plane and proceeded with our flight. All went well to Cairo, but after leaving Egypt we flew into a terrific electrical storm and the plane was buffeted so violently that quite a few passengers were sick. We lost an engine over the Mediterranean. When we got to Rome, to the relief of all on board, we changed planes and completed the journey without further mishaps.

In England we took the opportunity to travel around in a new Land Rover I had taken delivery of. Our impression of England was that there were too many people around at all times. This we were not used to and found it oppressive. In Africa it was easy to drive short distances and reach a place where you were completely on your own. No doubt there are a few places in England and Scotland where this was also possible, but we were not to find them. Part of our stay was with relatives on my mother's side and the rest of the time we rented a small place in Weston-Super-Mere. I had a total of six months leave, but after three months we returned to Kenya.

Back in Nanyuki things had changed considerably. The Mau Mau rebellion was now in full swing. Gangs were very active and I found myself being called out more and more to perform police duties. Once again I was patrolling the forest areas and tracking the gangs.

We constructed a wooden stockade around both the house and game scout quarters and reinforced it with barbed wire. We even built underground dugouts near the house in case we were overwhelmed by a gang we could not hold back.

There were reports of large terrorist gangs operating in the forest areas. The police built a post close to us in order to keep an eye on the local work force employed by the Forest Department. Many workers sympathised with the Mau Mau and from time to time they fed gangs who were passing through.

One amusing incident occurred about this time. A Police G.S.U. unit (paramilitary force formed solely to deal with incidents of unrest and to patrol forested areas) moved in and camped close by. In due course the European officer in charge asked if I could possibly shoot a buffalo for meat, as the Askaris were sick and tired of eating out of tins, especially 'bully beef'. I agreed to do this because I knew where a couple of bulls had been coming into a cypress plantation close to the forest station. These bulls debarked the young trees by rubbing their heads and necks on them to relieve the itching from lice. In doing so they killed the trees or broke them near ground level.

I loaded four or five dogs in the Land Rover, took a couple of game scouts and proceeded to the plantation where I hoped to pick up the tracks. The police officer followed in his vehicle. We left the vehicles close to the area where the buffalo had been doing the damage and proceeded on foot. The party consisted of myself, one police officer, one Askari and two game scouts with the dogs. We found the tracks of a bull buffalo which had come in during the night and followed them. After a while we got into *leleshwa* bush, which grew in thick clumps and was interspersed with open patches of grassland. My interest intensified as I knew buffalo often lay up in these clumps. My hopes of finding the buffalo improved as the tracks started to go round in a zigzag way and we passed a few old buffalo beds. The buffalo was looking for a place to lie up.

The dogs quickened their pace and showed that they were getting interesting scents. I went cautiously, holding my .470 double at the ready because I expected the dogs to start barking at any moment. We were halfway across a grassy patch between the *leleshwa* when the barking started. Moments later the bush ahead of us literally erupted. First two dogs came dashing out followed by a rhinoceros. Both the policemen turned on their heels and disappeared smartly into the bush behind us. The two game scouts and I were off to one side puzzling over the buffalo tracks. We stood our ground because it was obvious that the rhino would pass by and this it did, followed by a small calf and the rest of the dogs running with them.

After a while there was silence. We waited a couple of minutes and then whistled for the policemen. We received an answering whistle immediately. The European came into view looking very agitated and dishevelled. He had a narrow escape. As he was running away, he realised that the cow was right behind so he dashed around a bush to avoid her and ran smack into her calf. He put out his hands to ward off the calf, which promptly butted him into a bush where he landed on his backside. The calf then ran off after its mother.

After more whistling and calling, we received an answer from the Askari, who appeared minus his .303 rifle, which he lost while trying to get away from the rhino. We tracked the rhino and hoped that somewhere along the stampede route the missing rifle would turn up. By this time the dogs had lost interest in the chase and straggled back in ones and twos until they had all returned. We found the rifle hanging from a bush by its sling. As no shots had been fired, I suggested going back and picking up the tracks where we left off. The European policeman then said that there was no way he would hunt any more. He had had enough, and as far as he was concerned the Askaris would have to continue eating bully beef!

Soon after I returned to the Game Department in the Nanyuki Forest Station area, the police asked Don Bousfield and I if we would form a tracker team to operate in the Mount Kenya area on the northern side of the mountain, mainly in the Nanyuki-Timau areas. Don had been working at a tracker school in Nanyuki with Rodney Elliott, where they taught the art of tracking to the police, in order to improve their performance in the bush against the Mau Mau. By the time I arrived on the scene, Don and Rodney had already been involved in quite a few contacts. Don had recently been released from the cottage hospital at Nanyuki where he was recovering from chest wounds he received during an encounter with a forest gang. He had miraculously escaped from being killed.

Don was with a small group from the tracking school when they met a gang in the forest. With the first contact the gang scattered and fled. Don and an African tracker chased one member of the gang who was dodging between tall cedar trees. Eventually he disappeared behind a big tree. When Don and the tracker arrived at the tree, the terrorist stepped out from behind the trunk and opened fire at close range with a Sten gun. One bullet hit Don in the chest just above his heart while another cut a groove along the side of his ribs. The impact of the bullet and the shock knocked him to the ground. The tracker tried to shoot the terrorist with his pump action shotgun, but he never got a shot off because he panicked and forgot to release the safety catch or jammed the action. The Mau Mau fired a short burst at the tracker and fled.

79

The rest of the patrol ran up just as Don came to his senses and staggered onto his feet. When asked if he was okay, Don replied that he was and started to walk back. He then noticed blood coming out of the bottom of his trouser legs and promptly passed out again. He ended up in the hospital where I visited him and found him bright and cheerful, lying on his back with no pyjama top but a dressing over the wound. The rest of his chest was bruised black and blue by the impact of the bullet. Don had been wearing an army jacket with very large top pockets. In the pockets were maps folded many times like a wad or book. The doctor believed these maps had absorbed and turned the bullet, which would otherwise have gone into his chest and heart and killed him. He was a very lucky man.

In due course Don came out of hospital and we got our tracking team together. The various District Commissioners sent us numerous candidates from the Masai, Lumbwa and Ndorobo tribes. Eventually we selected six likely candidates, hoping to mould them into successful trackers. These gentlemen were completely raw from the African reservations and they knew nothing about firearms. The only weapons they were familiar with were spears and bows and arrows. We drew .303 rifles from the Police armoury, as well as ammunition and uniforms, and started basic rifle training with the .303 rifles. First they were taught how to aim and fire on the rifle ranges and later in a jungle course. We picked a path winding through an area of thick bush and trees. Every now and then we put up a target which the recruits would suddenly come upon as they rounded a corner of the path.

Don and I took turns having the recruits walk in front with the rifle held at the ready, loaded and with the safety catch on. The idea was that the recruit would get off a shot as quickly as possible when seeing the target after first slipping the safety catch off. With a lot of practice, most of the new members became pretty good and could hit their targets just about every time they fired. Afterwards we took them out tracking and found a couple who were very good at it. Then came the real thing. We tracked gangs several times and actually made contact a few times. Don and I moved from the Forest Station Game Headquarters at Nanyuki to a small cottage next to the Police Station at Timau. My wife and children also moved in, leaving the game scouts and dogs to occupy and look after the Game Department Headquarters.

The big day came when a flock of 300 merino sheep were stolen from a farm located high up on the side of the mountain. We were called out and picked up the tracks of the stolen sheep that were being driven along by about ten men. By evening we found ourselves high up on the moorland. We were not equipped to sleep out as we had no blankets or food so we decided to get back to the car below and return early the next morning when we would be prepared to stay out for a few days.

Darkness came and we stumbled down the tracks with no torch to guide us. It was especially dark that night. The worst moment came when we found ourselves on the edge of a ravine with fairly steep sides and realised that the car was across on the opposite side. A few moments before we stumbled onto a buffalo, which at first stood its ground snorting at us. We stood our ground too and waited anxiously to see what would happen. We could not see it, but the buffalo was making its presence felt. To our relief it eventually made off, and we heard it crashing through the bush.

We had to slide down the slope feet first in order to cross the ravine. I was leading and felt with my feet for any sudden drop. Fortunately a couple in the party had matches and whenever I put my feet out and felt nothing, a match was lit to establish how much drop had to be negotiated. It was a slow and painful process and seemed to take hours when in actual fact it took one hour. We reached the stream bed and started up the opposite slope. Going up was easier than going down and we moved a little quicker but the thorn bushes wrecked havoc with our faces and arms. With much relief we eventually reached the top and clambered into the car for the journey home.

That night we packed our rucksacks with extra ammunition, tinned foods, sleeping bags and warm clothing for the cold night that would fall in the high mountain areas. We managed to get a few hours sleep and awakened early for a half past five departure in the Land Rover. I don't know how we all managed to fit in, especially with all our gear, but we did. The vehicle belonged to Don who was being paid by the police for mileage we did.

We used the Hickson Track, which took us up onto the moorlands to the upper course of the Marania stream. Somewhere near this stream we stopped to unload our rucksacks and weapons. It was impossible to go any further with the car, so we proceeded on foot in single file, in the direction of where we left the tracks on the previous day. After three miles we reached the spot and picked up the tracks. The direction they took was generally towards the high mountain peaks. Whenever we came to the top of a ridge or a high position, we crept up and used our binoculars to look for any sign of the people we were following but all we saw were herds of zebra and eland.

The countryside consisted of open moorland dotted with patches of heath and heather and clumps of coarse grass. These clumps made walking difficult, particularly in the low lying wet areas. Each step required that one lift a leg over the tussocks and this made progress both slow and tiresome and the altitude made breathing difficult.

We had walked several miles by late afternoon when we arrived at a small lake or tarn. Here we stopped for a rest and tasted the water which was good but very cold because we had reached an altitude between 12,500 and 13,000 feet above sea level. I was aware of how quiet the atmosphere around seemed to be. There was an uncanny type of stillness. Occasionally it was broken by the cry of an eagle, an auger buzzard or the noise made by rock hyrax which were plentiful in the clefts of the rocks. We noted the beautiful iridescent plumage of the malachite sunbird, which flashed in the sunlight as it flew from one flowering plant to the other. They were noisy birds, making a continuous twittering. This was a pleasant sound which became quite natural in the mountain surroundings.

The tracks were heading to a place ideally suited for the enemy to ambush us. On our left was a high, steep stony ridge and on our right was a rock face about one hundred feet high. The top was a jumble of boulders and rocks providing plenty of cover for anybody. The tracks led up a slight slope between the pass made by the rocky cliff on our right and the steep ridge on our left. We looked through our binoculars for likely hiding places, but saw nothing suspicious. However we were uneasy and discussed the possibility of being ambushed, but decided that the people herding the sheep only numbered about ten, so we did not think there would be much opposition.

Albert had joined our party the night before. He carried a .375 H & H Magnum rifle in case we ran into rhino or buffalo. We carried a pack radio transmitter for emergency use in case of an injury or if the need for extra support arose. While we were resting we tried to contact Headquarters at Nanyuki, but when we received no response, we knew something was wrong with the set. After a quick examination we could not find the problem and decided that it would have to wait until we got back to base camp. Little did we know that if we had had a working radio, it would have been put to good use.

After a rest we continued tracking. We put our packs on our backs and slowly started up the slight incline leading into the pass. Don took the lead and I followed with the others all strung along behind. We all carried different weapons. The African trackers all carried .303 army rifles except an ex-army soldier who carried a Bren machine gun. It used .303 ammunition and could give automatic fire. Don favoured a M3 carbine, a semi-automatic that fired 30-30 ammunition. It was accurate to about 200 yards or perhaps a little more and was good at close quarters as well. I used a Beretta sub-machine gun, a relic of the Ethiopian and Italian campaign of World War II. This particular one was captured from the Italians. It had a lot of firepower and I carried several magazines which held forty rounds each.

We reached the pass with Don about five yards in the lead. We were walking slowly because we were soon short of breath at that altitude. Don reached a low outcrop of waist high rock and was going alongside it when, all of a sudden, there was a sharp crack and the pack on his back exploded. Everything burst out as the bullet fired from a 9 mm rifle hit him. (This we found out afterwards). The impact knocked Don to the ground and he fell behind the outcrop of rock. This saved his life because the shot was followed by a burst of automatic fire and I saw the bullets hit the rock. The firing came from the top of the cliff on my right and my first reaction was to dive for cover behind the same rocks.

Immediately the enemy started shouting, blowing whistles and shooting in an effort to make us panic and flee. We were made of sterner stuff and we all stayed put. A mass of objects were then thrown from the cliff down towards us. At first I thought they were hand grenades and shouted to our group to duck. After a few seconds I realised that they were only throwing stones. Don was trying to get the straps of his pack off his arms and Albert went to his assistance. I was relieved to see that Don was all right.

I cautiously peered up over the rock. Stones were still coming over, and I spotted a head showing over a rock. I raised my Beretta, quickly put a bead on the target and gave a short burst of fire. The head disappeared. I sprayed that whole cliff top from one end to the other. Meanwhile Don and Albert saw a terrorist wearing a white raincoat, standing on a big rock and shouting down to the others on the cliff. He was on the steep slope to our left, about 300 yards away. Both Don and Albert fired at him and were rewarded to see him come flying off the rock and disappear below.

We concentrated on looking for movement or heads showing on the cliff above and fired whenever we saw a target. During all this I looked back down the slope to see what the rest of our group were doing. I could not see all of them but the ones I could see were lying behind the rock outcrops and not shooting. They were either petrified or waiting for orders to shoot.

Suddenly the shouting, rock throwing and the shooting stopped and there was silence. Don gathered his things together and I heard Albert say to Don, "I can smell fish – they must have been eating sardines around here." Don replied, "Sardines be damned, those were mine and a bullet has gone through the tin." The bullet that hit Don's pack had also gone through a folded pullover which was now full of holes and looked as if the rats had been at it. There was also a toilet roll in the pack and the bullet ploughed through and opened it up like a flower.

We made a cautious retreat down the slope and decided to find another way around. Going further into the pass would have given the advantage to the enemy if they were still lying low. I stayed put while Don, Albert and the rest of the party pulled back. When they had gone a certain distance I moved back. At about 150 yards we stopped.

We sprayed the cliff again with automatic fire from the Bren gun but received no answering fire. We saw no movement among the rocks so we were unsure of whether the terrorists were lying low or fleeing. We tried once again to use the radio but could not raise Police Headquarters. Before leaving we had been promised assistance from the Air Force if we needed it. The terrorists would have been easy pickings from the air. As darkness was not far off and there was nothing more we could achieve, we made our way back to the car, planning to have another look over the area the next morning. The return journey was a little easier because the going was downhill and we had a torch. We reached the car at 10 o'clock that night.

The next day Police Headquarters sent a fresh group to the spot where we were ambushed. As we expected, the terrorists had fled but they did find two terrorist bodies. The sheep had been slaughtered in a cave. Apparently the Mau Mau were having a meeting of all the terrorist groups (approximately 300 members) in the area and the sheep were stolen to feed the entire entourage. We had managed to break up their meeting. Had the terrorists made a concerted attack and rushed us, they could have overrun us because we were hopelessly outnumbered. We would have accounted for a good number of them but I do not think we could not have held them back.

On the third day we went back to the area and picked up the Mau Mau tracks. We found the spot where they had spent the night on a bare hillside about eight miles from the contact area. They slept huddled up against each other in several groups and were too afraid of the security forces to use fires in order to keep warm. It must have been bitterly cold and I suspect they did not get much sleep because there was frost at that altitude.

With better equipment, such as grenades which could have been launched from the end of the .303 rifles onto the cliff, we could have achieved a demoralising effect on the ambushers. This extra equipment was originally requested but the police were unable to supply it. I may point out that the police were very poorly equipped for most of the Mau Mau emergency. The army received priority in everything even though the police were more effective and made more contacts.

Sometime later we were issued with grenade launchers but we never had the opportunity to use them. We found out afterwards that the wireless transmitter had a broken lead inside the base of the flexible aerial. The set had worked well right up to time when we really needed it. It is a peculiar fact that equipment often fails at the most critical moment.

The Mau Mau forest gangs had gradually antagonised the local population in the Kikuyu Reserve with their brutal attacks on the men, women and children in the villages. Anybody who did not give them full co-operation was punished. They believed that instilling fear into the local population would get them support but it backfired as more and more turned to the Government, supplying information or joining the Home Guard.

The Government concentrated the locals into well defended villages guarded by Home Guards. The village perimeters were fenced with barbed wire. Alongside these fences, ditches were dug and bamboo stakes with sharpened upright points were added to deter anybody trying to cross. Enormous ditches were dug along the bottom of the forest edges and along the Reserve boundaries. These were patrolled by the Home Guard with the idea of stopping the forest gangs from getting food or other assistance from the local Reserve population. These methods succeeded and the gangs were forced to subsist on the game they caught in pits and snares. On our forest patrols one noticed more and more pits, some big enough to catch elephant.

At about this time, I was notified by the Forest Officer at Ragati Forest Station that Kamino had been captured by a Mau Mau gang and had been taken into the forest on Mount Kenya. He was stationed at Ragati doing control work. Kamino had one weakness – liquor! He had gone down to the Kikuyu Forest labourers' village where they had brewed up liquor for him and got him drunk. (Most of the forest labourers were Mau Mau sympathizers.) Kamino had been assisting the security forces in tracking gangs in the area and the villagers had tipped off the local forest gang. They ambushed him on his way home when he was too drunk to offer any resistance.

He was never seen again and we learned later that he had been executed in the forest. I was sorry to get the news as I had done a lot of hunting with him and had found him very good with dangerous game. I never forgot his shot that saved me from being trampled by a cow elephant as it charged out of the bush behind me.

From 1955 onwards the gangs became less active as fighters and spent more and more time trying to find food. Security forces by this time were having increasing success using pseudo gangs recruited from ex-Mau Mau forest gangs. They entered the forests and made contact with the Mau Mau and then either shot the gangs or persuaded them to surrender.

Among these pseudo gangs were many Europeans who darkened their skins and dressed just like any forest gangster. One of the most successful was Ian Henderson, a senior officer in the police. He spoke fluent Kikuyu and could fool the locals easily, especially in the darkness. They could not tell that he was different from any of their members. I knew Ian well. In earlier days we both attended boarding school in Nairobi and his parents had a coffee farm at Nyeri.

It was now a matter of time before the Mau Mau defected and the incidents of violence decreased. Don and I gave up the police tracker team and returned to normal duties in the Game Department. Don married my sister, Anne, and they moved to the coast in the Lamu area where Don was stationed doing elephant control and anti-poaching work.

In the early 1930's a British Expedition visited the shores of Lake Rudolph and two of their members went across in a small boat to South Island. Their nightly fires were observed by the party remaining on the mainland and this confirmed that they had arrived safely. However, the two men failed to return on the expected day and were never seen again. The lake was fairly shallow and gale force winds were common, which made it treacherous for a small boat. The main party waited in vain for days and finally the men were presumed drowned while trying to return. A cork helmet washed up on another shore line sometime later and this confirmed their fate.

George and Joy Adamson made a trip to Lake Rudolf, also crossing by boat to South Island, a distance of several miles. There was a lot in the local newspapers and radio news about their trip and what they had seen as they were the first white people to return from the island alive.

After the Adamson trip, several of us decided to visit the lake and cross over to South Island. A party was organised consisting of myself, my two brothers, Don, Rodney Elliott, Theo Potgieter and Monty Brown. Monty supplied a ski-boat which he had built himself. We loaded two ski-boats onto trailers and all the remaining gear was packed into Land Rovers for the trip north via Maralal.

We passed between two mountains (Nyiru and Porale) which lie south of the lake in the South Horr Valley. Nyiru was fairly flat on top and covered with belts of bamboo and Kikuyu grass, the latter kept lawn-like by animals such as buffalo, bushbuck and native cattle. There were also giant forest hog living there. This mountain was hundreds of miles from Mount Kenya or the Aberdares and Mau ranges and was completely isolated by the Rift Valley. I wondered how it was possible for bamboo to establish itself so far from the other regions where it grew.

We left the mountains and we entered an area strewn with volcanic rock. There was a volcano named Teleki to the south of the lake which last erupted at the turn of the century. The route was pretty rough and wound its way down the escarpment through the volcanic rock. The area around the lake was moon-like, devoid of vegetation with only the odd thorn acacia struggling to survive.

When we arrived at the shore, a gale-force wind was blowing and we were forced to seek shelter in a gully nearby where we barely managed to put up canvas shelters for protection. The wind howled all night and in the morning I awoke to find sand covering my pillow. This reminded me of my army days in the North African deserts. Later in the day the wind died down and I wandered along the shore and climbed a rock jutting out into the water where I could see schools of tilapia fish. I put on a pair of goggles, dived to 6 or 7 feet and, to my horror, I came face to face with a crocodile. Fortunately the crocodile turned away and disappeared in a flash. Needless to say, I did not waste any time in going in the opposite direction and left the water.

We launched the ski boat and did a bit of trolling with spoons. We caught a few Nile perch, the biggest weighing 135 pounds, but we found they did not fight as well as the tiger fish on the smaller tackle.

The following morning we loaded our gear, bedding and food into the boats and departed for South Island. Theo Potgieter remained on the mainland to look after the vehicles. The trip across was uneventful. We went around the island and camped on the west side as the east side was very rocky and had no beaches. We found a suitable beach which also had a couple of acacia trees offering shade from the burning sun during the day.

During the day we saw many crocodiles sunning themselves on the small beaches to the south. Among them were some monsters. A couple of days later Don and I shot two, with the biggest measuring sixteen feet in length and five feet around the girth. The crocodiles had no fear of the ski-boats and a couple of times they swam across the surface towards the boat with the obvious intention of attacking the intruder invading their territory. We never waited to see what they would do with the boat if they caught up. The two explorers' boat may well have been attacked by a monster crocodile.

Besides the crocodiles, the island teemed with wild goats of different colours. They were in good condition with plenty of bush (although little grass) to feed on. One of the crocodiles we shot had eaten a goat which we found when we cut its stomach open. We also caught some very big Nile perch (over 100 pounds) and a rare golden coloured perch.

We had a very strange experience one night. There was a full moon and very little wind so the lake was calm. The boats were pulled well out of the water so that they would not float away. In the middle of the night we were woken by enormous waves hitting the shore. We rushed down to the boats and pulled them further from the water. Afterwards we pondered over what had happened and reached the conclusion that there must have been some underwater volcanic eruption.

In all, we spent ten days there. When we arrived back on the mainland, Theo told us that a crocodile had taken his little fox terrier. We decided to explore the south side of the lake and one day while we were exploring the south side of the lake along the shore, a big crocodile came swimming towards us. I turned the boat slowly to shore and came to a tongue of beach jutting obliquely out into the lake. I edged the boat into the narrow water behind it, putting the tongue between us and the crocodile. We got out of the boat and crouched behind it to watch the crocodile.

I had a loaded 8 x 60S rifle in hand. The crocodile started to cross the tongue of beach, still heading towards us. I fired one shot in the head and it stayed put with only a slight movement of the tail. When we skinned it, we dug a barbed spear head out of its body. There is a small tribe on the lake called El Molo. This tribe live solely on fish and occasionally they kill a hippo or crocodile. I assumed that an El Molo fisherman had put the spear into the crocodile.

We spent one night camping at the end of a creek. Our sleep was interrupted by the snapping jaws of crocodiles. This noise was made whenever they snapped at a fish. I have never heard them do this before or since.

The next day we cruised the south side of the island and encountered Turkana tribesmen bringing their cattle, camels and goats to water. When they saw the boat, they immediately started to drive their animals back into the hills in panic. They probably thought we were raiders from Ethiopia who had acquired motorised boats to come and terrorize them. To this day raiders descend from Ethiopia to wipe out whole villages and drive away the domestic stock. We turned back and while we were returning we had a mishap which could have been disastrous.

Don Bousfield with excellent tusks shot in the 1950s

Don Bousfield with an elephant shot on Game Control

Record Defassa waterbuck - Masailand, Kenya

Record Grant's Gazelle shot in Kenya

I was driving the boat and cruising parallel with the shore. Things were going fine until I made a slight turn and the boat almost capsized. We realised the boat was filling up with water but it was still floating so I gingerly headed for the shore. We barely made it before the boat started sinking. We pulled it ashore, removed the motor and turned the boat upside down for a hull inspection where we found that it had been bumped and a slight bit of the skin layer had lifted. The bottom layer was porous and a big patch of hull, which was like cardboard, had gone soft. As a result, it collapsed and allowed water to enter. Fortunately the hull had two watertight compartments, otherwise we would have sunk.

We now had to patch the boat before returning to camp, still some considerable distance away. Rodney produced a piece of plywood and some screws from his fishing box. We proceeded to repair the boat by punching screw holes in the hull with a Swiss army knife. Needless to say we kept very close to the shore, everybody being well aware of the great numbers of big crocodiles in the water and nobody wanted to swim. Eventually the boat made it back to camp.

We left the boat with Monty Brown for repairs. He was a fishery officer in the Game Department at Sagana and he rebuilt the boat in his spare time.

APPENDIX 1

COLONY AND PROTECTORATE OF KENYA

———— —— —.

SIR / MADAM,

I have the honour to inform you that, in accordance with regulations 630–636 of the Code of Regulations, I have made a confidential report on you for the *half-year/ one year/ two years' period ending ....3.1./.12/.55.........................

2. In accordance with regulation 633 (P) I am to advise you that I have –

†(a) said nothing in the report which requires, under the provisions of regulation 633 (K), to be brought to your notice;

†(b) made the following comments which, in accordance with the provisions of regulation 633 (K) I am required to bring to your notice : —

[handwritten] Thank you very much for the hard work you have performed in a very difficult & dangerous area both in hunting breed & terrorist. Gratitude is greatly appreciated for your loyal and hard work involving considerable bravery & fortitude.

[handwritten signature] F.C. Bartlett G.
Game Ranger.

I have the honour to be,
Sir / Madam,
Your obedient Servant,

[handwritten signature] William Vole.

*Delete as necessary.

†Delete either (a) or (b) as the case may be.

EIGHT

A New Era: Professional Hunting

Don resigned from the Game Department and started hunting professionally with Selby and Holmberg Safaris. I stayed on with the Department for a while but decided soon afterwards to take up professional hunting as there was better money to be made. The Game Department salaries were poor and with three children (two at boarding school), the cost of education was beginning to strain my limited resources. I enjoyed the work and the people, and the fact that our department was small (the whole of Kenya had only eight white field officers). William Hale, the Chief Game Warden, was a very good boss and I enjoyed working under him. He always stood up for his field officers and knowing you would get his support was a comforting thought. On numerous occasions the District Commissioner or the farmers complained that I did not deal with their various problems. However, I was responsible for an exceptionally large area and often received several requests simultaneously. I could only take one at a time with the result that, by the time I arrived in an area, the buffalo or elephant in question had done its damage and moved away.

I resigned from the Department in 1957 and was offered a job as a professional hunter with Ker & Downey Safaris in Nairobi. Before I left I made a trip to the Marsabit National Reserve in the company of Peter Jenkins and Bill Woodley, both National Park officers whom I had known for many years. The idea was to see the big elephant named Ahmed. The Marsabit area was unique in that the mountains were old, extinct volcanoes in the middle of arid desert country. The slopes of the mountain were forested and inside the extinct volcanic bowls, small lakes had formed. Elephants had moved in and were protected by the Administration. From time to time big elephant made their homes there. The first was Mohammed who eventually died and then Ahmed appeared.

Nobody knows where these big elephant came from but I suspect it was from Southern Ethiopia where big elephant did occur. Both Ahmed and Mohammed, when they eventually died of old age, were found to have recovered from bullet wounds. They must have led interesting lives.

My successor at the Game Department was David Allen. After I left, I rented a house on a coffee farm near Thika at Makuyu. The farm belonged to the Rundgren family. Peter and Rosalie Rundgren were once again our neighbours. Peter now managed the coffee farm having resigned from the Forest Department at Nanyuki, where they had been our neighbours when we lived on the mountain.

A warm feeling consoled me when I thought about the past eight years I spent doing game control. I managed to avoid injury to myself and the game scouts who accompanied me. This was partly due to having Wanyahoro as back up on most of my hunting excursions. We learned to work as a team and through the years relied on one another when dealing with dangerous game. He never let me down and always remained cool under pressure. It was a comfort to have such a reliable companion. We each had many narrow escapes from charging animals and always managed to survive unscathed. Maybe we were lucky or perhaps we had a good guardian angel – who knows? When I left the Department, Wanyahoro also decided to leave and work with me in my new professional hunting venture.

I received an official letter from William Hale, the Chief Game Warden, thanking me for my services in the Kenya Game Department. I kept the letter because I appreciated the kind words he personally added.

I was an assistant professional hunter to John Kingsley-Heath who showed me the ropes during my first safari. Professional hunting with clients was a different kettle of fish to what I was accustomed to as a game warden. I had to learn how to deal with clients and look after their needs in camp. Out in the field I had to advise the client on what to shoot. Most clients were not familiar with the different species of game and what to look for when judging trophy size. Some did not know the difference between a mature animal and an immature one. I had to point out the big heads and tell them whether it was record class or just average, and whenever possible what the size of the head might be – a fifty or fifty-two inch kudu or that the spread on a buffalo would measure forty-five inches and so on.

Then I had to get the client into position where he or she would be close enough to shoot. This often entailed careful stalking using all the available cover and while doing this keeping the wind in our favour so that the game would not pick up our scent. While approaching the quarry, we had to remind clients to move as quietly as possible so that our approach would not be heard. This was not always easy as many people were used to walking on city pavements and did not lift their feet high enough, with the result that they kicked stones or sticks lying in the path. To overcome this I walked ahead and pointed out any object which I thought they might not step over. Bushes had to be held aside so that clothing did not rustle as the hunter brushed past. Some clothing materials sounded like a canvas sail being dragged past a bush and consequently I advised the client what to wear. White or bright clothing was taboo because animals picked up movement much more easily. Neutral colours which blended in with the bush were best and soft materials made less noise. Rifle barrels and any other objects which reflected the bright sun had to be covered or dealt with to avoid reflection. A flash from a rifle barrel could be picked up over a long distance and immediately caught the animals attention. The rifle barrel problem was solved by carrying the rifle in a case and taking it out only when in position to shoot. The case was also useful when crawling on the ground as it prevented sand from getting into the barrel or action. Other solutions were to tape the barrel or to pull a tight fitting sock (made especially for hunting) over it. Later on, I carried a shooting stick for the client to rest the rifle on and make a steadier shot. To minimise wounding of dangerous animals, the closer to the animal we got, the better. If possible, long shots were avoided. Somebody else pulled the trigger and I only shot as a last resort, such as to stop a charging lion or buffalo.

I had no trouble getting a professional hunter's licence because I had considerable experience hunting dangerous animals in the years of working for the Government. I got my Kenya licence first and then my Tanganyika licence. Our first safari took place in Tanganyika with a party from California.

In August 1957, we left Nairobi with our clients for Arusha in Tanganyika, where we were to pick up our hunting licences. Both John and I used four wheel drive Land Rovers as hunting cars. Two Bedford trucks carried the staff and the camping gear including tents, beds, bedding, food boxes, refrigerators, spare fuel for the vehicles and drums of water. I borrowed a heavy .458 Winchester rifle to use in case of a charge from a dangerous animal but I was a little uneasy about using a magazine rifle, because I used double barrelled English rifles during all my years of game control. I handed in the Game Department's double when I left and, as it is always best to use what one is accustomed to, I decided to buy a good quality double when I returned from safari. The game laws in Tanganyika differed from those in Kenya. John Kingsley-Heath explained the laws and was available to clarify any points during the safari which made matters much easier.

Our first hunting area was at Mto Mbu in the Rift Valley close to Lake Manyara. We hunted lesser kudu and buffalo, and put out bait for leopard and lion. My client, Duncan O'Neal, was a lawyer and I found him easy to get along with. He had done quite a bit of hunting in the States and shot reasonably well. After we arrived in camp, we went out to sight in the rifles.

We managed to bag a buffalo quite easily and after removing the head and cape for mounting, put out the rest of the carcass for leopard and lion bait. A couple of days later we left camp early to check the buffalo carcass. I stopped the hunting car a good distance away in order to observe the flat-topped acacia tree where the bait was hung. I noticed some movement below the tree and saw two lionesses around the bait. We waited for a while to see whether there was a male lion around but after about half an hour I saw no other movement and decided to drive slowly towards the tree. When we were about one hundred yards away, the two lionesses became aware of our approach and slunk off. Immediately after they left we saw a leopard descending the tree. It was a young male and had obviously been put up the tree by the lionesses and was afraid to come down while they were on the bait.

We did not see any more lion or bigger leopard in this area but I managed to get quite a good lesser kudu for my client and John got an even bigger one, which ranked high up in Rowland Ward's Record Book.

We moved to Ngorongoro crater for a couple of days of photography. The crater is a unique work of nature. It is one of the biggest extinct volcanoes in the world. The bottom is several miles across and from the top of the rim to the opposite side is about fifteen to twenty miles. The rim is also quite high, 8,000 feet, with bamboo growing on much of the slope. We saw buffalo, elephant and rhino among other game. There was a lodge on the rim of the crater and National Park quarters were close by so we obtained permits to camp in the bottom of the crater and spent a couple of days observing and photographing game. To reach the track which led to the bottom of the crater, we drove along the rim to the opposite side, a distance of about twelve to fifteen miles. We passed through a thick forest and bamboo belt growing on the slopes. A lone bull buffalo and a few bushbuck were grazing between the belts of forest and bamboo. The nettles in the grass reminded me of Mount Kenya and the Aberdares ranges where similar vegetation grew. Quite close to the Ngorongoro is another volcano which rises out of the plains and stands on its own to the south of Lake Natron. It is still active and erupts periodically.

Eventually we reached the track which descended to the bottom and soon saw herd after herd of game scattered around. It was impressive. Most of the game was zebra, wildebeest, Grant's and Thomson's gazelle and Cokes hartebeest. There were three rhino standing on a hillside. We passed some ruins and John stopped to explain that when Tanganyika was a German Colony, two German cattle farmers owned the entire crater base. World War I changed all this. At the bottom of the crater, close to Soda Lake, we camped under some flat topped yellow fever trees (acacia).

Next day we travelled around taking photographs of game which included lion, rhino, buffalo, and even a herd of elephant tearing off branches of acacia and eating the bark. Among the vast herds of game were the Masai with their cattle. Masai often killed lion cubs in the belief that if cubs were allowed to reach adulthood they would prey on their cattle. Masai also speared rhino for sport or to prove their manhood then later on removed the horns to sell for a few shillings. Through the years Masai cattle herds have been an eyesore in this area. The authorities tried to keep the numbers down and even tried to expel them from the crater altogether but were unsuccessful because the area belonged to Masai tribal authorities.

Early one morning, we packed up and prepared to cross the Serengeti Plains National Park in order to reach our next hunting area adjoining the park. Here we were to hunt for lion, leopard, buffalo and a few species of antelope which we had not already collected.

With all the vehicles loaded, we drove out of the crater and around the rim, past the lodge and several miles beyond it to a road leading down the other side of the crater onto the Serengeti plains. The descent was tortuous and the trucks had to use the low gears. A few years later a truck from the same company went out of control and crashed at speed, killing several passengers. The driver failed to use low gear to keep the speed down and relied mainly on his brakes. Eventually the brake drums got so hot that the heat caused the brake fluid to boil and the brakes failed. The truck was travelling too fast for the driver to engage low gear and hence the vehicle went of out control.

At the bottom of the crater near the track was a site where archaeological excavations were taking place. There was a deep gorge and in its sides was evidence of prehistoric life. Animal bones could be observed still embedded in the walls of the gorge. Those bones included hippo teeth and crocodile jaws and teeth which indicated the area might at one time have been a lake. We spent a couple of interesting hours walking around.

Before we crossed the plains, we were lucky to actually see the yearly migration of game in progress. It was quite a sight for, as far as one could see, the plains were a moving mass of animals, mostly zebra, wildebeest, hartebeest and gazelle. It is hard to describe my feelings when I saw this for the first time. I wondered whether man would leave this area as it was for the future? There was already a tremendous amount of pressure on Government from the local tribes and their domestic stock.

Near the Seronera National Park Lodge and Headquarters we saw three different prides of lion quite close to the road and drove up to them to take photographs. They were not at all afraid of the Land Rovers and we got very close – only a few yards away. I realised they were used to cars and photographers. These prides were following the migrating herds. We also saw two males on their own, both with magnificent manes and so much alike it was obvious they were brothers. We stopped for lunch under some big trees and sent the trucks ahead to make camp. The lunch boxes were always fully stocked for the clients' different tastes. Later that day, we camped north of the Serengeti Park boundary in Loliondo area which was full of game due to its proximity to the Park.

The use of the areas adjoining the Park for trophy shooting was one way of controlling the Park's excess animal populations and of bringing much needed foreign revenue to the country. Shooting was controlled and professional hunting did no harm but later poaching in these areas by tribesmen living close by did create problems. They used wire snares, bows and poisoned arrows and even modern firearms. The Park staff were never able to fully control these poachers. I met Myles Turner, ex-Kenya game warden, ex-professional hunter, now turned park warden at Seronera who described the poaching. Unfortunately this was to get worse in later years.

We found our best trophies here. During the first few days we put out bait for lion and leopard and built blinds. Impala were numerous with some very good heads among the herds. One afternoon my client and I came across a big herd of males. Using binoculars, I carefully looked them over and noted three or four very good trophies. One in particular had a wide set of horns and I decided to try for this animal. We were about 200 yards away from the animals which were feeding and untroubled by our presence. I took my client's rifle out of the gun rack and handed it to him. Then I got the shooting sticks out as well as my heavy rifle which I always carried in case we stumbled on lion or other dangerous game. I worked out an approach along a watercourse covered with trees and bush. This took us to well within shooting distance. Wanyahoro carried the shooting sticks and I carried my heavy rifle. We had no difficulty in getting fairly close and from a new vantage point I looked over the herd to locate the big impala. After a while I saw him feeding close to three other males on the other side. A smaller animal was directly behind the male we wanted so we had to wait a while before shooting to avoid the chance of a bullet passing through one animal and into another.

We positioned the sticks and the client stood with his rifle resting in the fork. Satisfying myself that he had located the right animal in his sights, I told the client to shoot. The impala fell in its tracks. The horns measured thirty inches which placed them well up in the Rowland Ward Record Book.

A couple of days later we were driving around looking for signs of lion. Luck was on our side, for we came across a lone male lion about two miles from camp. He had not seen us, so we left the hunting car and loaded our heavy rifles. I carried the .458 Winchester that Don had loaned me. Wanyahoro carried my father's .425 Westley-Richards rifle as back up and the client had a .375 H & H Magnum. We made a careful stalk and came on the lion at about twenty-five to thirty yards. Fortunately he was lying down and looking away from us. Lions have very good eyesight and had he been looking our way, he would have seen us immediately.

I asked the client to use the shooting sticks. The lion's head was clearly visible and I told him to aim for the base of the skull. I had carefully explained the hazards of taking a head shot at a lion, especially one with a heavy mane. Many people neglect to take the mane into account and miss the skull because the bullet passes through the mane. This applies especially to a lion looking towards the hunter. The lion has little forehead above the eyes as the skull slopes backwards. Many hunters have learned the costly lesson of not shooting low enough and having the bullet clip the mane with no harm to the lion. The client made an excellent shot and the lion collapsed on the spot. This lion had one of the best manes that I have ever seen. After taking photographs, we loaded it onto the Land Rover and proceeded to camp.

Later that day we checked the leopard bait. We drove to within a suitable distance and observed the bait through binoculars. The bait had been covered with bush so that vultures could not see it. We never walked up to a bait to avoid disturbing any leopard that might be close by. One bait had been eaten so, after a rest at camp, we returned at 4 o'clock to sit in the blind and wait. Shortly after taking up our position, the leopard suddenly appeared at the foot of the tree and I indicated its arrival to the client using hand signs. We had to wait about ten minutes before the cat climbed up the tree and started to feed. I then signalled for my client to shoot. Once again he made a good shot for the big cat fell to the ground and did not move. In one day we had collected both a lion and a leopard. This ended a perfect safari.

I was happy with the results of my first professional hunting safari and was more confident that future ones could be handled as well.

97

When I entered the head office of Ker & Downey Safaris on my return from Tanganyika, the receptionist, who knew that I was looking for a heavy barrelled rifle, informed me that a Dutch bank manager had left his rifle in the safari company armoury and wanted to sell it. The rifle was a best quality .470 rifle which was an exact replica of the one I had been using for game control. The asking price was reasonable and I could afford it by using part of the salary from my first trip.

Without hesitation, I promptly paid the Hollander. I used this rifle on dangerous game for the rest of my professional career. It shot straight and never let me down. I am convinced that I saved my skin on many occasions by using the English double barrelled rifle throughout my Game Department work on control and during my professional hunting. This would not have been the case with a heavy magazine rifle. At close quarters in thick cover I could get two quick shots into a charging animal, each bullet weighing 500 grains. The rifle handled like a shotgun with a sliding safety catch which I automatically slid forward off safety as I raised it to shoot. I did not lower the rifle for the second shot but only realigned onto the animal without taking my eyes off it. The rifle had ejectors and there was always a spare round in my hand which could quickly be loaded in case a third shot was necessary.

Shortly after my return to Nairobi, I was offered my first solo safari. The trip was to take place in Kenya with a hunter from Connecticut, Henry Budney. At that time the hunting areas in Kenya were open because the territory had not yet been divided into hunting blocks. (This was to come about shortly afterwards.) Don Bousfield had given me some useful information on an area in the Narok District (Masailand) which had very little hunting activity and was good for lion, buffalo, leopard, rhino and other game. He mentioned the name of only one other well-known professional hunter who used the area for hunting. Throughout my professional career I always tried to find new areas with the least hunting pressure. This was important for getting good record class trophies. I often made my own tracks across valleys, through forests and bush in order to reach virgin territory and this frequently paid dividends.

As I was preparing to leave Nairobi with my client, I bumped into the professional hunter whom Don had mentioned. He asked where I was going and I answered truthfully, Masailand, and no more. He told me that he was also hunting in the Narok District. It crossed my mind that he would pitch up in the same area but I gave it no more thought.

Henry and I duly arrived in 'Don's area' and set up camp. The area was at a fairly high altitude with deep valleys, wooded hills and open areas of lush grassland. It was ideal cattle country and the Masai cattle grazed the area, but there were not many cattle herds around. There were buffalo, antelope and zebra herds to be seen which pleased me. Cedar, olive and yellow fever trees surrounded the camp. A strong stream flowed from a spring nearby and the clean, pure water was ideal for our needs. On the way to camp, in order to avoid disturbing the hunting area unnecessarily, Henry zeroed his rifles to make sure that they were shooting straight.

The first afternoon we went out on a recce, driving to some high ridges from which we could study the surrounding countryside. It was gratifying to see herds of buffalo, eland and zebra peacefully grazing out in the open. Seeing buffalo in the open was a good indication of an undisturbed area. In areas where there was heavy hunting, the buffalo moved into thick cover at first light and remain there all day, emerging again only at dusk. We also saw impala herds with some good heads close to camp.

Early the next morning we set out, taking lunch with us in order to spend the whole day seeking game. I drove carefully through the valleys as the grass was bumper high and it was difficult to see hidden rocks. Eventually, we came to the ridge where we had been the evening before. It was possible to see for miles into the great Rift Valley. To the south was Lake Natron in Tanganyika but it was obscured by a range of hills in the distance. We were looking at new hunting territory where I was sure we would find lion, leopard and buffalo. The side of the valley below us was steep for a vehicle's descent, but the four wheel drive Land Rover managed, though it took careful negotiating. We did a lot of manoeuvring before eventually finding ourselves at the bottom where we could get around to the virgin territory.

En route we bagged a good trophy-sized impala. After skinning the head and removing the skull and horns, I used the carcass as bait for a leopard. When we reached the valley floor, I looked for a suitable area in which to hang the bait and found a nicely branched tree. Thirty yards away was a thicket of heavy bush which provided cover for a leopard to lie up and watch his meat. This meant that he could stay close by and would most likely be on the bait before dark. We neglected to build a blind which could have been disastrous if we had caught a leopard feeding. However there was the odd clump of bush near the bait for us to hide in and watch the tree.

We tied the carcass onto a suitable limb or branch and covered it with bushes to prevent vultures from seeing it. Vultures have exceptionally fine eyesight, especially when it comes to exposed meat. In later years, I was baffled to discover vultures on covered bait and realised that these birds had spotted hyenas or other predators circling a baited tree. They then put two

99

and two together and decided that there was food around. This showed that vultures were not completely stupid.

We set off to the area where I had spotted buffalo grazing the previous evening and picked a suitable vantage point from which the client and I could glass the area. In Nairobi I had purchased a pair of Hensoldt (German made) binoculars. They were 7 x 50 magnification, and fairly long. To some they were considered cumbersome, but they suited me ideally and lay flat on my chest below my chin when the straps were shortened. These binoculars offered excellent vision and my eyes never tired even after hours of looking through them.

I caught a movement on the edge of a bush near a gully. This turned out to be a lone bull buffalo with a fine head. We made a good stalk and Henry shot it with his .458 Winchester Magnum. As it was fairly late in the afternoon, we removed the head and cape and took what meat was needed for camp staff. We tied the rest of the carcass to the foot of a tree and covered it to keep the birds off. I was hoping to attract lion. I used the Land Rover to drag the stomach contents to encourage any cats which might be nearby.

While we negotiated our way up the side of the valley heading for the ridge, the gun bearers on the back suddenly tapped on the roof. Wanyahoro said there was a bull buffalo lying nearby and it appeared to be injured. I took my heavy double and approached cautiously. The buffalo looked close to death and I signaled Henry to finish it off. Our postmortem revealed several wounds made by lions. The buffalo somehow managed to fight them off and escape, but the wounds were too severe and it was obviously dying.

We arrived back in camp to find another Land Rover. The visitor was none other than my Nairobi professional hunter. He was seething with rage and asked what right I had to be in this area and who told me to come here. He made it obvious that he regarded the area as his own private sanctuary. I did not reveal that Don had told me about it, but I did say that the area was big and there was plenty of room for both of us. He departed and moved several miles away. Afterwards I heard that he managed to get some good trophies – he was a good hunter.

The following morning we returned to the previous day's hunting area. From the ridge overlooking the valley, I glassed around the buffalo carcass and was gratified to see a big male lion appear out of a small wooded gully and approach our bait. He took a few mouthfuls, then suddenly left the buffalo and walked back to the gully to lie down. I decided that he had had a good feed and was not really hungry.

I wondered how to tackle the situation. There were several alternatives. Firstly we could find a vantage point close to the kill where we could sit and wait for the lion to reappear, but it could be hours before this happened. Secondly I could get my crew to drive the lion out towards where we would lie in wait. This method was often unsuccessful and we might scare the lion away for good. Then I noticed many vultures on the carcass of the buffalo we had put out of its misery. It crossed my mind that if we chased the birds off they would circle over our lion bait in the valley below and might even see the carcass on which the lion had been feeding. I knew that lion and leopard chase birds off their kill and this should bring our lion out into the open.

I instructed Wanyahoro to watch us while we moved down to take up a position close to the lion's lair. When we were in position he must chase the birds off the kill in the hope that they would fly over the area where the lion was resting. Henry took his .458 Winchester and I took my .470 and we proceeded down the slope, keeping to cover and concealing ourselves as much as possible so that the lion would not see us if he was watching.

We approached the crucial area with caution and came to within thirty yards of the bait. Here we hid behind a bush which allowed a good view of the lion if he came out. Soon the vultures were flying overhead and shortly afterwards the lion emerged from the bush in the gully and made his way towards the bait. I indicated to Henry to wait. The lion stopped short of the bait and looked up at the birds. He presented his body broadside, so I signaled Henry to shoot. He made another good shot and the lion fell in its tracks. It had a good mane and made an excellent trophy. In due course, Wanyahoro brought the Land Rover and, after taking some photographs, we loaded the cat and took it back to the camp.

After lunch and a short rest, we drove to where we had put out the leopard bait. Several hundred yards away from the bait I stopped the Land Rover and looked through the binoculars. The branch coverings had been removed and the carcass eaten. Then I spotted the leopard, stretched out asleep on a limb of the tree. We approached on foot hoping to get close enough for a shot. Fifty or sixty yards would suffice. We made a quiet approach. Every now and again I stopped to look towards the tree and the sleeping leopard, but each time he remained motionless. Eventually we were close enough but I decided to go another twenty yards until we were only forty yards away. Still the leopard had not moved, but I knew that if he put his head up and saw us, he would be gone like a flash. I indicated to Henry to shoot – he was using a .375 H & H Magnum. With his shot the leopard fell out of the tree like a sack of potatoes and never moved. It is often not possible to approach a leopard sleeping in a tree over open ground without his being aware of you. This area had been undisturbed by trophy hunters and that was why the leopard had not been on the alert. He was a big tom and had a fine coat. In one day we collected both a lion and a leopard, which took considerable pressure off the hunt.

As there were plenty rhino signs in the area, I decided to try for a suitable trophy. A few miles away there was a large area of bush and trees growing in a basin-like depression. This was the best area to seek out a rhinoceros. We did a lot of walking until we eventually found one. It stepped into view out of a thick patch of bush. The horns were long and I knew that it would make a good trophy, so again I told Henry to shoot. We were so close that he had no difficulty in dropping it with one shot from his .458 Winchester. The front horn measured twenty-seven inches.

We also managed to get other plains game such as zebra before we decided to move to another area to hunt elephant.

Our next hunting area was at Maralal towards Lake Rudolf, now called Lake Turkana. En route we spent one night in Nairobi. Maralal is similar to the Narok district, especially around the town, but to the north, there is an escarpment which leads to a dry sandy desert area. On top of the escarpment the view is breathtaking as you look over broken country into the Great Rift Valley, which leads northwards to Lake Rudolf. You can see some impressive mountains lying to the south of the lake, namely Mount Nyiru (2753 metres or 9032 feet high) and Mount Porror (2583 metres). The top of Mount Nyiru is plateau-like, with bamboo growing on it. Much of this area is volcanic. Teleki crater, which last erupted at the turn of the century, lies to the south.

We spent a few days in the high area near Maralal and then camped at the foot of a mountain just north of Baragoi. Julian McKeand, the local game warden, told me this area was good for greater kudu so we decided to hunt one and invited Julian to come along. Early the next morning we climbed the steep slopes and saw a few animals near the top, but no trophies. At about midday we spotted a good looking bull on the opposite hill. I proceeded with Henry, while the others stayed in position to watch us stalk the kudu.

The sun was very hot and our throats were parched, but we kept stalking, using cover and depressions for our approach. Kudu have excellent eyesight and we were extra careful. For the last hundred yards we crawled as there was no more cover. Eventually, we got to within about seventy or eighty yards and I decided that Henry must shoot. The kudu only went a short distance before he fell. We had an excellent trophy with fine horns. It was the first greater kudu I had ever hunted.

The plains in this region were home to herds of beisa oryx, Grevy's zebra, Grant's gazelle and gerenuk. The bush areas also had elephant. The

Grevy's zebra is the larger of the zebra family with big ears and very narrow stripes. We collected oryx and a Grevy's zebra. Each day we drove up the road towards Maralal looking for elephant. On the second last day we saw some bulls, one with good tusks of around seventy pounds each. When we approached, I noticed Henry was a little nervous - perhaps it was the sheer size of the elephant. I was surprised, as he had not shown this nervousness when hunting other animals. I took his arm as we approached until we were close enough to shoot. I had instructed Henry by drawing illustrations of where to aim. He elected to make a heart shot and, with the shot, the elephant rushed off and ran about seventy yards before collapsing. Thus ended a perfect safari.

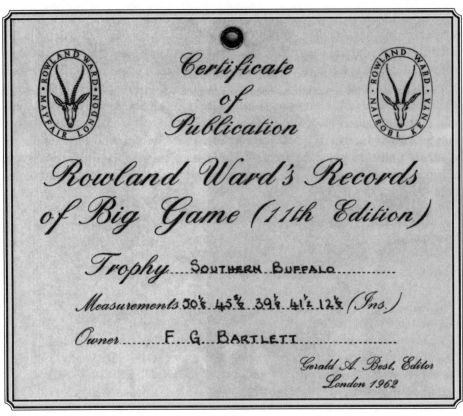

One of my four certificates from Rowland Ward for a 50 inch buffalo trophy.

Anne & Don Bousfield with the Nile perch they caught on Lake Rudolf, Kenya

Lion in Masailand, Kenya

Baobab tree damaged by elephant

On safari in the Northern Frontier District, Kenya

Lion shot during my first professional safari -1957

Mara Caldesi with her leopard

Bob Model

A sable taken by Don Bousfield in Kenya 1960

Bongo shot on Mount Kenya

NINE

LIFE IN THE SAFARI CAPITAL OF THE WORLD

My next safari was handled jointly with a second hunter. He was the senior hunter because he had been employed by the company for a few years and I was a newcomer. The party were Italians – a man, his wife and a professor friend. In later years I did many safaris with Carlo and Mara Caldesi and we became good friends. Carlo was one of the best hunters that I went out with. He had a lot of experience, having hunted all over the world. On this safari I guided Mara and the other hunter took Carlo. My dislike for the other hunter was instant. He was a little man and very cocky, ordering everybody around as if he was running a military show.

Our first hunting area was back at Maralal where we camped on the Lorogi Plateau. The camp was situated among dried up or very dry cedar trees, many of which were now dying and there was very little evidence of new growth. The fires, started by the local tribesmen, did not help matters as cedar trees burn very easily. The tribesmen kept both cattle and sheep and regularly burnt the grass so that their stock could feed on the new growth. The authorities tried to stop this burning but they were never successful.

The other professional hunter managed to get Carlo an elephant. One tusk was good, around eighty pounds, but it there was only a stump on the opposite side. Later on they shot a smaller elephant. Carlo took a side brain shot and the elephant dropped on its knees in an upright position. The body was lying on the lip of the escarpment. The following day I was asked by the professional hunter to take a few members of the staff to cut out the tusks and to retrieve the tail and feet. We had no trouble in chopping the tusks out but the feet and tail were underneath the body. When we rolled it over, the elephant just kept going. Its stomach was inflated with gas turning it into a rubber ball. It bounced down the slope uprooting trees, bush and rocks, and making a tremendous noise. In fact, the noise was so loud that a herd of buffalo across the gorge were put to flight in panic. The elephant fell at least 1,000 feet. We returned with the tusks but no feet or tail. Carlo decided that he must have the tail and a reward was offered to a local native guide to go down the escarpment and retrieve it. It took the local a full day to descend to the bottom and climb up again. In the evening he returned to the camp with the tail minus all the hairs which had come out during the elephant's momentous descent down the slope. Carlo wanted the hairs to make elephant bracelets – the tail itself was worthless!

I discovered a leopard had been feeding on one of my baits, so Carlo and I decided to sit up for it. We had already built a blind so all we had to do was to arrive in the heat of the afternoon and take up our positions. The sun was still up when we heard birds twittering and I suspected they had seen the leopard. Shortly afterwards I heard a body moving through the dry grass close to the front of the blind and I realised it was the leopard. Then we caught a flash of yellow as it moved past. It was so close. We froze. I don't know why the leopard did not see us in the blind because there were gaps in the bush that would have allowed him to do so. Over time I came to realise that most wild animals rely on movement to catch their eye. By keeping still a hunter can usually get away without being observed. The leopard jumped up into the tree and started feeding. Carlo made a perfect shot and we had our leopard – a big male.

We collected a few more species before moving to our next hunting area at Kinna, beyond Isiolo and behind the Nyambeni hills. I was still hunting with Mara, looking for both a lion and a leopard. One day while driving through the bush, there came the familiar tap on the roof. Wanyahoro told me he could see lions on a kill and they had not heard our vehicle. We loaded our rifles and proceeded on foot. There was plenty of cover for us to approach unobserved until we were close to the lions. They were busy on the kill, making a lot of noise as they fought over the meal.

We moved a little closer but still could not see any male lion. Suddenly there was a low rumbling growl and a lioness appeared out of the grass not more than twenty yards away. She had seen us and was very angry. She faced us with her tail twitching, and she started making short rushes at us. To make matters worse, a small cub ran towards us and disappeared into the low bush behind which we were standing. It was obviously her cub. I realised the lioness would charge any minute, especially if we made the wrong move. I quietly ordered Mara, who was standing directly behind me, to stand still. The lioness was now crouched down, growling constantly and swinging her tail from side to side. I knew that if the tail came up, she would charge. I whispered to those behind me to move back slowly, one step at a time. As we moved back the lioness made a short rush towards us and stopped again, lying flat and growling. After a short pause, we repeated the movement slowly backwards, and each time we moved she made another short rush. This scenario was repeated several times but the lioness always stopped short. Eventually we were far enough from her cub and she allowed us to move away. While we were going through these manoeuvres, I noticed that the male lion, who had suddenly popped his head up, was sitting like a dog watching us. There was nothing we could do. If we shot at the lion, the lioness would not hesitate about coming all the way. We had to leave them in peace.

I put up a zebra bait in another area, having first made a drag with the carcass to attract any cats around. We built a blind and made a path leading to it. All twigs and grass were diligently swept aside to allow for a silent approach. During the night I heard lions roaring in the direction of the carcass and decided to visit the bait early next morning. While it was still dark, we drove towards the area in the Land Rover.

About three quarters of a mile short of the bait, we left the hunting car and proceeded on foot. Two male lions started roaring, each one trying to out do the other - the noise was impressive. It was getting light and the horizon was red from the sun which would appear any moment. We silently approached the blind and took up our positions. As the sun was peeping over the horizon, I looked through the viewing hole. I noticed a lioness feeding on the bait, which was strung up in the tree. One male lion was lying beyond the tree, watching the proceedings. I started to look for the other male because I knew there were two, when suddenly I became aware of a movement just in front of the blind. It was the other lion who was not more than five yards away. I indicated this to Mara but she seemed to have difficulty in spotting it. After a long time she acknowledged that she could see him. She slowly pushed her rifle barrel through the hole and took aim. I moved to the entrance, ready to dash out as soon as the shot went off to check that the lion had gone down. It seemed ages before she fired. I kept looking back at her and wondering about the delay. Wanyahoro was standing behind her, and from the expression on his face, I knew that he was puzzled. Mara told me afterwards that the lion was so close she had difficulty with the scope - all she could see was the skin of the lion filling the whole scope. Eventually she worked out the head, put the cross hairs on it and fired.

With the sound of the shot I dashed out of the blind, my .470 rifle at the ready. The lion was no longer visible. I then heard another shot which was fired from inside the blind. I ran past the front of the blind and saw the lion running away so I fired and dropped it. Wanyahoro told me that Mara's shot had not connected with any vital spots and the lion had jumped up and run into the blind! As its head burst through the side, Wanyahoro was ready and fired immediately. He hit it in the body, but once again did not anchor it. By this time I had been right around the side and front before I spotted the lion and managed to fire the fatal shot. The lion was old but the mane was that of a typical scruffy N.F.D. lion (N.F.D. standing for Northern Frontier District). The manes in this area are seldom good and some males have no manes at all.

We loaded the lion onto the Land Rover, then examined the bait and I noticed that leopard had also had a meal off it. I decided to return in the afternoon and try for leopard. We took the lion to camp, had a short siesta after lunch and then drove back to sit up for the leopard. As usual we parked well short of the bait and walked to the blind. When we were a few hundred yards from our destination, I heard growling and saw two male leopards fighting over the bait. One of them did not want to fight because he always gave way whenever the other got too close. They were coming towards us so I quickly put the shooting sticks up to provide Mara with a steady rest for her rifle as she prepared to shoot. The leopards kept coming and I could see both of them clearly but they were so preoccupied with their own quarrel that they were not paying much attention to anything else. I told Mara to shoot as soon as she had a clear broadside shot but she never did fire. The leopards passed very close, not more than twenty five yards away, and eventually disappeared behind a big clumpy bush to our left.

When I asked Mara why she had not fired, she replied that she could not see them. She was a very short woman, about five feet tall, and I stood six feet and one inch. The extra foot gave me enough of an advantage in seeing the leopard which she could not. I quickly grabbed the shooting sticks and moved towards the big bush where I had seen the cats disappear. I moved around to the side of the bush and I walked into the backside of a big bull elephant, busy feeding in another bush. We could still hear the leopards growling beyond the elephant but what amazed me was that he took no notice of the cats and merely carried on stuffing his face. We backed off quietly until we were far enough away. I told Mara that we would try again in the morning because the leopard who won the argument would not come back until dark.

The next morning we left camp in the dark and settled in the blind as we had done the previous day. When I looked through the hole in the blind I saw the leopard lying at the foot of the tree. Mara waited until the cat stood up, and then she shot and killed it. Throughout my years of collecting lion and leopard, I had as much luck on bait in the early morning as I did in the evening. Getting the leopard ended a successful safari and the next day we returned to Nairobi.

Before long I returned to the Kinna area with another safari. This time my clients were a film director and his actress wife. They wanted to shoot the cats and a good elephant.

I went out with Pat, the film director, on the first afternoon to sight in the rifles and make sure that after his long trip to Kenya, the firearms were still shooting accurately. Pat had trouble zeroing in the light rifle which he would use if we found a leopard feeding on bait. His shots were all over the target and he kept altering the scope adjustments. He was not much of a shot and did not go about sighting in properly. I suggested that he let me have a go but he refused. Eventually he claimed to have the problem sorted out satisfactorily but this was only because he had hit the bull with the last shot. I suggested he fire again to confirm the last shot but he refused once again. I hoped he would not have to shoot a leopard and consoled myself that if he did get a shot at the cat, he would miss it cleanly. That same afternoon we managed to shoot two animals but both were wounded and I had to finish them off. We put the carcasses up for bait before heading back to camp.

During the next couple of days we hunted elephant and saw a lot but nothing worth shooting. However, we got a lesser kudu. They make a pretty head mount and their skin is very attractive, with vertical white stripes down the side. We eventually had a leopard feeding on one of the baits and we sat up for it one afternoon. The leopard arrived very late, just as the sun was disappearing over the horizon. He settled down to feed, broadside to us presenting a perfect target. With the shot the leopard leapt off the limb, jumped to the ground and disappeared into the grass.

At the sound of the shot, the gun bearers and Wanyahoro drove up. I was not particularly happy with the reaction of the leopard when it was shot. I had the impression that the bullet hit too far back, possibly some-where in the guts. Such a shot was bad news in a follow up. Not only does the wound make the animal extremely bad-tempered, but in the event of a charge it does not slow its speed one bit.

When Wanyahoro came up, we went in the direction where the leopard had disappeared into the grass. I was armed with my .470 double loaded with soft nosed bullets. Wanyahoro carried a 12 gauge shotgun, whose barrels were both loaded with ssg. The client came along and carried the rifle with which he shot at the leopard. Immediately we spotted drops of red blood mixed with spots of watery blood and small traces of stomach content. The leopard had received a gut shot. I explained this to Pat and told him that if we got up to the leopard we would more than likely be charged.

Tracking was not easy because we could not see the leopard's tracks in the grass and had to rely on the spots of blood. We tracked for about 400 yards and the leopard was still going but it looked as if he had slowed to a walk. I was in front of Wanyahoro and another tracker. Pat followed in the rear. I was all eyes for any sign of the wounded animal and the two Africans behind did the tracking. I felt sure the leopard would seek refuge in any thick patch of bush ahead. Darkness came and the visibility deteriorated sufficiently to call it a day and continue in the morning. I tied my white handkerchief to a dead tree close by so that we would know where we had turned back. That evening back in camp, Pat asked me what the chances of finding the leopard were. I was sure we would find it, but if it died during the night the hyenas would probably get it first. I was still angry with him for not letting me zero in his rifle to make doubly sure that it was shooting straight. I was not convinced that he had done it properly. That night I slept uneasily and was pleased when the tent African brought my tea as the sky started to change colour when the sun rose above the horizon. After a very hasty breakfast, we headed straight for the area where we had stopped the previous evening.

I drove slowly until the white handkerchief on the dead tree came into view. We disembarked and loaded our rifles. With the safety catches returned to safe positions, we proceeded to track. We had worked twenty to thirty yards when we came on the leopard. It was dead and hyenas had ripped open the hindquarters and ruined the skin. All we could get was a head mount. We looked around the area and noticed that the leopard had lain up couple of times, moving around from one place to another. Obviously it h suffered a lot of pain before dying. It was still alive when we turned back th evious evening and, had we come on it, we most certainly would have bee ed. Luck had been on our side but we lost a good skin through the f de and carelessness of a 'know it all'.

A cou of days later, while we were driving around, we spotted three elephant bu moving through thick thorn bush. One had good tusks. We stopped, hurr lly got out and with our heavy rifles, we quickly followed the elephants, whi h by this time had moved off. After a few hundred yards, we came upon th elephants. They had stopped to listen and had their trunks up, obviously esting the wind for danger. One of them was big and well worth shooting. We manoeuvred to get close enough and Pat shot at the big bull. The elephant went a short distance and collapsed. When we examined the tusks, I realised we had a very good trophy, although one tusk was a little bit shorter than the other. Elephants use their tusks for digging up roots when feeding and this results in one being worn shorter than the other. Just as humans favour one limb, elephants will use the same tusk frequently with resultant wear.

We took the inevitable photographs, as well as some Polaroid pictures. The African staff were delighted because it was the first time that they had seen instant pictures. The next day the camp staff chopped out the tusks and brought them in. When we got back to civilisation (being Nairobi), we had them weighed. They were 110 pounds and l00 pounds respectively.

For my next safari, I took out a young couple who had previously hunted in Moçambique. Before we left Nairobi, we were talking in the office of the manager of Ker & Downey Safaris, Ronnie Stevens. The client said, "I want to make it clear that my professional hunter does not shoot at any of the animals that I will hunt on this safari!" The manager's reply was, "You should leave it to the discretion of the professional hunter." However the young man was insistent that I did not shoot under any circumstances. I was uneasy about his request and thought it over before I decided that I would not shoot unless it meant life or death.

This client thought he knew everything about hunting and throughout the safari ignored my advice, with the result that he did not do as well as he should have. To start with, while hunting elephant in the Tana River area of Garissa, I explained very clearly what he should do when we got up to elephant and how to go about shooting it. One of the most important things he was to observe was not to shoot at an elephant if there was another standing behind it. This was to avoid a bullet passing through one elephant and hitting the one behind as well.

Well ... we walked up to four bulls, one of which had good tusks of around eighty pounds each side. Eventually we manoeuvred close enough to shoot and I told him to wait until the big elephant was clear of the others, but he would not listen and immediately fired at the bull. He hit it low, near the foreleg, and the bullet went through and hit the elephant behind. This was clear from where I was standing. I told him to shoot again, which he did and the second bullet raised dust on the shoulder. I knew that it had hit

111

home. All four elephants took off with a rush but I knew the big bull would probably only go a short distance. After about eighty yards he started to slow down until he stumbled and fell. The other three kept going. I followed the tracks to see if there was any blood and sure enough the gun bearers picked up drops of blood. We followed the spoor for several miles and there was a little blood all the way along. We decided it was not serious as the wounded animal was managing to keep up with the others. We made our way back to the dead elephant, took photographs and left instructions for the gun bearers to cut out the tusks and remove the other trophy parts needed by the client.

I told the client that we had to report the wounding of an elephant because it was required by law. This meant a drive of about seventy miles to Garissa, where the game warden, Ken Smith, was stationed. I filed a written report with him and sent a copy to the Game Department Head Office in Nairobi before returning to camp. I had known Ken Smith for many years before he joined the Game Department. We met when he was a farm manager on a pineapple estate at Kilifi. Rodney Elliott and I once stayed with him during our local three weeks leave. Kilifi is on the coast and offered excellent spear and deep-sea fishing. Rodney and I spent most of our leave fishing in the channel among the coral heads.

The trip to Garissa took the whole day and this did not please the clients because it meant that we could not hunt that day. I realised that the man was not a true trophy hunter but merely wanted to shoot everything on his licence, regardless of whether or not it was trophy quality. In spite of this, I managed to get him a good lesser kudu and a buffalo with a forty five inch spread during the next few days.

We moved to Mount Kenya to continue the hunt. Once again I had trouble with the young man. A couple of days after we arrived in the new area, we were driving up a mountain track in a bamboo forest early in the morning when we suddenly spotted a male lion walking ahead. I stopped the Land Rover and watched the cat until it walked around the next bend and disappeared from sight. We then left the vehicle and followed on foot.

The young chap was using a .375 H & H Magnum and quickly loaded it. I took my heavy double and we followed the track. As we walked around the bend we saw the lion about sixty yards ahead. He was walking very slowly but he must have sensed our presence or seen a movement out of the corner of his eye, because he suddenly turned, stood broadside and looked right at us. I told the young man to shoot, which he did. The lion dropped but started to roll around on the ground. I felt sure he would get up, so I told the young man to shoot again. To my astonishment, he slung the rifle over his shoulder, turned his back on the lion and started to walk back to the Land Rover remarking, "What for, one shot is enough!" The lion suddenly sprang up and bounded away into the bamboo. I turned on the young man and the look I gave him was enough to express my thoughts. He knew exactly what I thought of his stupid behaviour.

We followed the wounded lion which was not bleeding too badly. Utmost caution was required because the short heavy bamboo afforded the lion all the cover he needed and gave him the advantage. We put the lion up twice but all we heard was a growl and a crash of bamboo as he departed. He never charged. Several hours later we followed the spoor down a deep gorge into the Sirimon River at the bottom. The water was crystal clear and very cold at that altitude. The tracks went up the side of the gorge along a narrow game track. About halfway up I decided that the lion was showing no real ill effects from the bullet wound. In fact, he was going strong so I called off the search and lost another trophy unnecessarily.

As the safari progressed, I grew more and more disillusioned with the client. The young man had four buffalo on his licence and he wanted to continue to hunt them. I told him not to shoot another unless it was bigger than the one he already had but he made no comment. On one occasion we saw a lone bull grazing in a grassy clearing across a valley and walked across to have a closer look. Once again I told him not to shoot unless it turned out to be larger than the previous one. When we got closer I looked through my binoculars and reported that it was an old bull, smaller than the one he had. I started to walk back expecting the client to follow when I heard a shot. He dropped the buffalo with a neck shot. Angrily, I asked him what he wanted it for and he replied that he did not want it. I was not prepared to waste the carcass and instructed the gun bearers to cut it up and load it onto the Land Rover. I left the client in camp and took the meat to the family farm a few miles away where I knew Albert would use it. There was no more hunting that day, much to the displeasure of the clients.

I decided to see the safari through as we only had two more days to go to the end. We went hunting the next day and the young man shot at an immature male waterbuck without me telling him to do so, but fortunately he missed. We had words and I was told by his wife that they had paid a lot of money for the safari and would shoot everything on their licence, regardless of whether or not they were going to take it as a trophy. I tried to explain that it made sense to shoot good trophies and the animals needed for meat, but not to shoot animals we could not use. I suggested they leave the animals they would not utilise for another hunter, especially the young immature males which would in later years grow up into good trophy animals.

We continued to drive up the forest track. I was still seething when we came around a corner and saw a small herd of buffalo disappear into the forest. The client jumped out, took his rifle and said he wished to follow them. I very reluctantly agreed (remembering he had four buffalo on his licence). The buffalo took a well worn game track up the slope and we came up to them after a few hundred yards.

They did not seem to have been much disturbed by us and were walking very slowly. A big bull stood at the rear of the herd. His massive horns protruded a good distance from his sides. At the top of the slope he suddenly turned round and looked right back at us. He was big and I knew that he had a spread of over fifty inches, which would have taken him well up in Rowland Ward's Record Book. Anyhow, he had seen enough of us and disappeared from sight. The clients were a little way back with their heads down and did not see the buffalo. I was relieved because I did not want the young man to get the big bull after the way he had been behaving.

Sometime later we came upon the buffalo in thick cover and a young immature bull got our scent and crashed past. The client then shot and killed the smaller buffalo without my telling him to do so. We ended the safari badly. I was pleased to get back to Nairobi and spend a few days with my family before starting out again. I heard from Albert that he had been called out by a farmer to deal with a lion that was killing his cattle. The farm was close to the area where we had lost the wounded lion. Albert shot the lion and when he examined it, he found a bullet wound in the neck from which it had recovered. It was without a doubt our lion.

The young man had the audacity to tell the manager of our company that he would like to return for another safari. However, the next time he wished to hunt with Eric Rundgren. Eric was a very good professional hunter and I knew he would never tolerate such a client. I would not have taken him on another safari under any circumstances.

I had the good fortune to be invited to lead a 35 day safari for the collection of small mammals for the American Museum of Natural History in New York. This included rats, mice and all other small creatures, including a rare striped hyena. In the safari party were Robert Model and Henry Blagden, both young men who had recently finished their university studies and whose wealthy families had sponsored the safari for the Museum. The Museum sent a young trainee to help with the preparation of the specimens.

We started on the Aberdare Mountain range and Mount Kenya collecting rodents and other creatures such as the tree hyrax, as well as small carnivorous animals like mongoose and jackal. The tree hyrax has a startling cry when it calls at night. It is a loud screech, and the sound gets softer as it reaches the end of it's call. To any stranger it can be quite frightening.

We collected a beautiful black and white Colobus monkey with its long flowing coat and bushy tail. The young man from the Museum worked hard, even at night, skinning specimens with the aid of the camp staff. Henry, Robert and I could not get used to the fact that this young man seldom washed or showered. He even came to the dinner table with blood and gore on his hands. It obviously didn't bother him. Bob and Henry were forever playing practical jokes on him with no effect.

Many of the animals we needed were nocturnal and these we caught with small traps or shot at night. Some, like the striped black and white rat, I had never seen before. We moved towards Lake Rudolf, to an area north of Maralal, where we found a striped hyena and an aardwolf, both rare animals. For some of these specimens we needed a special permit from the Game Department called a Governor's permit. One day I was sitting on a rock looking for rock hyrax when I noticed quite a few hyrax making alarm calls. Something was upsetting them. Eventually I made my way down and found a big puffadder had killed a fully grown hyrax and was almost finished swallowing it. I was amazed because I thought this was beyond a puffadder's capabilities.

Our next move was to Garissa on the Tana River. We collected a few night flying bats, most of which were taken with shotguns using a very light shot. The bats flew around our camp catching insects which were attracted to the lights. This shooting was similar to bird shooting and our skills improved rapidly with practise.

We spent some time at a place called Bura near Garissa. Near our camp we watched a big crocodile swimming upstream with a goat in its jaws. It had caught the goat earlier at a watering place. The croc was taking its meal upstream to hide it in its lair. These lairs were frequently found in hollowed out places under river banks where water eroded the earth and formed natural under-water caves. The reptile ignored all the humans on the bank and made steady headway upstream until it disappeared from sight.

From Bura we moved north toward the Somali border. Here we found another pastime shooting ducks and geese in the water pans, now full from the rains. The ducks made a nice change in our diet. We also shot many

115

beautiful vulturine guineafowl which abounded in the area. These are the most colourful of all the Guineafowl species with their vivid blue feathers and white streaks around the neck. Near one of these water pans we saw a big elephant bull with an enormous single tusk which I estimated at around 150 pounds. It was quite a sight and we watched it for long time.

Eventually we moved to the coast and camped on the beach under some coconut groves in the area south of Malindi called Watamu. Here we collected elephant shrews, the largest of the shrew family (a rodent). It lives in the Arabuku Forest and catches insects found under dead leaves. I collected them by moving slowly through the forest while listening for the shrew digging among the dry, and therefore noisy, leaves. When I spotted one, I used a shotgun loaded with very light shot. There were many shrews in the Arabuku Sokoke Forest and I found well worn runs on which they scurried to and fro. This area had thick bush and afforded a home to many species of animals, including red duiker and bushbuck, which we also obtained.

We did quite a lot of night shooting. The young museum assistant had grown a rather tatty beard and was nicknamed 'Scratchmo' by Henry and Bob. One night he insisted on accompanying us, saying that he was a good shot and could add some valuable specimens. That afternoon Henry and Bob doctored the shotgun shells, emptying out most of the shot and replacing the end wads. The night shoot came about and we drove out to the forest area with the spotlight. The assistant fired shot after shot with no results while Bob and Henry added to his discomfort with cutting remarks. This went on until the assistant accidentally tilted the barrel while reloading and a couple of loose pellets fell out, hitting the cab of the Land Rover and making an unmistakable sound. One wad came out of the front of the shell and the young man realised at once that a trick had been played on him. He was so angry that I don't remember him going out again.

My next safari was the result of a recommendation by Pat, who had shot the big elephant. His friend also wanted a big elephant. By this time Kenya had been divided into hunting blocks. This idea was good because it meant that once a block was reserved, no one else could hunt there.

I reserved Block 29 towards the coast, because it was good elephant country and I hunted elephant there with a fellow officer, Julian McKeand, when I was on local leave from the Game Department. Both of us had licences. We spent a couple of days at Makindu and J.A. Hunter kindly gave us accommodation. We hunted the area along the Athi River without much success. One afternoon we moved to the area now called Block 29. We used a Land Rover and a three-quarter ton trailer in which we carried food, extra petrol, water in a forty-four gallon drum, bedding, tents and two African gun bearers – Wanyahoro and one other (I cannot remember his name).

We left the main road outside Kibwezi and headed in the direction of the Athi River. There was no track to follow so we had to pick our way through the bush. We were crossing a dry sand river on the way down when I heard a sound, as if a stake had punctured the tyre and air was escaping. The sound came from the back and I put my head out to check the wheel when I saw a rhino bull bearing down on the rear of the vehicle. The sound I heard was not a tyre deflating but the puffing noise the rhino made while charging! The brute was close and looked as if he would hit the vehicle any second. I quickly slammed the car into first but missed the gear and there was a horrible grating noise which unnerved the rhino for he swerved away and ran off into the bush.

We arrived at the Athi River late at night and chose two enormous trees to camp under knowing their shade would be welcome in the heat of the day. The Land Rover was unloaded and all our gear was scattered around. When everyone started to itch, we realised that we were covered with pepper ticks. We moved all our gear to bare ground away from the grass growing under the trees. Fortunately, we had some aerosol spray and quickly killed the ticks.

Julian and I put our camp beds under the full moon, ate a quick meal of tinned food and tea, and settled down for a night under the stars. The night was very hot, being the middle of the dry season and blankets were unnecessary. White cotton sheets more than sufficed.

In the middle of the night Julian heard a noise close by. He sat up with the white sheet draped around him and saw a rhino standing at the foot of his bed. The rhino got a shock at seeing the white apparition loom up right under its nose, gave a loud snort, wheeled round and went puffing off the way these animals do when alarmed. Julian had a good chuckle and eventually settled down to sleep.

Twice more during the night the rhino came back to check up on what he had seen. The first time we heard him approaching because he was feeding on tasty twigs and making a lot of noise while slowly progressing towards us. We threw a couple of hefty pieces of firewood in his direction and he departed, puffing and crashing through the bush. The second time he came close again but this time he got our scent and departed for good.

117

We hunted out of camp on foot. Each morning we departed at 6 o'clock after the usual hasty breakfast and coffee. We walked either upstream or downstream parallel to the river until 1 o'clock in the afternoon, when we rested for half an hour and then made our weary way back to camp, arriving at dusk. We saw a lot of elephant and, one morning fairly soon after heading downstream from camp, we shot an eighty pounder (approximately 80 pounds each tusk).

On one of these daily trips we came across a young bull elephant that had been pinned down by an enormous baobab tree and killed. In times of drought elephants strip the bark off the tree and eat it. They also dig out chunks of the trunk of the tree with their tusks and eat the soft, pulpy wood filled with moisture. It is common to come across baobab trees devastated by elephants. Some of these trees look like pictures I have seen of trees eaten away by beavers, gradually chewing a ring around the trunk until the tree falls over. The elephant will work a baobab in very much the same way and often the tree is so undermined that it will collapse. Nearby we found another good elephant bull and shot it. Julian and I both got our elephant.

My American client (recommended by Pat) and I made camp in Block 29, not far from the Athi River. John Dugmore, who was then a young apprentice hunter, was with us to help wherever necessary and to learn the ropes. His duties included driving the client's wife around viewing game.

In Block 29 we looked around for a day or two for a big elephant without seeing anything worth shooting although there was plenty of traffic between our hunting block and the adjoining National Park (part of Tsavo). The Athi River was the northern boundary and a dry river bed near Mtito Andei formed the eastern boundary. The other boundary was the main road from Nairobi to Mombasa. Across the main road was Block 73, with the Chyulu Hills dominating the area. It had been closed for hunting for many years but I knew that it was about to be reopened very shortly.

I also knew there was a waterhole across the main road on the edge of this area and, one day in passing, I decided to call in and see what animals were drinking. We left the Land Rover short of the hole and walked in on a lone bull elephant. I was amazed at its enormous tusks which reached down to the ground. They were very thick and I estimated the weight around 130 to 140 pounds each. The skin on his head was sunken in many places and his backbone protruded which indicated that the animal was very old. The elephant had not heard us and we watched him for many minutes. It is difficult to describe my emotions when seeing such a big tusker. The main feelings were a combination of excitement and awe as I looked at something so unusual. I had seen bigger elephants in previous years, some in the national parks, but this time we were close with an unobstructed view and the wind was in our favour.

I was faced with a dilemma. We did not have the necessary Game Department's permission to shoot but the client was now excited and ready to shoot. I decided to travel thirty miles to the nearest telephone and call the Game Department in Nairobi. This we did and permission was granted so we rushed back and reached the waterhole one and a half hours later only to find the elephant had moved off. We picked up the tracks heading in a westerly direction but after a while they were lost among the many tracks of elephant herds in the area. The bush was very thick due to the late rains and the leaves had not fallen to the ground making visibility difficult. After many hours of fruitless searching, we gave up and headed back to camp.

Block 73 was small but it had plenty of elephants, and some big tuskers, which now and again roamed out of the National Park. There were also buffalo and lion. Some of the buffalo had very big trophy-size heads, two of which we collected on a safari I did with Bill Jenvey, a fellow professional hunter, but that is another story. A few years later Wakamba tribesmen moved into the area and chopped down all the hardwood trees in order to make charcoal, most of which was shipped by dhow to the Persian Gulf. The bush was cleared and huts sprang up along with cultivated lands. In a few years there were no wild animals to be found here which was sad. I hated to think about it.

My disgruntled client made his feelings quite plain. He maintained that we should have shot the elephant and then made the necessary arrangements afterwards. A few fellow professional hunters might have done just that. I consoled myself that I had adopted the right approach in the matter because I did not want to run foul of the authorities and lose my licence. We did not see that elephant again but we did shoot a bull with tusks of about eighty pounds each side. The tusks were good but this did not please the client who had to be satisfied with tusks smaller than those of his friend, Pat.

The following day, I took some of the camp staff to cut out the tusks of the elephant. We returned to find that the client had departed in a huff. John Dugmore drove both clients back to Nairobi where they caught the first plane home. I was relieved that the client did not get the big tusker as he had an unfortunate attitude.

Shortly after the elephant safari, I went hunting with Robert (Bob) Lee, whose main trophy was a bongo, a shy elusive antelope. I selected Mount Kenya for the hunt. Kenya, at that time, offered more variety of animals than most hunting areas in Africa. I always enjoyed hunting here because of the diverse vegetation and climate. Some game inhabited the desert areas, others preferred the dry thick bush, the bamboo forests at high altitudes or the plains. In the course of a 30 day safari, it was possible to change one's scenery to see all the vastly different areas. The bongo, in my opinion, was the most difficult animal to hunt. It had everything in its favour and was a challenge to any hunter. I looked forward to the hunt as the difficult ones were often the most enjoyable.

Our first camp was about eighty miles from Nairobi near the Regati Forest Station. This was below the bamboo belt which started at about 7,600 feet above sea level. The climate was cold, especially at night. We were hoping for rain to soften the ground and make tracking easier. Tracks in this forest stayed fresh for many hours and it was always difficult to gauge their age. Night rain made things much easier because it obliterated the existing tracks and allowed the hunter to establish the animal's lead. It also softened the fallen bamboo leaves which made it possible to walk quietly. Unfortunately the wet and cold made it miserable for the hunter. Each time you brushed the bamboo or branches, water cascaded down onto your head, neck and shoulders. It was impossible to keep your feet dry, so you had to be content to stay wet all day. Bamboo grew on all the steep slopes of the valleys and even on the ridges.

Bongo travelled great distances, crossing several valleys, rivers and streams, and in doing so they did not always select the easiest of gradients. If the ground was wet, it was slippery as well. It was difficult to follow quietly as you often lost your footing and started to slide. It was natural to grab at the nearest bamboo for support, causing one bamboo stalk to bump against another and make a loud crack, which seemed magnified in the stillness around. Any self-respecting bongo for miles around was alerted. The only consolation was the knowledge that other inhabitants of the area, such as Colobus and Sykes monkeys, also made noises especially when jumping from tree to tree. Going down a steep slope was much easier than climbing up the next one and the high altitude made you short of breath. The heavy cold weather clothing meant that you perspired while climbing, then got cold when resting at the top of the ridge. After a few minutes it was imperative to get up and walk to prevent getting a chill.

In every likely place where bongo might be hiding we walked as quietly as possible, pausing frequently to look and listen. This animal has

On safari with Alberto and Teresa Bailleres. Their photographer is on the left.

One of the camps used during the Bailleres sixty day safari

Alberto Bailleres took three of the big five during his first safari in 1961

Alberto Bailleres with his elephant

Truck overturned on safari in the West Lake District, Tanzania

Mount Kilimanjaro viewed from the main road en route to the coast

My trackers had a narrow escape from this elephant which was wounded by poachers with poison arrows and finally shot by Dr. Lindgens

Good buffalo shot by Dr. Lindgens in Masailand, Kenya

extremely good hearing, sight and smell, just like its cousins the kudu, nyala, bushbuck, eland and sitatunga. But the bongo's senses are even more acute as it keeps as far away as possible from man, its worst enemy. Later in my career I discovered many areas where bongo could be found.

On the first day it was possible to find many tracks, but as the days went by, fewer and fewer fresh tracks were found, until usually after three or four days no more could be seen. This happened at our first camp because the bongo detected our scent and moved to another area many miles away. It was then imperative to move camp so we packed up and moved to the area above Embu. We used a forest track constructed by the security forces during the Mau Mau rebellion. It followed the ridge between two valleys and eventually we reached the bamboo belt where we made camp.

The first morning we departed by hunting car but soon realised that it would be better to proceed on foot. We had not gone far when we came across fresh tracks of a herd of bongo, probably seven or eight in number. We tracked a short distance and heard the familiar bamboo crack. A body was moving just ahead and we felt sure that the bongo were close. We moved as quietly as possible. This was difficult, but the bongo were making just as much noise. They were feeding in the thick cover and did not hear our approach. A bull passed through a gap in the bamboo, and two cows followed. I alerted my client to watch for the animals crossing the next gap. By now we were in a crouching position which made it easier to see under the heavy bamboo foliage. As the first animal appeared, the client shot and it dropped in its tracks. I thought it would be the bull because he was leading, but was disappointed to find that we had bagged a big cow. Perhaps we were too anxious and should have waited for all the bongo to appear. However, the client was happy to get a bongo, and this eased my disappointment at not getting the male.

After this we moved to Block 29, on the Nairobi/Mombasa road. For his elephant hunt the client brought a very expensive, double barrelled best grade .470 calibre English rifle. It must have cost him a lot because it was gold plated. He had recently received it from his gunsmith, barely in time for the safari, and was dying to try it out. It shot very poorly on target. One shot was close to the bull but the other barrel fired almost a foot high at fifty yards. Normally the range for elephant shooting is forty yards or closer, so I was a little worried about what would happen when we had to shoot an elephant. I was surprised that the English gunsmith was not able to regulate both barrels. Up to this time, my experience was that all the English heavy doubles were very accurate. At a later stage I heard that due to declining demand for these rifles, many of the good gunsmiths had retired and the

121

younger generation were not prepared to spend the years of apprenticeship required to become proficient at their trade.

We saw elephant bulls during the first three days but nothing worth shooting. On the fourth day we found a very old, lone bull. His head was sunken and his tatty ears had been torn by the bush when running away from danger over the years. His tusks were short but exceptionally thick and I suspected he would be a good trophy. The client made a good shot and he fell on the spot. The tusks weighed around 95 pounds each. The safari ended satisfactorily and we returned to Nairobi.

TEN

A MEDLEY OF EXPERIENCES

I was on safari in the Maralal/Samburu district with a Mexican client. I enjoyed hunting in this high altitude area because the daytime temperatures were cool and pleasant (unlike the areas located nearer the coast). These areas were noted for having elephant carrying heavy ivory and tracking them usually took place during the heat of the day with the discomforts of thirst and sweat flies.

Maralal forest areas have a predominance of cedar and olive trees growing among thick bush, along with much open grassland. There are many valleys and dry water courses covered in bush. The bush is ideal for leopard and a variety of wildlife such as impala, Grant's and Thomson's gazelle, warthog, dik-dik, vervet monkeys, baboon, porcupine, game birds and other small animals that augment a leopard's diet. Elephant, buffalo and rhino roam in the forests. To the north of Maralal, at Porror, it is possible to look down towards Lake Rudolf and the great escarpment of the Rift Valley. This is a wonderful view.

We were after leopard and I was happy to be in this block because I knew our chances of getting a big male were good. During the first few days of the safari we shot a number of trophy animals and used the carcasses as bait. We arranged the bait in carefully chosen places. First we needed a tree with a suitable limb or branch to tie the bait on. The tree should, if possible, be close to thick cover so that the leopard could lie up, and watch his meat and keep vultures and other birds such as crows and hawks from feeding on it. The birds stayed away from the meat if they saw the cat on guard. We then built a blind about 40 or 50 yards from the tree. I always tried to plan a good approach so that the leopard did not see us getting inside the blind. This was important for an early morning approach. I also considered the direction of the prevailing wind because leopards move away quickly when the wind is unfavourable and they get the scent of the hunter. Some professional hunters say that leopards have a poor sense of smell and that the placing of the blind in this regard is not important. I know that a leopard relies mostly on its eyesight to catch movement but I also know it can smell.

We checked all the baits every day and it was about 5 days later that we found one had been eaten. This particular one had been half eaten and, by the deep scratch marks on the tree trunk, the cat appeared to be a big male. That afternoon, the client and I cautiously approached the blind and patiently waited for the cat. We waited until dark but he never arrived. Obviously, he had a good meal earlier and was not hungry, so I decided to make a morning approach. We left camp in the dark about one hour before light and drove to the bait. A good distance away we stopped and continued on foot as usual to avoid disturbing the leopard. We made a silent approach and when it was light enough, I peered through the porthole at the bait and saw the leopard sitting on the limb next to it. He was facing towards us, having finished feeding and was busy licking himself. His next move would most likely be descent and departure.

By now the light was good enough to shoot but I was worried about letting my client take a chest shot. A leopard's chest is very narrow and I had experienced clients wound leopard because they had not taken into account the angle of the body on the limb. Their bullets had gone into the chest, raked along the side and exited behind the shoulder, completely missing both the heart and the lungs. However, I decided to let my client to shoot. He had, after all, shot well up to now using a .300 Weatherby Magnum. He got into position and fired. I expected the leopard to fall out of the tree like a sack of potatoes, but to my vexation it sprang off the limb going away from us, hit the ground and disappeared in a flash. I dived out of the blind and ran towards where the leopard had gone. I was armed with a double barrelled 12 gauge shotgun loaded with buck shot. The next thing I saw was the leopard coming towards me at speed. I fired quickly but the shot hit the ground and threw dust into the leopard's face. It swerved and disappeared into a thick bush. It disappeared so quickly, there was no time to fire again so I ran around the bush hoping to get another shot when it appeared on the other side. The leopard beat me and had already disappeared into the forest beyond.

In the few seconds when it first appeared, I noticed that one front leg was swinging uselessly, obviously broken. What surprised me was the speed at which it moved on three legs. I would never have thought it possible. Wanyahoro soon joined me. He was carrying my .470 double which I exchanged for the shotgun. I felt more at home with the trusty heavy rifle.

We immediately took up tracking. There was quite a bit of blood on the ground so it was easy to follow. We had not gone more than seventy yards when I heard the leopard growl and immediately went down on one knee to get a better view under the low bush. With that the leopard appeared only five yards away and coming down the path in full charge. I fired one shot and managed to hit his head which put him down. When we skinned the leopard, we found that the soft nose bullet had smashed the skull to pieces. I realised how lucky I had been for had my shot failed to stop the leopard, I would have been mauled. A leopard can do a lot of damage with its teeth and claws in a very short time, and it is doubtful that Wanyahoro could have come to my assistance in time.

Up to now I had been taking safaris mainly in Kenya and northern Tanganyika but had never hunted sable or roan. The most popular areas used by my fellow professional hunters for hunting these animals was southern Tanganyika. I was not familiar with them and, when John Kingsley-Heath kindly offered to show me round, I accepted eagerly. We met in Dodoma, a town in the centre of the country located on the main railway line from Dar es Salaam to Kigoma on Lake Tanganyika.

I travelled from Nairobi in the Land Rover and arrived the same evening John did. While we were having a drink he told me that he and his gun bearers had a narrow escape from a charging elephant the previous day. They were tracking four bulls and finally came up to them in a thick patch of bush. (This area was near Simba Nguru, where there was the lone grave of a white man buried many years ago. No one knew how the man had died.) They manoeuvred close enough to see the ivory and John found that one of the bulls had very good tusks – over 100 pounds. One of the askaris (a name given to young bulls guarding a big one) got their scent and promptly charged. John did not want to shoot the young bull so he fired a shot over its head. This turned the elephant slightly off course and it charged past them, stopped and came back. This was too much for the gun bearers and they fled. John nearly had to shoot but fortunately the animal turned and followed his companions. When John met up with the gun bearers, he found that the one carrying his .470 double had fallen and broken the stock.

After spending the night in the hotel, we departed for Simba Nguru as John still wanted to fill his elephant licence. The day following our arrival, we went out looking for signs of elephant. It was not long before we found fresh tracks of bulls and started following. The two gun bearers went ahead tracking and John and I followed. We had not gone far when the trackers rounded a bush, turned and charged back nearly knocking John over and going past me at speed. I raised my rifle expecting to see an animal coming after the trackers, but nothing happened so I walked up to the bush and peered around to see what had put the two trackers to flight. There, about ten yards away, was a bull elephant with his head in a bush feeding. He obviously never heard the commotion behind him. The two trackers were still jittery from their experience a couple of days back. John and I retreated a short distance and rejoined the two trackers. John asked one of them to climb a tree and see whether he could spot the jumbos. In due course the man reported that he had seen three bulls moving towards a thicket ahead. We followed and found them in very thick bush. The wind was not constant so we had to wait it out until afternoon when the elephants emerged after their midday rest period. When it got cooler at about 4 o'clock, the elephants would start feeding again.

We followed as soon as we saw they were on the move again, waiting for our chance to catch them in an open area where we could see their ivory. Eventually we spotted one carrying respectable ivory and John shot it. Later he weighed the ivory and told me that they were seventy-five pounds each. We looked around and saw plenty of kudu tracks but none of sable.

From Simba Nguru we drove back to Dodoma and then to Iringa. From here we planned to drive westwards with the idea of crossing the Ruaha River (which would be fordable as it was at the end of the dry season) and then joining the main Mbeya/Singida road. This would take us through new game country. At Iringa we filled up the petrol tanks and left for the bush. Shortly after leaving Iringa on the main road, we took a side road. After about eighty miles, the track ended and we took off across vast flat plains consisting of black cotton soil. In the dry season it has many cracks which made it rough going for the vehicles. That evening we reached the banks of the dry Ruaha River and slept on the river bank while lightning flashed in the night sky. The rains were not far off. It was late October and they usually started early in November. Once the rains started, the river would flood and it would be impossible to cross.

In the morning we drove up and down the river until we found a passable crossing. We had a little trouble but eventually both vehicles got over and we drove upstream for quite a distance but saw absolutely no game. We did come across a crocodile hunter's camp but the hunter was away hunting and only two Africans were in the camp.

We left the river heading west and hit a road which eventually led through some villages but again saw very little game. John told me that the locals hunted with muzzle loading black powder guns which accounted for the lack of game. John had been a district officer in the Tanganyika Adminis-tration (before he took up professional hunting) and knew most of the territory. Southern Tanganyika had been plagued by man-eating lions for many years because the locals shot most of the game, with the result that a population of lion was left with not much to feed on. The lions took to killing domestic stock and when that failed, humans. The locals had a habit of visiting neighbouring villages for beer drinking sessions and then collapsing in a drunken stupor on the road back home. When a lion came across a body on the ground, it made an easy meal for a hungry fellow. This was one way for a lion to become a man-eater.

John and I eventually hit the main Mbeya/Singida road. On the way back north, we stopped at a couple of villages where John introduced me to men who could guide me to areas for sable and kudu. After this trip, I made many recce trips looking for new hunting areas. This was a vital part of a successful professional hunter's work.

Shortly after the recce with John, I took a safari for sable, kudu and roan and selected the area west of the Mbeya/Singida road and south of the Rungwa River for the hunt. We used an old abandoned road built by the Germans before the First World War and had difficulty crossing the various rivers because the bridges had long since ceased to exist. These wooden bridges had been burned out by seasonal grass fires which the locals started every year. At every crossing we had to cut away the river bank to allow our vehicles to cross.

At one place we camped for five days and, while my crew was busy making a crossing, we hunted an area with a lot of game. Here we shot a forty-five inch sable, placing it well up in Rowland Ward's Record Book.

We first saw the herd of sable with the accompanying bull while driving through *miombo* woodlands. The herd was feeding on new green grass growing in the wake of a recent fire and the black bull clearly stood out from the brown cows and calves (in Botswana the cows are often as dark as the bulls). His horns were thick and long in comparison to the cows and I knew he was a good trophy. I was very excited because it was the first sable that I had hunted.

In fact, the sable were tame and unconcerned at the sight of our

127

vehicle, which I parked behind a big anthill. We stalked the herd and after a few hundred yards my client was close enough to shoot. I pointed out the bull who was trailing the herd. One good shot dropped the animal in its tracks. I felt quite sad to see such a noble beast lying on the ground.

We also bagged Lichtenstein's hartebeest and buffalo. I put up some leopard baits and very shortly had two leopards feeding off them. We bagged one good male and my second client shot at and missed another. The second leopard made a remarkable leap from a high limb where it was feeding to the ground. This high limb was the only one suitable for the bait, but it was a good eighteen feet above the ground. After being shot at, the leopard jumped, spreading all four legs out and keeping perfect balance, and landed on all four feet whereupon it immediately dashed off into the bush.

We crossed the river and our next camp was on top of a big hill in an area where huge mango trees grew around a spring. The trees made an excellent camping site as they provided shade for our tents and the spring water supplied our drinking needs. There was a good view of the surrounding country and we had the benefit of the slightest breeze, especially welcome as this was the hottest time of year. Another benefit at this high elevation was the lack of tsetse flies. It was a different story whenever we ventured down into the bush below where tsetse flies were abundant. They made life uncomfortable whenever we ventured from the vehicle. We wore tightly woven long sleeved shirts and long trousers to protect ourselves as the little pests could bite through thin material. Insect repellent had little effect and after a while the flies ignored it.

From our hilltop camp we ranged below into the surrounding bush and shot a good roan antelope and another sable which was not as big as the first but, nevertheless, a presentable trophy. We shot another buffalo but could not find any kudu, so we decided to move further north to the Rungwa River. En route we encountered two bull elephants crossing the road. One bull had magnificent tusks – well over 100 pounds. The clients wanted to shoot it but, as they did not have a licence, I had to say no. Before we left Nairobi I asked them whether they wanted to shoot elephant and they declined. It was their own fault.

In Rungwa there was good sign of lion and leopard, so we shot a zebra and used it for bait. In due course we visited the bait and found that two male lions had eaten quite a lot. That evening we sat in a blind but the lions did not reappear. The tsetse flies gave us a hard time. They were a nuisance as it was difficult to sit quietly and still when they were around. The sting demanded instant attention and the lions may have come close enough to hear all the swatting.

The next morning we revisited the bait and found that the lions had another meal. The tracks revealed that they had recently departed. I felt certain that we could track them and stood a good chance of getting one. When I put the idea to the two gentlemen, they declined, saying that they both had bad hearts and the doctors had warned them not to do too much. Reluctantly I gave up the chase. Needless to say we did not get a lion. We were still looking for kudu but we did not find any and moved to an area near Kondoa Erangi.

The move occupied a whole day and eventually we arrived near a sand river with lots of reeds. There were plenty of kudu tracks in the river and we felt our chances here were good. The first night a drama unfolded. At midnight my headman and staff brought in a porter who said that a cobra had spat in his eyes. I made a weak solution of permanganate of potash crystals and water to bathe his eyes. He was in a lot of pain. While I doctored the patient the others told me what happened. It was usual for the staff to lay out their bedding on the ground and to put a mosquito net over it. This man had just completed this when he heard something rustling in the grass next to his net and, thinking it was a rat, he put his head up and the snake spat through the mosquito net into his eyes. The next morning I drove him to the hospital in Kondoa where the staff washed his eyes with milk. Today I am told that the proper treatment is frequent bathing of the eyes with water.

During the following days we scouted the hills early in the mornings, climbing before sunrise to any likely vantage point and using our binoculars to look for kudu. We saw them every morning and eventually shot two nice trophies. These animals are very wary and have excellent eyesight, hearing and scent. To crown it all their bodies are well camouflaged. Foreigners always have trouble seeing them. Stalking kudu requires time and patience. I found that early mornings and late evenings were the best times to make an approach because the kudu were moving around and feeding. At this time they were preoccupied whereas in the midday heat kudu were typically lying up in a thicket, and it was difficult to sneak up without being seen. They were usually standing still or lying down and any noise made during a stalk was easily picked up. This also applied to bongo.

I got both gentlemen up to kudu every day in the Kondoa area, but the sight of these animals gave them buck fever with the result that there were quite a few poorly aimed shots. Fortunately, towards the end of our safari, they calmed down and managed to shoot two kudu. Our 35 day safari was over, so we packed up camp and returned to Nairobi.

I completed a successful 30 day safari with a couple from Philadelphia who shot some very good trophies. I was back in Nairobi, seeing them off at the airport and making arrangements for my next safari which was due out the next day. The hunter, Dr. Lindgens, was from Germany. I knew from reading the correspondence that our office had with the Doctor that his main objective was to shoot a big elephant. Once this was accomplished we would hunt other game. I would have preferred four or five days at home before starting again. This would have given me time with my wife and children, but it was not to be.

I made my way to the Ker & Downey office in the main centre of Nairobi where our manager, Ronnie Stevens, was having a conversation with an elderly bespectacled gentleman who turned out to be my client. He was overweight and did not look at all healthy. I remember thinking at the time that the Doctor would find the going difficult as most elephant hunting in Kenya involved a lot of walking under trying conditions. I thought we would have to be lucky to get a big tusker. I knew from past experience that the average elephant hunt in Kenya, especially if one is after big ivory, involved tracking twenty or thirty bulls before a suitable one was selected, and this was in a good hunting area. I consoled myself that a good area had been reserved for the forthcoming hunt and hoped we would do all right.

A short while later we left the city and headed for the Thua River in the lower Wakamba tribal area, east of the Tsavo National Park. I drove the Land Rover and the Doctor travelled with me. There were two gun bearers, who would also do the tracking, in the back with the rifles, ammunition, personal effects and a lunch box and drinks. The Bedford truck was loaded with all the essentials for a luxury safari from our store. Among this were two large crates containing 144 magnum bottles of champagne that had been especially shipped out. The truck also carried the rest of the African staff. I found out later that my client drank champagne and very little else, from morning to night. It was a new experience for me. The Doctor had his own vineyard in Germany and I suspect that was how his fondness for champagne came about.

En route to our hunting area we stopped to engage a local guide who had good knowledge of the Thua. I had used the local on a previous hunt and found him to be worthwhile. I rather suspected him of doing a little poaching as a sideline because he looked the type that might indulge in it.

An hour later we reached the Thua River and the crew put up tents under some big shady trees growing on its banks. Two men shovelled away sand in the river bed to a depth of about three feet and water started to percolate into the hole. The water was clean, having been filtered through the sand, and would serve our needs during our stay in the area.

The river was a fair distance from Tsavo Park and the Tana river. It was the only watering place for many miles around and, as it was the dry season, I knew bull elephants would be using the sand river to quench their thirst. In the dry season I seldom found cow elephant herds in the area. I suspected they preferred the lush bush of the park and the Tana river, and only moved into the Thua when it rained. Typically bulls watered at night and then moved away into the bush as far away as fifteen to twenty miles from the river.

The first morning we left camp early and drove up the sand river. It was heavy going for about four miles until we rounded a bend in the water course and came upon a watering place. There were elephant droppings around but nothing fresh. Elephants make these drinking places by digging in the sand until they create a depression, and when it is deep enough, water percolates into the hole. An elephant will spend hours standing by the hole until its thirst has been quenched. A bull drinks forty to fifty gallons of water at a time and this will suffice for two or three days before he needs his next drink. In the hinterland this water will be supplemented by chewing succulents that contain moisture such as wild sisal (*sansevieria*). Other game also make use of these drinking places.

As there was no fresh sign at the hole we drove further upstream to another drinking place. We examined the ground around the hole, and immediately spotted the fresh tracks of a recently departed bull. The sand was still falling back into the water. The elephant must have heard the approaching vehicle and been frightened away. The tracks in the sand were big enough to warrant a follow up so I sent our two gun bearers and the local man to track the bull. It was a common practice for professional hunters to use two or more groups of trackers to scout out big bulls. These trackers were seldom armed because it was usually possible for them to get close enough to see the ivory from a safe distance and then return to report to the waiting hunters. It was not considered dangerous because they were experienced in the bush and knew their limitations. One of my trackers was named Kamanzi, but I have forgotten the names of the other two. I instructed them to meet me back at the water hole as soon as they had seen the bull's ivory. I then drove off, accompanied by the Doctor and my head gun bearer Wanyahoro, to examine other drinking places further up river. We drove for several miles and came to other water holes, but found no fresh sign so I decided to turn back to see if the others had better news.

We arrived to find only the local guide standing there in a highly excited state. There was no sign of the other two. Obviously something had gone wrong. The guide said that we must go at once to where they had found the elephant because it charged them and he was sure it caught the others. I asked him to explain more slowly exactly what had happened. The men followed the tracks for only a short distance when they heard the bull in a thick patch of bush just ahead. They stopped and waited because the wind was not constant enough to approach any closer. A short while later they heard a noise and looked up to see the elephant charging and closing fast. They all got up and ran, but the two men fell down right in the bull's path. The local tracker ran as fast as he could and when he was some distance away, he realised that the elephant was not following him. He decided to climb a tree where he could see from the top branch that the bull was charging around, making a lot of dust and tearing up bushes. He was sure it had killed the other two men.

My opinion was that the elephant might have caught one but not both. In any event we waited a while longer to see if anyone turned up. It was only a few minutes later when the two trackers came into sight. Both were very excited and I asked them how they had managed to escape from the elephant. Kamanzi said that they were sitting down waiting for the wind to change direction when they suddenly heard a noise and looked up to see the elephant very close and coming fast. It did not make any trumpeting sound as elephants normally do when they charge. He got up to run, but ran into the other tracker, and they both fell down in front of the beast. He found himself underneath the elephant but managed to get up and dash off through the bush, running until he realised the elephant was no longer following. He saw the other tracker, who also got away unscathed, and they made their way back to the river where we met.

The Doctor and I got our rifles and went to the place where the elephant had tried to kill the trackers. We found Kamanzi's jacket on the ground but the elephant was gone. The jacket had been pulled off when he fell and had a long tear in it. What really caught my attention were two parallel grooves on the ground, each about three yards long. These had been made by the tusks when the bull tried to impale, but somehow miraculously missed, the two men. It was difficult to see how they managed to escape injury. I decided to track the elephant and discover the reason for its unusual behaviour.

The sun was well up and it was going to be a hot day. Yellow-billed hornbills were making a lot of noise which was usual on a hot day. It was going to be a test for the Doctor and I wondered how he would cope. We picked up the tracks of the bull and soon got onto a well worn elephant path. These paths have been made over hundreds of years and sometimes

132

extend for many hundreds of miles. They become more numerous near watering places. We made our way slowly, following the tracks of our bull. Along the way we came across many branches stripped of their bark and left lying on the ground. Elephants eat the bark and discard the rest. There were also elephant droppings along the path. We tracked for three hours before the bull left the path and headed for some tall trees and bush in the distance. I felt sure that we would find the elephant there. Our pace had been slow as the Doctor set his own pace but did manage to keep it up which surprised me. The only sign of wildlife other than elephant was a predominance of little dik-dik antelope. They are no bigger than a rabbit and are usually seen in pairs. They are browsers, and if undisturbed, it is possible to see them feeding off the leaves and tender shoots of bushes. These little creatures have regular runs and tend to use the same places to go to the toilet. Their tiny droppings eventually become small mounds which can be seen at regular intervals and this is one way of marking their territory. Whilst tracking the elephant we noticed quite a few of them darting from the path and disappearing in a flash.

A short distance after we left the main path I noticed a branch broken off a commiphora tree. It was freshly broken by the bull we were following. He had eaten very little and discarded it after walking a short way. This was strange because elephant are very fond of commiphora. It is a soft wood tree with a lot of moisture in its branches, and elephant chew it the same way humans chew sugar cane. There were no leaves on the trees because it was the dry season. The commiphora looked dead but within a few days of rain falling they would all spring into leaf and change the whole picture of the countryside. We came to the tall trees and found that the elephant had carried on until the spoor entered some low thick bush. Suddenly, I saw the elephant, standing still, its back showing above the bushes. He looked very thin and reminded me of the term 'razor back hog'. We stopped to look while I tried to decide on an approach, when he suddenly charged across our front and stopped about seventy yards away to our right. I remember saying to the Doctor that I was sure he would come looking for us. I did not know whether he heard us or got a faint whiff of our scent because the wind at the time was not constant. It was obvious he knew we were around.

Suddenly, the elephant spun round and came straight for us. I thought his action peculiar, and not what I remembered during earlier charges from elephant. He made no sound, and came fast with his front legs bowed, his head held low and his ears out. I told the Doctor not to fire until the elephant was close. He appeared to cover the ground in no time and was suddenly only twenty five yards away. The Doctor fired and I saw dust fly off

133

his head. The shot was too high. The elephant hardly faltered in its charge. I quickly aimed for a frontal brain shot and the bull went down in a cloud of dust. I ran around and put a shot into the back of his head. We examined the body and found a couple of places where blood had run down over the skin and dried. When the trackers removed the skin, we discovered discoloured flesh underneath. This was caused by poisoned arrows. After cutting away the flesh we found the first arrow head and several more later on. The poison on the arrow heads had not been potent enough to kill, but the elephant must have suffered in agony, which accounted for its aggressive behaviour. Both tusks were over 60 pounds each. At that time a good trophy elephant was considered 80 pounds or more but the Doctor told me he was well satisfied because he had enjoyed the hunt and it would make a good story back in Germany. I was told by some local Africans who came into the camp that the elephant had killed one of the poachers when they followed up after wounding it. The bull eventually turned on them and ran down one of their numbers.

The Ker & Downey Safari office in Nairobi informed me that my next safari would be with Ted Philpott from Indianapolis in the United States. He was seventy-two years old and, because of his age, I might battle to get all the trophies he wanted. When I met him at the airport, I also had my doubts. However, I did not have much to worry about, and we managed to get good trophies as the safari progressed. Ted shot well and he was easy going, putting no pressure on me to produce the goods in a hurry. Over the years I found that a calm client with confidence in my ability ensured that the safari went well and good trophies were shot. The worst thing was to have a client who doubted my ability. I became over anxious and invariably made mistakes which I would not normally have made. I am sure most professional hunters would agree with me on this.

I guided some anxious clients who wanted to shoot the first animal that they saw right at the start of the safari. When I was confident that a bigger animal could be found before the end of the safari, I always advised the client not to shoot. On many occasions the client insisted he shoot and invariably a larger animal was seen at a later stage.

Ted and I hunted elephant in the Voi area. He could not walk far, so I used the Land Rover to get him close to the animals. Only the last few hundred yards of our approach was made on foot. After much looking and driving, we found the tracks of a large herd of bulls. I left Ted in the hunting car and proceeded with my trackers and gun bearers on foot. Several miles later we caught up with the bulls. It was midday and they were resting under trees. The herd had split into small groups with four or five elephant under each tree. I looked at the nearest group and saw a couple of seventy to eighty pounders, and decided to fetch Ted. We drove to within half a mile of where I left the animals and parked under a big shady acacia tree. We continued on foot and found the bulls close to where I had left them. The wind was steady, so we moved down wind of the animals, looking at the different groups to find the largest tusker. Eventually I spotted one elephant whose size dwarfed all the others. When I approached him, I was amazed to see an enormous tusk. It was beautiful, thick and protruded about eight feet from the lip. I estimated the weight around 150 pounds, but when I looked for the other tusk, it did not have one. The tusk must have broken off, no doubt in a fight many years back. I suggested to Ted that he shoot the one tusker and then we would get a second elephant licence to hunt another with two tusks. He declined because he wanted an elephant with two tusks for a head mount which was to be included in a private museum he was starting at home. We settled for a two tusked seventy pound elephant. I would dearly have liked to see the tusk of the big elephant and to know its exact weight. It took a lot of work getting the head skin off the elephant. I wanted it done properly because it was my first head mount.

We moved to Masailand, Block 60, in the Mara area where we bagged a big male leopard on a bait and also a big Defassa waterbuck. While we were hunting for buffalo, I had some excitement with a bull. I left the Land Rover to walk around and look for tracks. Fortunately I took my .470 double because I walked onto a bull lying down in a thick belt of bush. The buffalo got up and took off when it saw me. I noticed a spear shaft sticking out of its side when it turned, so I ran after it and burst out of the bush to see the bull running across the open. I dropped it with a neck shot. The spear shaft had broken and splintered but was still attached to the blade. When I examined the wound, I decided that the bull had been speared the previous day and would have died after a few days – a long and painful death. I was surprised that the bull had not charged on sight. A gut shot made most animals very angry and aggressive and they usually charge on sight. However, animals are individuals and their temperaments vary: one charged on sight and another ran like a coward.

We found the buffalo was a very good trophy with a thick boss and a forty-six inch spread. Ted wanted it for his museum, so I asked the game warden for permission to keep it and he consented. We shot another buffalo

135

but it was not as big.

The following year, Ted came out with his wife and we hunted Tanganyika, starting off in the southern part of the country for kudu, sable and roan and ending up near Fort Ikoma for lion. Fort Ikoma had been built by the Germans when they administered the territory. They lost Tanganyika after World War I and the fort gradually fell into ruins.

The lion was bagged quite easily, once again with the aid of a poacher. We shot a hartebeest for bait and I had it in the back of the Land Rover. I was driving around looking for a tree in which to hang the bait with a good approach to the blind when I spotted a suitable one and stopped the hunting car underneath it. We were standing around the car when I heard a lion growl in the thick bush nearby. Ted and I got our rifles and circled round the patch of bush from the rear. We made a cautious approach taking one step at a time, stopping and listening. We heard another growl which gave us an idea where the animal was lying up. After a few yards we saw the lion. It was lying down facing away and we moved slowly round to get a shot at its flank, being careful not to make a noise to attract its attention. After sometime we were in a position to shoot. Ted fired a shot and the lion rolled over.

After taking pictures we loaded the animal into the Land Rover and went back to the camp well satisfied. The lion had an excellent mane. My skinner found an arrow head in the animal's flank. The arrow was poisoned and the lion was half dead when we shot it. The growling was caused by the painful wound and the poison. We were lucky to come across it when we did. Had we found it a day later, the skin would have been spoiled.

We returned to Nairobi well satisfied with the results of our safari. A couple of years later I sadly received news of Ted's death. He was a grand old man and we had become good friends.

136

Big lion shot by Kay Pickering on a 'camel and horse' safari in Barsoloi, Kenya

I shot this buffalo with a spear sticking out of its side on safari with Ted Philpott

Herb Klein on safari in Tanzania

Carlo Caldesi with his record size rhino shot on Mount Kenya

Carlo Caldesi with his giant forest hog taken in Kenya

Carlo Caldesi with his leopard taken on the Aberdare Mountains

My big forest elephant

Don Bousfield and Kirk Douglas on safari - Kenya 1962

Don Bousfield with Al and Becky Woodward and their French PH in the C.A.R.

ELEVEN

NEW CLIENTS AND GOOD FRIENDS

Carlo Caldesi, my Italian client and friend, returned many times. He was a first class sportsman with extensive worldwide hunting experience. For his next safari he wanted to hunt rhino, lion and elephant. The safari started on Mount Kenya, high in the bamboo belt. After a few days we found a bull rhino and Carlo shot it. The rhino ranked well up in Rowland Ward's Record Book.

Another time Carlo, accompanied by his brother, and I hunted in the Laitokitok area near Mount Kilimanjaro. Early one morning we heard lions roaring and went looking for them. We spotted the fresh tracks of two males in the sand and started tracking. Within a short time we saw the lions and I pointed out the better of the pair. Carlo was a first class shot and had no difficulty in dropping it. The lion had a black mane which was not very long.

After the lion hunt we saw some bull buffalo feeding in the long swamp grass. The animals' backs could be seen above the grass, but not the heads because they were feeding. We approached quite close but it was only when the animals put their heads up to look at us, that we could evaluate them. Immediately I saw one very good buffalo with a wide spread. I told Carlo to shoot and once again he dropped it where it was standing. It had a forty-seven inch spread – a good trophy.

When judging the size of a buffalo, the only way to ensure accuracy is to wait until the buffalo faces in your direction. It is even better when the nose is pointing at you and the animal is looking directly at you. A sideways view does not allow a proper judgement. I found this also applied to kudu. However, with sable and roan, the best position for accurate judgement is side on.

On yet another hunt Carlo wanted to shoot a big forest leopard and the area I chose was the north side of the Aberdare Mountain range, right up in the bamboo. For bait we used bushbuck and giant forest hog, which abounded in the area. Bushbuck males were usually very dark with good trophy heads, so we kept the horns and used the meat for bait.

At high altitudes where the temperature was cool and it often rained, carcasses took a long time to rot. As it is this rotting smell which attracts the cats, it was usual for several days to go by before the leopard came to the bait. We also dragged the stomach around to help entice the leopard.

One day I drove up the forest track which ran along a ridge. I had a bait high up in a tree in the valley below. It was easy see down into the valley glades from the ridge so I stopped the Land Rover, looked through binoculars and saw a big male leopard standing at the foot of the tree. He circled several times and reached up as if he wanted to climb up. The bait was about ten feet up on a spreading branch and the cat could see it clearly. After several minutes the leopard disappeared into the surrounding bamboo. It occurred to me that the big cat either thought the tree was too difficult to climb or that he was not very hungry.

After a discussion with Wanyahoro, we decided to find an easier tree to bait. When we got down to the tree we found deep scratch marks on the trunk where the leopard had tried to climb and failed. The main reason for placing bait high up in trees was to make them inaccessible to hyenas. Any meat on the ground was eaten by hyena long before a lion or a leopard found it. We found a suitable tree lower down in the valley. It was leaning at a forty-five degree angle and was easy to climb, even for handicapped or lazy leopard. I found that the female was a better climber than the male and took this into account when placing bait. We placed the bait in the tree and then dragged the stomach around. We also built a blind sixty yards away with a good approach up a slight depression, which meant we could get inside without the leopard seeing us.

The following morning we found the bait partially eaten. In the afternoon, at about half past three, we cautiously entered the blind. Brian, my youngest son then aged eight, was with us. After an hour the leopard, a big male and most likely the one we saw the day before, came out and lay down close to the tree. I had a whispered conversation with Carlo who assured me he could shoot it on the ground. The shot required great accuracy because the animal was facing head on and did not offer a big target. Carlo aimed for the head and the animal never knew what hit him. He used an 8 x 68 Magnum rifle which has a flat shooting and hard hitting bullet.

This was one of the largest forest leopards that I ever shot with a client. I guessed its weight at well over 200 pounds, possibly 220 pounds. The tail was short, having lost about one third of its length, so it could not be

138

measured from nose to tail. The animal was too heavy to carry out and we skinned it on the spot and carried the head and skin back to the hunting car. The largest, or should I say longest, forest leopard that I shot was in the company of Don Bousfield in the Aberdares. It measured eight feet three inches, though it was not nearly as heavy bodied as Carlo's. Don found a big leopard later on, also in the Aberdares. It was shot by his client, Prince Hohenlohoe and measured eight feet seven inches.

The main diet of the big forest cats in this area was bushbuck, duiker, young giant forest hog, bush pig and young buffalo, with lesser stuff thrown in. We hunted giant forest hog and bagged a big male. These pigs are quite impressive with their size and ugliness. Some weigh nearly 500 pounds but their tusks are not as long as warthog tusks.

Shortly after hunting with Carlo, I had another client, C.C. Adams, who was also an excellent shot. He used a .300 Weatherby Magnum. We started the safari by shooting plains game and I vividly remember him shooting a Thomson's gazelle at 500 yards. He usually picked a flat anthill or a mound, lay down and shot from a prone position. Later in the safari we had a big forest leopard in the fork of a yellow fever tree and all we could see was the head and chest and this same client refused to shoot it.

We arrived in Masailand from Nairobi and camped at the bottom of an escarpment near a river. Once the camp was up, we went out shooting and promptly shot a fine waterbuck. The staff skinned the buck and put the carcass, skin and head in the back of the truck.

The truck driver was a city African who was scared stiff of the wilds and decided to sleep in the cab of the truck. In the middle of the night I was awakened by him banging on the cab with his fists. I got my torch and went over and asked him what all the noise was about. He said something had jumped into the back of the truck and then jumped out again when he started banging. I shone the torch into the back of the truck and saw that all the meat and trophies were uncovered. I told the driver to cover the heads and skins, which included the Thomson's gazelles we had shot that afternoon en route to our present camp.

At about 4 o'clock in the early morning, I was again awakened by the driver banging on the cab. I took my torch and went across. He said that the animal had jumped in again. I looked in the back and could not see anything amiss. At first light I went over to the truck and saw the tracks of a big leopard. Further on there were marks where something had been dragged away. I followed the drag with my gun bearers and found the backskin of the waterbuck wedged in the fork of a tree. There was another drag nearby which we also followed. It crossed the shallow, fast-running river and we found more drag marks on the other bank. These led into a thick patch of bush on the river bank and here we found the hind leg of the waterbuck lodged in the fork of a big yellow fever tree.

I sent back to the camp for rope to secure the leg to a limb of the tree. In due course we tied it securely or so we thought, and I instructed the camp crew to build a blind on the opposite bank. This gave us a sixty yard shot. Then we went lion hunting. Shortly after leaving camp we located lion tracks and followed them into a gully with high banks on either side. Eventually it narrowed right down and we walked up a narrow water course with high walls on both sides. Our progress was purposefully slow because we were hoping to get close to the lion or lioness without them being aware of our approach. On my right, in a washed away cut leading into the main stream bed, I suddenly saw a lion's tail. The animal was lying down and only its tail was showing. The body remained hidden behind a bend in the river bed. It was very close – probably five yards. I stopped short and was thinking what to do next, when a lion growled and both of them took off up the cutaway. We never had a good enough view to allow for a shot before the lion got our scent. We followed for a short distance but both animals went fast and far and we reluctantly returned to camp.

I was told by the camp staff that they saw a leopard jump into the tree while they were building the blind. He tried unsuccessfully to remove the bait but retired to the bush below when the activity of blind building disturbed him.

In the afternoon we went to the leopard blind and waited for the cat to show up. At about 5 o'clock the leopard jumped into the tree and I advised C.C. to wait until it went out onto the branch and offered a broadside shot. While we were waiting, a Masai came by driving a herd of cattle. He was whistling and making all the noises that are usual while driving cattle. The leopard promptly disappeared into the bush below and we settled down for another wait. The sun was just going down when the leopard reappeared. Once again he sat in the fork and looked around.

I suggested that C.C. take a shot at its chest. He whispered back that he was afraid to wound it and would rather wait for it to go to the bait. We settled down and hoped the leopard would move out. Instead of doing this, the animal climbed up higher into the tree and disappeared amid the foliage. It did not reappear before darkness fell and we returned to camp. The next morning we entered the blind while it was still dark. When it was light enough to see, I noticed that the bait was gone. The leopard had chewed through the ropes and taken the leg. We continued to wait, hoping to see the leopard, and as the sun was coming up, he reappeared from behind the foliage. He was carrying the leg in his jaws and quickly moved down the tree and disappeared into the undergrowth. We went across and tried to find where he might have hidden the leg but we had no success. The leopard had disappeared with the leg.

Early the next morning we saw a good rhino bull and went after him. C.C. was armed with a .470 double rifle which he had hired from a Nairobi gun shop. It was not long before we caught up with the rhino but we had to walk quickly to get close enough to shoot. In doing so we made too much noise and the rhino heard us. He trotted a bit then started to walk but every now and again he stopped to listen. We quickened our pace and closed the gap to forty yards when the bull stopped once more and turned broadside to listen. I told C.C. to shoot. He put the rifle up and fired. The beast dropped but immediately started to roll around as if he wanted to get onto his feet. I told C.C. to shoot again because the rhino was trying to get up and would be off in an instant. Nothing happened so I glanced towards C.C. and saw that he had broken the action and was trying to reload. I said, "Hurry up and shoot." With that the rhino was on his feet and disappeared from view before either of us could fire.

We started tracking straight away. There was little blood, a drop now and again, but the tracks were easy to follow. After about 400 yards we came upon a rhino with his head in a bush and his hindquarters towards us. It was a bull and he was not feeding but, in fact, he swayed a little on his feet. I thought it might be our rhino because the animal was obviously in pain but I told C.C. not to shoot. While we were looking at him, the rhino suddenly became aware of our presence and spun around. His horns were about the same size as the one we had shot at and I still thought it was our rhino. The bull came towards us so I told C.C. to shoot and the bull fell on the spot. When we looked at the beast, he only had one shot in him and, try as we might, we could not find any other bullet holes. I knew there must be a shot in the shoulder area, probably high enough to temporarily disable him, but we could not find it.

We looked around and sure enough we found the tracks and spots of blood going past the unfortunate rhino. We followed the tracks again. The animal was trotting at high speed and, because of its weight, the tracks sunk into the ground making them easy to follow. After about one mile, we came upon a group of hysterical Masai women trying to round up their donkeys, most of which had just thrown their loads. The rhino had trotted right through the column and caused chaos. We could see no casualties and quickly bypassed the scene, having ignored the jabbering women who obviously blamed us for their misfortune. A couple of hours later we found the rhino in the middle of a huge overhanging bush. He was barely visible because he was lying down and we had to get really close to be able to see him properly. We crouched down and waited until I could confirm either blood or a bullet wound. I did not want to shoot another 'wrong' rhino.

It was now midday. The sun was beating down and we felt really uncomfortable and thirsty. The beast was also uncomfortable and kept rolling around. One minute it was lying down, next it was up and exposing its side. Eventually I spotted a line of dried blood down its side. It had been shot too high. I nodded to C.C. and whispered to him to shoot. With the shot, the rhino was on its feet and came straight towards us. I quickly fired into its chest and C.C. fired again. The rhino slithered to a halt only two yards from us – dead.

After this I had to report to the game warden, Major Temple-Boreham. I went to his headquarters with the horns of the beast we had accidentally shot and a written explanation. I left them at his office as he was away at the time. Later I received a cable saying that my explanation was accepted.

We moved to the Meru area on Mount Kenya for buffalo and another try for leopard. Our bushbuck trophy provided the bait. A day later we came upon a herd of buffalo moving into the bamboo. We moved around the edge of the bamboo and saw a small buffalo calf a few yards away. The calf spotted us, started to bawl and with that the mother came dashing out and confronted us. She stopped and shook her head. I stood my ground because I knew that if we moved back, the mother would charge. The calf moved off into the bamboo and, to my relief, the mother finally followed it.

I wanted to get ahead of the buffalo to see if we could find a big bull but it was not to be. We walked right into the cow again. This time she did not hesitate and came at full speed. Out of the corner of my eye I remember seeing the trackers and C.C. taking off. Then everything happened quickly. I had no choice but to shoot. My first shot was in her chest. Immediately I switched to my second barrel for the head and neck. With the second shot the buffalo collapsed and came skidding towards me. I threw myself backwards and sideways to avoid the body, tripped over a tussock of grass and landed on my back right in the middle of a lot of stinging nettles. I was up in a second but the buffalo was dead. C.C. fell face down, also in the stinging nettles. Within a short time the trackers returned. The next day we found some buffalo bulls and C.C. wounded a bull. We followed him for hours only to hear him go crashing off. Eventually we lost the buffalo and gave up the chase.

We moved around the mountain hoping to change our luck. While hunting in some forest glades we came across a bull eland. C.C. wounded the animal which took off up the mountain and soon disappeared into the forest. We followed a good blood trail for hours. Late in the afternoon we arrived on the edge of the moorlands with the eland still going strong and we had to turn back. On the way back there was a violent thunderstorm with lightning. We were thoroughly drenched and once were nearly struck by lightning. We came across a rhino track which was so fresh that water was just starting to run into it. The rhino must have passed ahead of us.

The storm cleared and the sun came out as we were going through a patch of heath. The trackers walked ahead, going downhill at a fairly good pace when I saw them stop and start to move back. I heard Wanyahoro tell them to stand still but they ignored him and with that an old buffalo cow charged and Wanyahoro also had to run. The trackers, followed by the buffalo, came towards me. I had to shoot and dropped the cow. I had now shot two cow buffalo on one safari. This I had never had to do before, nor have I had to do since, in many years of hunting professionally.

C.C.'s safari ended. I concluded that he was a very unlucky hunter. Some have good luck and some less so, but I have never witnessed anything like C.C.'s bad luck.

Don Bousfield and I did quite a few professional safaris in Kenya and Tanganyika, but in the off season when we were not taking out clients, we did our own private trips. Don and I had become good friends. We enjoyed being out in the bush, looking for new hunting areas and making a little extra money. Don had also become part of the family when he married my sister, Anne.

We hunted zebra for their skins in the Isiolo area, with the permission of the game warden, George Adamson, and also in the Masai area with the permission of the game warden, Major Temple-Boreham. The zebra in these areas bred to such numbers that the local tribesmen complained about the competition for grazing.

Experience taught us how to select the best skins out of the herd. We used binoculars to carefully choose the black and white stallions (the males had the best skin contrast, whereas the mare was usually much browner).

We avoided animals with lumps, torn ears or bare patches on the neck, as those indicated fighting scars. A short mane usually meant an old stallion with the probability of scars and so it was also rejected. Our target animal was a black and white male, with a clean skin and a longish mane.

These hunts improved our skills in many ways. Our shooting became more accurate and we were able to take longer shots, sometimes up to 500 yards (usually from a prone position). We became skilled at picking out the stallions from among the mares and most of all we became very good at skinning. After a while we could get the skin off, clean with no fat and meat, in a matter of minutes. The skin was washed to remove any blood, immediately salted and left to dry in the shade.

Don and I often took our children on these zebra shoots because they enjoyed going out into the wild as much as we did. Don's son, Keith, was a very bright two year old and after a while he became bored. One day young Keith had been out all day with Don and his skinners while they shot. Late in the afternoon Don and his crew were skinning a zebra when Keith suddenly said to Don, "When is this all going to stop?" Don replied, "What do you mean?" Keith answered, "All this killing of zebra!" The shooting must have made quite an impression on Keith because he never took up hunting. Today he works for a National Park in Australia.

My two elder sons, Cecil and Richard, always gave a helping hand with the skinning. We often had Don's three nephews, Brian, Massey and Colin, with us. They also lent a helping hand with the skinning. We had to stop these operations when the rains started in earnest. On one trip, the first heavy rain made the ground soft and waterlogged in many places. The following day we only went a few hundred yards because one truck sank down to the axles in spite of having four wheel drive. Getting the truck out was a tedious process. Each wheel was jacked up and logs carted by the second vehicle were placed under the wheels. Sometimes the truck went only a few yards before sinking in again and the tiresome process was repeated.

On this occasion we spent the night out on the plains with intermittent rain storms bringing more and more water. We put up a large tent and slept on camp beds which was fortunate because it rained all night and water ran through the tent like a river. The next day we managed to get over the plains on to a hard road and out of the area.

Not long after this Don and I camped way up on the Aberdare Mountains. We were looking for places to hunt bongo with our clients. Keith was with us on this trip. One cold evening we were sitting around a camp fire. Keith had been caught telling Don a lie and Don reprimanded him saying, "Keith, you will NOT go to heaven if you lie." Keith's reply was, "Good! I like it better here!"

Our favourite rifles were magnums. We liked their flat shooting qualities over long distances because we often made long shots. I used a Weatherby .300 Magnum and sometimes a .300 H & H Magnum. Don used a .300 H & H bull gun (a target rifle with a thick barrel). He had the barrel rebored to a .300 Weatherby because he liked their ammunition. The bullets were usually 180 grain Noslers, which held together on impact and gave maximum penetration. Soft nose bullets on the .300 Weatherby were poor performers on zebra, sometimes exploding just after impact under the skin with no penetration, and this usually meant we would have a wounded beast. We always had scopes fitted to these rifles.

Most of our better skins were sold in Nairobi and fetched 150 shillings each. After we deducted the Government dues, petrol and oil for the vehicles, salaries for our native staff, salt for the skins, food and rations, we still had a bit of a profit.

Years later Don had a bad accident with the bull gun. He was with an African assistant on a private ranch shooting zebra from a Land Rover. He aimed at a zebra, pulled the trigger and nothing happened. He thought the gun misfired, ejected the round and pushed another into the barrel. When he pulled the trigger this time, there was an explosion and the whole action blew up. The bolt went through the roof of the Land Rover, parts of the breach and stock shattered his elbow, and both his eardrums burst but his eyes were all right. The African assistant drove Don back to the farm house and from there Don went to the hospital. Several operations were required to remove bits of metal and bits of stock from his arm and the bones were reset. Don was very lucky because he regained the use of his arm and elbow with a lot of therapy. A Sikh doctor grafted bits of vein from his wrist into his eardrums and he also regained his hearing.

Our best and most exciting hunts were for forest elephant. At that time we could each buy four forest elephant licences at twenty-five pounds each (500 East African shillings). We hunted forest elephant mainly on Mount Kenya. It was exciting because most of the time we came on the elephants at very close range in bamboo, sometimes when visibility was only a few yards. Often we got right up to an elephant and saw only its feet while the upper body remained hidden by the thick foliage.

One day we camped in the bamboo belt above Embu on Mount Kenya. We left camp on foot with quite a large party including John Russel (who later became a professional hunter and years later died from a heart attack), Cecil (my eldest son) and about four African staff to assist with chopping out

145

the tusks and the skinning of the ears and feet of the elephant we shot.

We progressed up and down valleys, in the bamboo and along glades for a few miles when, suddenly, in a large patch of cabbage weed between the bamboo belts, we came across the tracks of two elephant bulls. They had either heard us or got our scent because we could see from their tracks, which were sunk deep into the soft ground, that they were running. We had not heard them.

Don and I went ahead with the rest of the party trailing a few yards behind. We went through cabbage weed which was taller than our heads and after a couple of hundred yards, came to the edge of the bamboo. Don was leading and stooped to pass under some overhanging bamboo. Immediately he darted off to one side, went round a thick clump of bamboo and stopped. Realising that something serious was afoot, I followed. As we stopped and crouched, there was a rustling of leaves and a huge body appeared opposite us and stopped only yards away. It was a bull. He had heard us approaching and came to investigate. The animal was so close that I could see the white tips and the dark stained thicker portions of the tusks. Most of the head and parts of the shoulder were showing. I glanced at Don who nodded and put his rifle up to shoot. I did the same and since Don was clearly aiming at the head for a brain shot, I decided to go for the heart. The animal was obviously listening but he could not see us.

Don fired immediately after putting up his rifle and I did likewise. The reports from the two rifles seemed almost as one. The elephant dropped with a crash and ended up on its side. Had he fallen towards us, we would probably have been pinned down by the bamboo that he would have pushed over with its falling body. All is well that ends well.

Don and I were examining the ivory when our party came crowding in. Cecil said that when they saw Don and I dash off to one side and then heard the elephant's approach, they took off away from the scene. After the rifles were fired, they stopped to listen and decided to come back when they did not hear the elephant. Cecil was then twelve years old and really enjoyed all the excitement of the hunt. He had no trouble in keeping up with the grown-ups.

The tusks were good for a forest elephant and weighed about fifty pounds each. We did shoot bigger ones at a later stage. The rest of the day was spent cutting out the tusks and skinning the feet and ear (we could only take one ear as the other was pinned underneath).

I was always amazed at how easily these large animals traversed the steep slopes even when the ground was wet and slippery in the rainy season. Don and I often hunted these elephants in the wet season when we were not occupied with clients. These big animals had very good balance. This was most evident when I was hunting many years later with a fellow professional hunter, Tony Seth-Smith. We were on the Mau range in the bamboo belt, following four bull elephant and trying to get close enough to see their ivory. The elephants had big feet which made it more interesting. The wind was very bad, switching around as it often does in the forest. As a result, the elephants eventually got our scent and took off with us following quickly behind. We came to a steep slope and were amazed to see the elephants had gone down so rapidly. We found that they had slid down the slippery ground on their haunches while in a sitting position with the two front feet straight out in front. It looked like bulldozers had gone down the slope, taking everything with them including some enormous fallen tree trunks. This rapid descent continued right down to the bottom where the elephants had simply regained their feet and continued their headlong flight. I noted elephant doing this on two or three other occasions. Anybody who thinks elephants are slow and clumsy had better think again.

I discovered that forest elephant did not move much in heavy rain. I often picked up tracks that were made before the rain and followed them to the place where the elephant had waited for the rain to stop before moving on. Even then the tracks made after the downpour continued only for a very short distance before we came on the elephant.

One day Don and I were coming back towards camp after walking miles in an unsuccessful search for elephant. We came across a black river duck swimming in a small pond in the middle of a clearing surrounded by bamboo. Since there was no meat in camp, Don decided to shoot it. He was armed with a .458 Winchester rifle which would make mince meat of the duck so he decided to shoot it in the head or neck. We made a bet – I bet that he would miss. Don lay down, took aim at the duck and fired. We were both amazed to see it floundering in the water, having been shot in the neck. I should have been more careful in taking on a bet because Don was very knowledgeable about firearms and always made sure that his rifle shot spot on. On another occasion I saw him shoot a suni which is the size of a rabbit, with the .458.

One day while we were out hunting we heard an elephant feeding in a big patch of short but thick bamboo. We realised that if we went into the bamboo, it would be impossible to see the ivory with the visibility at a couple of yards. We decided to remain in one place and sent two gun bearers around the back of the bamboo to give scent to the elephant. We expected the elephant to come out in our direction. This worked perfectly and the elephant came through the bamboo very cautiously. We watched his

147

progress, noting the shaking bamboo tops. He stopped for what seemed like ages just inside the edge of the bamboo, testing the wind and listening. Eventually he stepped out and walked towards us. He was a young bull with small ivory. We stood still and let him come right up to us. He only saw us when he was about twenty yards off. He stopped and his head came up with his ears out. He made a couple of quick steps towards us, shook his head violently and his ears came forward in a very aggressive manner. These actions were repeated twice but we stood still. The elephant could not understand our behaviour and this broke his nerve because he suddenly turned and walked away from us, slowly at first for about fifty yards, and then he ran away fast. Standing up to dangerous animals works most of the time even with lion, buffalo and elephant. However this does not work with wounded animals that are enraged because most will charge on sight, especially if pressed.

Sometimes I hunted elephant without Don's company, taking only Wanyahoro plus a couple of locals to help. I shot my forest elephant with the largest ivory on such an occasion above Embu. We left our camp in the bamboo and went west along the side of the mountain. After walking for about two hours we came across big bull tracks that were made the previous day. It had rained during the night but we could follow the tracks quite easily. After about a mile, we came on a place where the elephant had stood around during the rain. We picked up fresh tracks leading away and it did not seem long before we heard bamboo breaking ahead on a lower slope. We advanced slowly and only when we were very close could I see the elephant, and every now and again a lot of ivory sticking out. The tusks looked impressive for a forest elephant.

We waited for the elephant to turn its body so that I could get a shot. The wind was switching around a bit and I hoped that the animal would not smell us. Suddenly he got our wind, turned and started off. I knew I had to shoot quickly if I was to get this elephant. I put my rifle up and went for the shoulder. At the shot, the elephant really got going and I managed to fire a second shot into its hindquarters, high up near the kidneys, but he kept going. I caught up with him on a steep slope. He had slowed down, obviously feeling the effects of his wounds. I managed to get in another two shots which put him down.

This elephant had the biggest tusks I had seen on a forest elephant.

Later we weighed them at 85 and 83 pounds. Much later Don shot a big bull above Chuka that weighed 96 pounds but it only had one tusk. Don came across this elephant in fairly open forest and shot it in the brain with a 7 mm Rigby rifle loaded with solids. Don liked to read all of W.M. Bell's books on elephant hunting. Bell, commonly known as 'Karamojo Bell', was an expert shot and only used light calibre rifles, the .256 and 7 mm being his favourites. I was not with him on this occasion. Years later I happened to come across an enormous skull and when I turned it over I heard something rattle in the brain cavity. I had my Africans cut open the skull and inside the brain chamber I found the bullet. A local told me that Bwana Donna (that's what the Africans called him) had shot the elephant. I knew then for certain that it was Don's elephant. He had told me, after shooting the single tusker, that he tried a W.M. Bell shot for the brain with his 7 mm.

Once again I was out with Wanyahoro and two locals. We decided to investigate a new area on the mountain close to the Castle Hill Forest Station, between Karatina and Embu. On this trip I also wanted to hunt a bongo if one came across my path, although elephant remained my first choice. We picked up the tracks of a bull bongo in the soft ground (it had rained during the night) and got right up to the bongo but, in spite of moving as quietly as possible, the animal heard us. There was a crash of bamboo a few yards ahead and we knew it was him. We picked up the tracks again and followed for at least a mile before coming to a place where the bongo had stopped and taken up a position behind a big tree with a fork in it. From here the bongo could look back and see any enemy approach. Sure enough he saw us as soon as we came into view and he took off once again. We realised that following any further was a waste of effort.

This goes to show how difficult and wary bongo are. I always considered a bongo hunt the most difficult of all. The area we went through while hunting the bongo had giant camphor trees which grow only on the south east slope of the mountain. I sometimes stopped to rest at the foot of these trees and smelt a bit of bark. The camphor in the bark came through quite strongly. This part of the forest, with its indigenous trees, was natural and unspoilt. I wonder if that area is still the same today. I often hear stories about the clearing of the indigenous forest to make way for pine plantations or cultivations for the local tribesmen.

On our way back, we heard an elephant breaking bamboo. We made a cautious approach but just before reaching the animal, the wind gave us away and we heard it crashing off. We quickly followed and soon came on its tracks sinking deep in the ground, indicating that it had made a hasty retreat. The tracks were big enough to follow so we trotted after the bull and continued the fast pace for quite a distance until I noticed that the elephant had slowed to a walk. I turned to Wanyahoro and told him that we should now go cautiously because the elephant was not running anymore. We went a little further and came through the thick bamboo belt into a small clearing about twenty yards across.

There was the bull elephant facing us. His head was up, his ears were standing out and he was looking right at us. Wanyahoro whispered that the tusks were not big enough. I estimated that they weighed about forty pounds. We usually tried for a minimum of fifty pounds for a forest elephant. I whispered back to him, as he crouched next to me to move back slowly and I would follow. As soon as Wanyahoro moved back and away, the elephant made up his mind to charge. I was still crouched down and had to shoot from that position. I went for the frontal brain shot and fired at the elephant only ten yards away. The bullet went straight to the brain, the head jerked up and he collapsed in the upright position with the legs folded underneath. This bull gave me no alternative but to shoot in self defence. The tusks later weighed 45 and 44 pounds – not good, but not bad either.

TWELVE

New Experiences in Botswana and Kenya

In 1963, Ker & Downey Safaris asked Don and myself to drive two Bedford 4 x 4 trucks and a Dodge Wagon to Botswana. The trucks were loaded with all the equipment needed for a safari. Harry Selby, who had rejoined Ker & Downey, was to initiate hunting safaris in that country. My wife accompanied us as far as Southern Rhodesia where she joined the Kenya National hockey team on tour. We also had the African staff who would be working for Ker & Downey in Botswana with us. The trip was uneventful but very slow because the Dodge Wagon could hardly go over thirty miles an hour. At night we camped along the side of the road.

One afternoon we stopped on an escarpment overlooking the Zambezi River. Don decided to play a prank on the African staff. Next to the road were huge pieces of fossilised wood. They were strewn around the slope and looked like ordinary wood. Don told the Africans that we needed firewood for the night's stop and asked them to load some onto the trucks. When they went to pick up the fossilised wood, they were unable to do so because it was as heavy as a rock. The expression on their faces was comical. Don then explained to them what the pieces were. After picking up genuine firewood, we turned around and backtracked to the Victoria Falls turn off which we had overshot. The safari staff with us were amazed at the impressive sight presented by the Falls.

South of the Falls we turned off the road and headed for the Bechuanaland border which we crossed at Pandamatenga. Bechuanaland later became independent and is now called Botswana. My first impression was of the soft white sand and the dryness. Good roads soon became sand tracks which required a 4 x 4 vehicle. The Bushman Pits road was both long and hard going. Very few vehicles had been along it for some time. We saw very few wild animals and no humans on this stretch. Early one morning the

151

cook was crouching behind a bush when a cobra spat in his eye. We doctored him and continued on our way towards Maun.

After we handed the trucks over to Harry Selby, Don and I decided to explore the Okavango Swamp head waters. We were keen to see sitatunga which were numerous in this area and we had heard that big heads were common.

We got a lift to the head of the swamp and made arrangements to accompany Bobby Wilmot's crocodile hunters. The Okavango River is large with its sources in the Angola Highlands. It in turn is the main source of the Okavango Swamps. The water is very clear, probably because it runs through sand for most of its course, and it is easy to see tigerfish and bream swimming around. The river flows at about five miles an hour and it is usual to see islands of papyrus reeds floating down with the current. Where the river breaks up into channels lower down, these islands eventually stick in the narrows and soon the reeds take root and block the water course.

At the head of the swamp, Don and I were met by a young crocodile hunter who worked for Bobby Wilmot. We left the next day by boat and the river soon broke up into channels. It was very easy to take the wrong water course and get lost, so it was important to have a local who knew his way through the swamp. We hit a blockage and the boat crew was kept busy cutting, slashing and pulling the reeds to make a passageway. This happened several times throughout the day until we eventually reached an island where there was an established camp.

When darkness fell we went out in the boat with a spotlight powered by a twelve volt car battery. The crew held barbed spears and with a little luck, bream would be on the menu for supper and breakfast. The bright light picked out fish swimming in the clear water and our expert crew speared enough fish for our meals. I tried my hand at it and found it very difficult. I was told to aim below the fish's gills in order to hit it in the centre. The water did altered our perceptions and aiming low made allowances for this. After several tries, I eventually succeeded.

The next morning we made an early start and went downstream by boat, hoping to catch the sitatunga feeding on burnt patches of grass along the bank. The locals burnt the reeds periodically to improve their chances when illegally hunting animals with dogs. Sitatunga usually fed in the early mornings and again late in the afternoon. We saw several during the trip, including a couple with good heads. After a few days we were more than satisfied with what we had seen and returned to where we had started our swamp trip.

The young crocodile hunter was due to take us to Maun in his Land

My sons, Richard and Brian, on safari shooting for the pot

Lion posing for us in Masailand, Kenya

Unusual zebra shot by Don and myself

Don Bousfield and Jock en route from Kenya to Botswana

Victoria Falls

Page Brown with his giant forest hog shot on Mount Kenya

Buffalo shot by Page Brown in Masailand, Kenya

Good impala shot by Page Brown - Masailand, Kenya

Page Brown with his beautiful tusks,
Kenya 1963

Marge Brown - siesta time on safari,
Mount Kenya

Rover. Don and I were appaled at the poor mechanical condition of his badly neglected car. One main leaf on the front spring was broken and the tyres were flat. Don offered to change the front spring but the crocodile hunter said he did not need any help because he had been a mechanic in Bulawayo (Southern Rhodesia).

We eventually left and, after forty miles, we had a flat tyre. We jacked the car up and found the spare tyre was also flat. We pumped up the spare but found it was losing air from an unrepaired puncture. We offered to fix the tyres but the young man had no patches. All he had was a pump and water. Don came up with the idea of taking out the valve core, unscrewing the handle and plunger of the pump, filling it with water, replacing the hand and plunger and forcing the water into the tube with the pump. Eventually we had about a pint of water in the tube, we replaced the valve and pumped air into the tube. The tyre held up because the water inside the tube sealed the puncture. We went a further 80 miles and had to repeat the operation on another flat tyre. We travelled another 180 miles with the tyres holding up then, twenty miles short of Maun at 9 o'clock, disaster struck. The rear wheel and half shaft came out of the differential and we came to a halt.

We had neither food nor bedding, so Don and I decided to walk to Maun. A young coloured man, who was also a crocodile hunter, came with us. It was a bright moonlight night and we could see well enough but it was difficult walking in the soft sand. Luckily it was cool and we were pleased not to be walking in the daytime heat. We started at about 9 o'clock and eventually reached Maun at 3 o'clock in the morning. The local hotel manager kindly gave us a room and some beers which went down very well.

After a couple of days rest, we went up the other end of the swamp to the Kwaai. There we saw herds of red lechwe, sable, buffalo, elephant, wildebeest, roan and lion, as well as quite a few other species. When we returned to Maun, Don and I decided that we would spend a season in Botswana one day.

Don and I both resigned from Ker & Downey Safaris when we returned to Nairobi. We joined White Hunters Safaris who offered us a better deal as they were keen to have us.

Before leaving Ker & Downey, we did one final safari with David and Julie Dorn, in the Wakamba country down on the Thua River. This was a sandy river bed in the dry season but sometimes became a very large swollen river when the heavy rains came. This we experienced towards the end of our stay in the area. In the dry season the elephant dug for water just under the surface of the sand in the river bed. In the morning we picked up tracks in these drinking places and followed them to the feeding grounds, sometimes fifteen to twenty miles away.

Before we managed to shoot an elephant, the rains came with a vengeance and we experienced four days of torrential rain which brought the river down in flood. One evening there was a slight lull between rain storms. I put my gas lamp outside the tent on the ground so that the insects, which had come out in droves with the rainfall, would be attracted to the light and stay outside the tent. When I came back after dinner, the light was burning with myriads of insects all around but what attracted my attention was an enormous black scorpion gobbling up the insects on the ground. For a while I watched the scorpion partake of this feast. I went to bed and before I fell asleep the rain came down heavily again. After four days the rain stopped and when the sun came out, we packed up and moved out.

We left about mid-morning and right from the start we had trouble. The ground was saturated and the four wheel drive Bedford bogged down. We had two of these trucks with us and they kept sinking down to the axles. The only way we got them out was to jack up each wheel with Tanganyika jacks. They lifted the body a considerable distance and once the wheel came up, we cut logs and packed them in the ruts. Each wheel was treated individually. We put chains on all four wheels to give better traction but, whenever we hit a soft patch of ground, the trucks got bogged down anyway. We also used hand operated Terfor winches for an extra boost. These winches were anchored to a tree about thirty yards ahead of the bogged down truck. The other end of the steel cable was attached to the truck's front bumper and two men worked the handle. Sometimes the winch pulled the truck forward out of the quagmire but quite often the truck did not move and the winch pulled the anchor tree out roots and all. It took us two days to travel twenty miles before we got onto firmer roads and away to another hunting area.

I spent seven years with Ker & Downey. The first few years were very happy but thereafter I became disenchanted with the company and it did not take much for me to move to a new company offering better prospects.

After joining White Hunters, Don and I did quite a few double safaris together. These took us all over Kenya and Tanzania (both of which had become independent). We found two serviceable ex-army Bedford 4 x 4 trucks in very good condition and two radio transmitters with a very good range which allowed us to contact Nairobi via the telephone system and get any number in the country. We sometimes made calls from Southern Tanzania, a distance of 800 miles away. Colonel Robert Caulfield, our manager in White Hunters, was efficient and capable.

During my numerous safaris with overseas clients, I made many friends and among them were Page Brown and his wife Marge. Page was a good hunter and fisherman. Marge was not interested in hunting but enjoyed the outdoors and the wildlife.

One of my safaris with them started on the south side of Mount Kenya. We were looking for bongo. We arrived at midday and made camp. In the afternoon, after zeroing in the rifles, we walked up into the bamboo, looking for signs of bongo but saw nothing fresh. The next day we packed up camp and moved around the mountain to hunt above Timau. Page noticed that the ring on the eye piece of his binoculars had come unscrewed. We had no idea where it had been lost.

High up on the mountain, in green park-like areas among tall cedar trees, we hunted bushbuck and shot two good trophies. Here the males are usually jet black and quite impressive, although some are brown with white spots, almost like a deer. On a subsequent day we ran into giant forest hog and Page took a big boar. These creatures, the largest of the wild pig family in Africa, are quite ugly. Most of the time they live in the bamboo belt, rooting and feeding on succulents. They live in large family groups and I have seen as many as twenty feeding in an open glade, although old boars are often on their own. The best way to hunt these animals was to look for evidence of their presence in the area, and then to slowly walk around the various glades in the evenings and early mornings, with the hope of coming across them feeding in the open.

We put up bait for leopard in the most likely areas next to game tracks. One bait was eaten after a few days, so I picked a good vantage point and built a blind. After we finished building, I realised my gold signet-ring was missing. I was not aware that it had slipped off my finger because it fitted quite loosely and I resigned myself to its permanent loss. It could have been

155

lost anywhere, even while walking in the forest during a hunt.

We sat in the blind one afternoon and before the sun set the leopard appeared. Page shot it on the ground before it had a chance to climb up to the bait. We took pictures before we loaded it onto the vehicle and I then dismantled the blind with the help of a couple of Africans. Most professional hunters took down their blinds and cut down their bait for two reasons. Firstly, to remove the evidence of a lion or leopard for the benefit of the next professional hunter. Secondly, old hanging bait and dried branches of blinds were an eyesore.

While I was busy destroying the blind, Page suggested that my signet-ring might have come off during the building process. I looked among the loose leaves which had fallen onto the ground and soon saw something shiny and yellow. What luck! It was my ring. The ring had belonged to my father and my mother had passed it on to me when he died, so it had great sentimental value.

We moved on because Page wanted to hunt greater kudu, gerenuk and Grevy's zebra. We drove 120 miles to the Maralal area and camped near Baragoi on the banks of the sand river. The surrounding area was volcanic with rock strewn everywhere. The area was hilly and dry, and the vegetation was mostly acacia bush and trees, all covered with some sort of thorn. Kudu and gerenuk are browsers and they fed off this bush. At first glance it was impossible to imagine anything living off this vegetation but somehow they managed. There was an escarpment close by which led down to the Great Rift Valley. From a vantage point, I could see Mount Nyiru to the north and beyond it was Lake Rudolf in the Rift Valley. Along the slopes of the escarpment we hunted greater kudu. Early the first morning we struck it lucky and managed to stalk and shoot a kudu male. I skinned the kudu and carried the head and cape back to the hunting car. The gun bearers returned for the meat.

A few days later we shot a gerenuk (Waller's gazelle). This is an unusual looking antelope with a long giraffe-like neck. It often stands on its hind legs, rather like a goat, in order to feed off the upper branches of a bush. We also shot a Grevy's zebra, with its typical, handsome narrow black and white stripes. They are the largest of the zebra family and have enormous ears like a mule.

We packed up camp and moved back to Mount Kenya to have another try for bongo. The first evening we were walking slowly through the bamboo, looking for tracks along a trail. I was in the lead and noticed something unusual. I picked it up and there in my palm was Page's eye piece from his binoculars. What incredible luck! We had not known where to look for it because we had no idea where it had been lost. It was a million to one chance and we stumbled onto it by accident.

Page did not get the bongo that trip but he did shoot one when he came out a year later. For this safari we set up camp on Mount Kenya. It rained during our first night which was good for us because the ground was soft and this made tracking easy in the morning. However, we were uncomfortable because we were soaked as soon as we started walking. It was cold but walking up and down the steep hills kept us warm. We soon came across the fresh tracks of a lone bull bongo which we naturally followed.

After two hours we came into a valley. The tracks led towards some big trees ahead and as we got nearer, I suddenly spotted the outline of an animal standing with its head hidden by a tree trunk. I looked through my binoculars and saw white stripes down its side which confirmed it was a bongo. Its body looked dark because it was in the shadows but I could not see the head which was hidden by the tree trunk. I had to make a quick decision. I was tempted to approach a little closer but the wind was not steady and there was a chance that the animal would get our scent. The distance was seventy to eighty yards and I decided Page should shoot from where we were standing. With his .375 H & H Magnum, Page made a perfect shot and the animal dropped in its tracks.

We were disappointed to find that it was a cow bongo. The bull had joined a small herd of about seven to ten animals and just beyond the dead animal, were signs of where the bull had been lying down with the rest of the herd. We were lucky to get a bongo but unlucky not to get the bull.

I was staying in the New Arusha Hotel, having completed a safari with clients in Tanzania. We were due to return to Nairobi the next day. While I was in Arusha, I received the terrible news that Don and his gun bearer. Omari, had been killed. Don was motoring from Timau to meet his client in Nairobi where they would begin their safari. At Karatina they were involved in a collision with a train at a level crossing. The visibility was bad at the time because it was raining and Don did not see the train until it was too late. It was terrible that his life should have ended in this manner, especially when he had escaped death so many times before. One day when we were sitting around a camp fire high up in the forest on the Aberdare Mountains, Don made a remark which I often recalled. He said that he would not like to live to an old age where he would be too feeble to enjoy life and do what he liked most. I am sure that The Maker took him sooner than he would have chosen. Many times in later years I was to miss Don's companionship and good humour. We had good times and lots of laughs together. Through the years I learned a lot from him, especially when it came to firearms because he knew far more about them than I did.

After Don was killed I became friendly with Tony Seth-Smith who farmed at Molo. Tony was a professional hunter and a good one at that. We both worked for Hunters Africa and enjoyed bongo hunting. Tony offered to show me areas where it was possible to hunt these difficult animals on the Mau range of mountains.

Bongo are mainly browsers, feeding off the leaves of certain plants and tender shoots of bamboo tips. They have a liking for charcoal on burnt tree trunks, obviously getting some sort of benefit from it, and they also frequent natural salt licks.

Tony and I hired several African porters to carry our food and tents. This was easier walking than on Mount Kenya or the Aberdares. The vegetation was mainly bamboo interspersed with tall trees but there were also thick patches of tall plants, like holly, which I had not seen elsewhere. There was also a tall plant with a seven year life cycle. Hunting became much easier during the dying-off period of this plant because the visibility improved, making it possible to see the bongo while tramping through the bamboo.

I noticed large, unnatural, circular mounds overgrown with bamboo. When I inquired about them, Tony told me that a few hundred years ago this whole mountain range was open grassland occupied by a tribe that kept cattle, sheep and goats. In the side of the slope, this tribe excavated a huge round hole large enough to accommodate all their livestock with an opening on the lower side. This was the only access. In the side wall of the excavations they dug out a shelter large enough for the inhabitants to escape from the rain and cold. These caves were comfortable and warm and protected both the livestock and the natives from other marauding tribes or predators such as lion and leopard. Apparently there was a lot of tribal fighting at that time. Eventually this particular tribe was forced to flee and went elsewhere, probably south to Tanzania. With their departure, bamboo encroached and covered most of the Mau mountain range, including the mounds.

I hunted for bongo with Bill Spencer who was another good client. For this safari, we hired porters and walked into an area where I had previously seen good signs of bongo. We hunted for several days, often getting close only to hear the all too familiar sound of an animal crashing off through the bamboo. Once I actually saw our quarry. Bill and a tracker were in the lead when the tracker crouched down and pointed. From my position behind them, I saw the bongo get up from where it was lying and slowly walk off. Bill never saw the animal because the bamboo obstructed his view.

This type of hunting was very rough and it entailed walking from morning to evening, up and down slippery slopes. The hunt took place in the rainy season when the ground was soft and it was possible to track easily. At that time of year, the moist bamboo leaves on the ground did not make a noise when stepped on. The hunters were constantly wet and water cascaded down our neck every time a branch was disturbed in passing. Our feet and socks were soaked immediately after setting out in the early morning and stayed that way for the rest of the day.

Besides bongo quite a few other animals such as buffalo, elephant, waterbuck, bushbuck, giant forest hog, bush pig, leopard, lion, yellow-backed duiker and monkeys are found on the Mau ranges. The yellow-backed duiker, the largest of the duiker family, were difficult to hunt as many sportsmen have discovered. They used a series of beds in patches of giant holly to lie up in. When they were disturbed, they quickly moved from one bed to another. We were not successful on this hunt but Bill came back again to hunt with Tony and shot a bongo bull.

I had heard good things about the safaris now being conducted in Botswana. The country had only recently been opened to overseas clients. In 1963 Hunters Africa Limited started operating in Botswana. For political reasons, White Hunters had changed their name to Hunters Africa Limited. Jacky Blacklaws and John Lawrence were among the first from Hunters Africa to hunt in Botswana. Other Kenya companies also started conducting safaris in Botswana at about the same time. The operation entailed taking a truck, which carried all the safari equipment, and a hunting car plus about ten crew and motoring through Tanzania and Zambia into Botswana, crossing the Zambezi River via ferry at Kazungula. Then at the end of the season, which usually lasted from after the rains in May until November, they returned to Kenya. Our company had its main base at Kasane, not far from Kazungula. There was a small hotel, owned by Lollie Sussens, on the banks of the Chobe River where all the petrol and safari provisions were purchased.

A couple of years later, Jacky Blacklaws contracted sleeping sickness when he was bitten by an infected tsetse fly and died. The tragedy would not have happened had Jacky sought medical attention as soon as he got sick, but he lay for about ten days in camp thinking he had malaria. Eventually he went into a coma and was flown in a light aeroplane to Livingstone Hospital where he died the next day. I knew of several hunters who contracted the disease and recovered, but this was only after being treated by a doctor during the early stages of the disease.

In 1967 I took my crew, truck, hunting car and necessary camping gear and drove to Botswana. Hunting here was a new experience. Most of the concession areas were flat, covered primarily by woodland with intermittent belts of mopane and teak trees. Only four wheel drive vehicles were able to negotiate the tracks in soft white sand. There were very few landmarks and I took to wearing a compass on my belt which I used frequently. In the swamps there were many sitatunga and big herds of red lechwe, as well as hippo and crocodile. Fishing was good in the channels of the Chobe swamp.

We had three concessions. The first was Bore Hole 2, an area south of Kasane bordered in the east by Rhodesia and in the west by the Chobe National Park. This area was named after the local water well and it was good for sable, antelope, gemsbok (oryx), roan, tsessebe, buffalo, elephant, kudu, lion and eland. The second area lay about one hundred miles west of Kasane and it was called Kachikau after the main village in the area. It bordered on the Chobe swamp in the north and Chobe National Park in the south. It was good for sitatunga, red lechwe, lion, buffalo, sable, roan, impala, bushbuck, elephant, zebra, wildebeest, tsessebe and kudu. The camping site on the Chobe or Linyanti swamp was called Saile. This area was full of tsetse fly and it was here that Jacky Blacklaws picked up sleeping sickness. One of my trackers also got sleeping sickness and I took him to the local hospital for immediate treatment where he recovered. The third area was Kwando, lying between the Linyanti and Okavango swamps with the Silinda Spillway as the southern boundary and the Caprivi strip as the northern boundary. This area was, for all practical purposes, inaccessible and we did not use it very much. In later years I built a bridge over the Silinda and made a camp at the Kwando River.

Hunting here was a little different to what I had been doing in East Africa. For one we hunted sitatunga in the swamps using a flat bottom boat powered by an outboard motor. A platform was built on the boat to allow the client and professional hunter to stand about eight feet above water level. This enabled them to see over the tall reeds on the sides of the channel and spot sitatunga. Hunting for sable and buffalo was a little like hunting in Southern Tanzania – driving around in the woodlands until game was spotted. A successful stalk usually achieved the desired results.

Gemsbok (oryx) were hunted on the vast plains near Bore Hole 2. These plains extended from the Rhodesian border for forty miles and averaged about twelve miles wide. The ground was black cotton soil with wide cracks on the surface which produced an uncomfortable ride when driving. Speed was very slow because of the rough roads and most progress was at walking pace, in low gear and four wheel drive. We all loathed having to hunt the area and hence the plains ended up being aptly referred to as the 'haemorrhoids'. This title I thought very apt!

Gemsbok hid out in the islands of Mopane trees dotted in the middle of the grasslands. They were very wary and it was essential to spot them before they were aware of your presence. I made use of climbable Mopane trees from which I used my binoculars. Sometimes I stopped the hunting car and stood on it to try to spot these ellusive animals. Once spotted, a good stalk was the order of the day.

Lion were usually tracked because Botswana lion and leopard were wary of bait. This was due to the local tribesmen using traps with steel jaws. When professional hunting safaris started, the government put a stop to the use of these traps in the concession areas. It was not until ten to twelve years later when a new generation of cats was born, that baiting worked.

My first hunting season in Botswana was very successful and at the end of October I packed up my gear and crew and returned to Kenya. I decided to return to Botswana permanently as soon as possible but this did not happen until 1969.

I was on an elephant safari with Ted Philpott in the Voi area in Kenya. We left camp before sunrise and headed for a big mountain nearby. Our plan was to climb to the summit and glass the flat bush below hoping to see elephants. When we arrived at the base of the mountain, I left the hunting car and the client, and then climbed up the slope with Wanyahoro and two other trackers. (The client was an older man, not very fit and unable to climb very far.) I handed my .470 double to Barissa, a Liangullu, who worked for me. Little did I realise how I would regret not having that rifle.

The climb was difficult and slow because the slope was steep and we had to stop many times to catch our breath. Dawn was breaking and the horizon was turning bright red. It would not be long before the sun appeared. We were halfway up the slope and in 30 minutes it would be light enough to spot any elephant moving in the bush below.

When the sun appeared over the top of the mountain there was a crash of bushes and a rhino came puffing and snorting down the slope in my direction. I was partly blinded by the sun and the rhino appeared as a huge mass coming right at me. I held my hand out hoping that Barissa would give me my rifle. At the same time I glanced over my shoulder only to see Barissa taking to his heels down the slope with the rifle. I noticed a large flat rock, about table height, to my left. I stepped behind it just as the rhino arrived on the other side and found myself looking across the rock at the rhino, which had by now skidded to a halt on the opposite side. For seconds the rhino glared across at me. I was trying to decide what evasive action to take should the rhino come around the rock or clamber across the top to get at me. It seemed like an eternity before anything happened. Suddenly the rhino spun around and went trotting off, still snorting and puffing, and disappeared round the side of the hill. Barissa came back up the hill with my rifle. From that day onwards I never let anybody else carry it.

However, I did get caught once more a couple of years later and it happened so easily. My clients, a married couple, were after a leopard in the Samburu area near Maralal. One day a Samburu came to our camp and told us a leopard had killed a calf near his *manyatta* (a dwelling built in the same manner as the Masai dwelling, usually a wooden frame plastered over with a mixture of mud and cow dung and with a heavy thorn bush enclosure for domestic stock). We all got into the hunting car and drove to the *manyatta*. When we arrived, my client started to take some photographs. I asked the Samburu where the leopard had made the kill and he pointed to a patch of thick bush about 300 yards away. I understood that it was on the edge of the bush and followed him. Wanyahoro and a couple of trackers came along, and after we had gone a short distance, I noticed that Marjorie, my client's wife, was also with us. I had not taken my rifle because I thought it would not be needed.

When we reached the bush, the Samburu went in and set off along a game path. I asked him again where the kill was and he replied that it was very close. Now I was worried that I did not have my rifle but decided against sending for it as the Samburu had said that the kill was nearby.

We proceeded through the patch of bush and came to a little opening where a big bull elephant was walking across the far side. We stood in a group watching it walking peacefully along when it either heard us or got our wind, for it stopped, spun round and charged. I shouted to everybody to run. The others took off while I waited to see whether the elephant would come all the way or stop, but he just kept coming. I decided it was also time for me to take off as the elephant was moving fast. I came through the patch of bush into the open to see Marjorie on the ground with Wanyahoro holding her by the arm to help her along. I ran up, took hold of her other arm and said "Run." Somebody shouted, "Here comes the elephant!" We partly dragged Marjorie along and ran as fast as we could. I expected the elephant to be on us at any moment but when I glanced over my shoulder, I saw that the beast had stopped at the edge of the bush and was turning back. We watched it disappear and then walked very shakily back to the car. I never failed to carry my rifle again. It was a hard lesson.

My last safari in Kenya was nearly a disaster. Bob Model and Anne were out on their honeymoon. Bob had been with me on another safari years before when we collected specimens for the American Museum of Natural History in New York. We were hunting elephant on the Tana River. The Tana had a lot of thick bush, called riverine bush, growing along both banks. In the dry season this bush was home to many different species including elephant, buffalo, leopard, lion, rhino, lesser kudu, giraffe, oryx and waterbuck.

One morning while we were walking through a particularly thick patch looking for elephant, I heard an animal moving through the bush on our right. I thought it might be an elephant, so the party waited while I went to investigate. I backtracked a short distance only to see a rhino step onto the path we had just been walking along. As soon as the rhino came onto the path, it put its nose down and started trotting along following our scent. I had experienced this before, so I knew that the rhino was hunting us.

I ran back to our party and told them to get behind a tree because a rhino was coming. We had a local Somali with us as a guide and when he heard me say a rhino was coming, he promptly took off. Anne saw him run and she followed him. Bob ran after her to stop her. They all soon disappeared. With that the rhino went charging past me and was soon out of sight.

Bob appeared next running back towards me with the rhino close behind him. As he was now directly in the line of fire, I could not shoot. I just stood and waited. A few seconds later, when Bob was about 15 yards from me, he turned and the rhino lunged at him but fortunately did not connect. Bob stumbled over a log and fell flat on his face. The rhino passed right over him, went on a couple of yards and suddenly spun round (a rhino is very quick on its feet for a big clumsy looking animal, contrary to what many would think). The beast, intent on attack, headed back towards where Bob was lying. I now had a clear shot and managed to drop it. Bob jumped up and the only injury he sustained was when he fell over the log and took the skin off the front of his shins. When the whole party reassembled, Anne got a good telling off from Bob because he was angry with her for running off and endangering both their lives. She should have stayed close to us.

I had shot the rhino without a licence and had to report to the nearest game warden, Ken Smith, who was stationed at Garissa, a small administrative centre about seventy miles up river. He instructed two game scouts to return with me to the scene of the shooting and retrieve the horns. Ken also asked me to submit a report to the Head Office in Nairobi. (The law allows one to shoot, in self defence, an animal which attacks.) We did not shoot an elephant on this safari because we were after a big tusker and did not see any worthwhile trophies.

I was on safari in the Voi area with an American client. We climbed a hill in order to get enough height to look down on the surrounding flat bushland where we hoped to see lesser kudu. We eventually found a suitable place to sit and use our binoculars. It did not take long to spot a lesser kudu bull accompanied by four or five females, all peacefully feeding off the bush and unaware of our presence. We also saw two rhino sleeping in the shade of a tree not far from the kudu.

The kudu were about one hundred yards off so I told the client to shoot. He made a good shot and the bull went down. I switched my binoculars to the rhino, expecting to see them get up and run off, but I was amazed to see them still sleeping. There was no reaction. We decided to shout and made enough noise to get them moving. At the sound of our voices they stood up, ran off and were soon out of sight. We then went down to pick up the kudu.

On a later safari I was hunting in Tanzania with a Mexican client. We put out bait for leopard and after a few days we had a take on one of them. A good blind was prepared with the usual quiet approach. We sat all afternoon but the leopard did not come. We returned early the following morning hoping to catch the cat feeding.

Before daylight, we drove to the blind but stopped about half a mile short of our destination. We walked the rest of the way, following a path that had been marked at intervals with white toilet paper so that we could see our way easily in the dark. Before we reached the blind, with the sky changing colour on the horizon where the sun would soon appear, I saw the big body of an animal feeding off the bushes of the blind. After watching for a while, I realised it was a rhino. We had to stand still and wait for it to finish. Meanwhile, daylight was coming quickly and I was able to see the leopard on the limb feeding on the bait. I was worried because we were right out in the open and if the leopard saw us, it would be gone in a flash.

After what seemed like hours, the rhino moved out of sight. We moved up, and took our positions in the blind. I kept looking at the leopard which was so busy feeding that it did not see us. Eventually, with the sun showing on the horizon, there was enough light for the client to shoot. The leopard was broadside and reaching down to get at the meat when the client fired. It fell out of the tree like a sack of potatoes.

It hit the ground and started growling and trying to get up, but was unable to do so. We thought the leopard had a broken back or the bullet had just touched the neck vertebra. If it was a temporary paralysis, there was a possibility that it would get up and take off so we had to move up and finish it off before it regained mobility. We moved out of the blind quickly and started towards the cat when I saw the rhino reappear from our right. It was walking towards the leopard. We stopped and watched to see what it would do. The leopard was still growling and struggling to get up when the rhino reached it. The rhino looked as if it wanted to smell the cat, but stepped back when the leopard took a swipe with its front paw. The rhino circled around, keeping a respectable distance, then walked away heading off into the bush. Before it had completely gone out of sight we got close to the leopard and my client fired another shot. The rhino just kept walking away as if nothing had happened. I was puzzled that it had not reacted to the sound of the rifle shot and remembered the lesser kudu hunt when the two sleeping rhino had not reacted to the sound of a shot. The only reason I could think of for the lack of reaction, was that their intelligence was so low they associated it with thunder in the rainy season. They were the most unpredictable of the dangerous big game animals.

A few years previously, we shot an elephant with tusks that weighed ninety-eight and ninety-five pounds. On that safari we nearly had a mishap. I was hunting with a client in his seventies, tracking bull elephants into the thick riverine forest. When we got up to them we found they had joined a big herd of cows with calves. In very dry years many animals, including elephants, collected in the riverine bush and it was not unusual to find cows and bulls together.

Fortunately, we came on the bulls as they stopped in a small clearing. The elephants were all around and I could hear branches being broken and tummies rumbling from the left and the right. The biggest bull presented a good broadside target so I told my client to aim at his shoulder. When the shot was fired, the big bull took off and in a second was lost from view in the thick foliage. I knew he was well hit because I had seen dust fly up from his shoulder. We followed as quickly as possible.

I was leading with the client and Wanyahoro and the other trackers were about five yards behind when I heard an enraged scream from an elephant which I realised was very close. I stopped and turned to see the client on the ground and about five yards from him a really angry cow elephant and its calf. Wanyahoro dashed forward, took hold of the client's arm and dragged him to the safety of a nearby tree. I thought the cow might have to be shot but she suddenly spun around and departed after her small calf. To this day I don't know why she had not gone for my client when he was lying on the ground. It was a close call and I was relieved at not having to shoot her. We collected ourselves and continued on the bull's tracks. We found him collapsed on his side, resting against some saplings and quite dead. He had very good tusks, ninety-eight and ninety-five pounds respectively.

THIRTEEN

A New Challenge

In 1968 I hunted again in Kenya and Tanzania. Then in February 1969 I sold my house in Nairobi, packed my gear and paid my Kenya crew. It was a sad moment because some of my Africans had been with me for many years. Most of all it was sad to say farewell to Wanyahoro. We had grown up together and we had been inseparable in all the years of hunting in the Game Department and later during my professional hunting in Kenya, Tanzania and Uganda, as well as one season in Botswana. We had many narrow escapes from charging lion, leopard, elephant, rhino and buffalo. I was lucky to have had such a person with me and it was a very sad day when we parted.

At the end of 1969, I purchased a plot of land in Victoria Falls and built a house. My wife had come down by ship from Mombasa to Beira, bringing her car with her. She and my daughter, Elizabeth, motored to Victoria Falls. This was a suitable base because it was only forty miles from Kasane, with a good tarred road between the two towns. The house was completed by the end of year. In the garden we had lovely teak trees (*baikiaea pluijuga*) for shade. Nearly all the Victoria Falls houses with gardens had these lovely trees.

I moved my operation to Botswana because I saw a good future ahead. Professional safaris were relatively new and the country had a lot to offer with its many species and quantity of game. I also liked the fact that Hunters Africa had concessions in sparsely inhabited areas, with a lot of territory where there were no villages for many miles around. Botswana had this advantage over the game countries to the north, many of which were so over-populated that the game was being squeezed into smaller and smaller areas.

Our concession areas were both varied and interesting. The northern one bordered on the Chobe and the swamps while the other, south of Kasane, was dry with thick belts of mopane trees. The swamps were home to the much prized sitatunga and big herds of red lechwe as well as hippo and crocodile. There was good fishing in the channels and lagoons. Lions inhabited the various islands, living on sitatunga and red lechwe, but the males here were smaller in body than their mainland cousins. The leading edges of their manes looked shaved as a result of their continuous passage through the reeds. These swamp lions must have done a lot of swimming to get over the deep water channels to the islands. On several occasions I also came across leopard on the islands. I have often heard it said that lions and leopards do not like to swim, but in Botswana they adapted to swamp living and did a lot of swimming. Bull elephant also lived on the bigger islands, some of which were a few miles wide, and they crossed deep water with no difficulty. On quite a few occasions I watched elephant crossing deep channels with only their trunks showing above the water like periscopes.

When I started hunting in Botswana, I found it easy to lose my sense of direction because the country was very flat and there were no hills to use as landmarks. It was necessary to carry a compass on my belt whenever I ventured into the bush. I had to acquaint myself with the various tracks and remember which direction they took. When heading off on foot, I had to remember whether I was east or west of the track, so that when the time came to return I could just take a compass reading. The prevailing winds were useful because they were reasonably constant and as a result the ant hills usually leaned to the west.

Lion and leopard did not feed on bait because they were trapped by the locals. The best way to hunt them was by tracking which was fairly easy because most of the country had a lot of soft sand. We soon realised that it was not good to get close to lion too early in the morning because they were awake and alert, and saw us approaching in time to slink away. The best time to approach was during the hottest time of the day, usually between 1 and 3 o'clock in the afternoon, when they were sound asleep. I often approached to within a few yards of a sleeping lion. It was easy to spot the male if he was accompanied by females. The wind direction was also important because a lion picked up human scent even when it was asleep.

I used the movement of the sun to good advantage when hunting lion as it gave me a clue when lion were very close. Lion often lay down at the edge of the bush to take advantage of early morning sun. They then moved a couple of times as the sun got too hot. Eventually they moved to the shade of thicker cover for the final resting place of the day. When I came across the place where lion had rested initially, I instructed our tracking party to move

Don Bousfield

Barissa who died tragically when he fell off a truck

Don Bousfield with his leopard taken in Kenya 1964

Bill Spencer with his buffalo in Kenya

Fine lion taken by Bill Packer in Kenya

Dr. Frank Serena with his elephant, Kenya

Vincent Andrus with his lesser kudu in Kenya

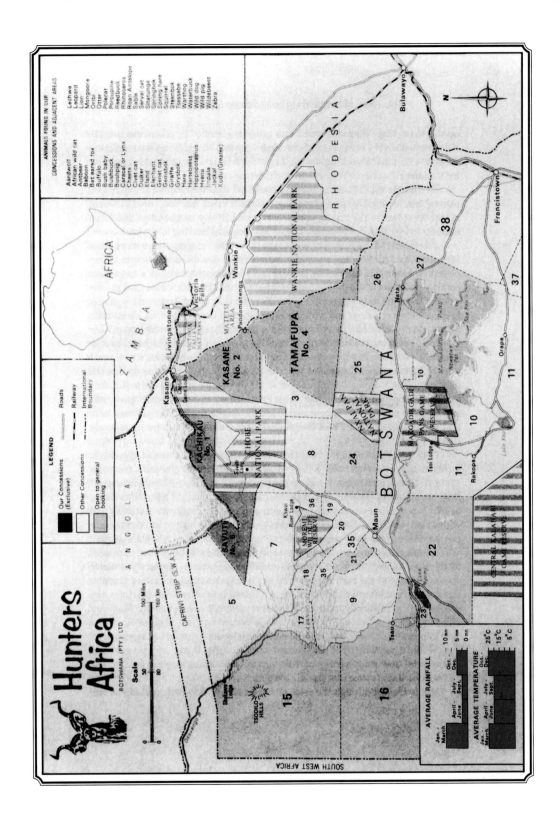

Map of Botswana showing the concessions

as quietly as possible and every lying up place in the area was inspected closely with the use of binoculars. This was repeated every few yards as we moved along the tracks. I always found this type of hunting exciting and interesting, and no two hunts were ever the same. Not all were successful because there were times when either the lion got our scent or heard us or even awoke and saw us approaching.

The closest I ever got to a sleeping lion was about five yards. I had a client from Houston, Texas and we were hunting on the Kwando. This is an area which has the Kwando River as the eastern boundary and the Okavango Swamps on the west. The Caprivi strip lay to the north. We found the morning tracks of a big lion and then returned to camp where we waited for midday before we went back to follow the tracks. By then I hoped the lion was sleeping.

We started tracking and after a few miles came on a place where the lion had rested in the early morning sun. I cautioned the trackers to slow down and be on the lookout. Minutes later we found another place where the lion had lain down and yet another place where he had moved into the shade. By this time we were moving a step at a time and straining our eyes looking for the lion which we knew was very close. We were in mopane woodland with odd clumps of thick bush interspersed throughout. The grass cover was not too high, but high enough to screen a sleeping lion and we were able to walk quietly. I had my Bushman tracker, Samson, in front doing the tracking and I was directly behind him with Pat on my heels when I saw the lion really close lying in short grass. Samson had not seen it because he had his eyes on the ground. I put my hand on his shoulder and gently pulled him back. When he saw the lion his eyes widened and he moved back without making too much noise. I looked back at Pat and indicated to him to step to my right. All this time the lion remained sound asleep. His hindquarters were towards us with his head facing away. This body position was not ideal for a shot.

Pat put up his rifle and looked through the scope. He was using a .375 H & H Magnum rifle and I had my .470 double barrel rifle loaded with soft nosed bullets. I realised that Pat had not seen the lion because he had the rifle pointed to the far distance and was moving it around from side to side. I squeezed his arm to get his attention and pointed down to where the lion was still peacefully sleeping. Once he had seen it and he took aim.

The lion's sixth sense must have started working, for he suddenly put his head up and looked right back over his shoulder at us. I actually saw his eyes suddenly change and imagined his brain starting to click. I hissed to Pat, "Shoot." What seemed like ages passed before there was a bang. The lion did a somersault and landed on his feet facing us. Years of experience told me that he was about to spring at us, so I shot him through the head. When we examined the body, we found that Pat's bullet hit the lion's flank, raking forward. Pat said that when he looked through the scope, all he could see was skin. He could not tell what part of the body he had his sights on, but when he heard my urgent request to shoot, he just fired.

The Bushmen told me that the lion in this area were very bold and there had been cases of man-eating. This was borne out when I was building the Kwando camp. I selected a site on a high bank with a beautiful view overlooking the river and the swamp, with the Caprivi on the other side. The camp was built from mopane poles and the roof thatched with grass from the area. The walls were plastered with mud and painted with white wash. While building the camp, I placed my camp bed and mosquito net under a tree on the bank overlooking the river. To keep the building crew fed, I shot an old buffalo bull. The local Bushmen and their families were attracted by the meat and soon moved in. There must have been fifteen to twenty people and they put up the typical Bushman dwellings which consisted of bent branches covered in grass making a low dome-shaped hut. However many of them slept out in the open next to campfires. It was the dry season and, being summer, dwellings were not really necessary.

One night I heard a lot of screaming and shouting from the Bushman camp. I thought it was a domestic quarrel but the next morning some Bushman families came over supporting an old man with a wounded leg. He told me that he was sleeping next to a camp fire when a lion crept up, fastened its teeth onto his leg and dragged him off. He screamed and his wife jumped up and hurled a burning fire brand at the lion which promptly released the Bushman and ran off.

After giving him a shot of penicillin, I disinfected the wounds, put pads over them and bandaged the leg. I subsequently heard that he recovered from the wounds and I also learnt that he was the local witch-doctor. So much for the powers of witchcraft! I followed the lion to see if I could shoot it. By the size of its tracks, it appeared to be a lioness. After following the tracks for a short distance, we came to the place where it joined up with another lioness and a young male. The trail continued downwind. That day the wind was very strong and hardly varied. The lions consistently kept downwind, which made it impossible to get up to them because they got our scent every time we got close. I eventually abandoned the chase.

One month later, in a camp run by another safari company about twenty miles south on the Kwando River, a lioness killed a Bushman, dragged him off and started to eat him. The camp staff alerted the professional hunter, Bert Milne, who drove out and picked up the lioness in his headlights. The beast was feeding on the body when he shot it. I am convinced it was the same animal that attacked the Bushman in our camp.

I often listened for lions roaring at night and took careful note of the direction the sounds were coming from, especially the last call in the early morning. Then at first light I drove in that direction and looked for tracks. This turned out to be very successful and I followed on foot on foot when I found fresh spoor.

On one occasion I had two German clients on safari and one of them only wanted a lion. This gentleman was an important man in the West German Government and I did my best to get him what he wanted. We were using the Chobe safari camp, close to the Savuti River which flowed out of the Linyanti Swamp. To improve the chance of finding a lion, I left the two men in camp, took my Land Cruiser and prepared to sleep out close to the Savuti River and listen for lions roaring.

I headed for a likely area and set up my camp bed next to the Cruiser. That night I put up my white mosquito net and attached it to the top of the vehicle. I always used a white mosquito net when in a lion area because old-time hunters always said that a lion was reluctant to attack a person sleeping under a white net. The lion could possibly scent a human under the net but could not be sure whether the human was awake or asleep. A lion also did not like to attack an object it could not see clearly. I am sure there was some truth in this and it was confirmed by what happened later that night.

The two trackers, one of whom was Samson (the Bushman), moved a short distance away, set alight a huge dead tree which had fallen down and made their beds close to the fire. I had a cup of coffee and ate a couple of sandwiches. The cook had prepared more than was necessary, so I gave most of the sandwiches and coffee to the two trackers and I went to bed. A couple of hours later, I heard a pig squeal and a lion grunt nearby. Then I heard a couple of hyenas making nervous laughs which they often do around a kill. I was sure that the lions had made a kill and I fell asleep.

At first light, I got up and walked around. After a few paces I noticed fresh lion spoor and from the tracks I saw where a male lion had walked right up to where I had been sleeping, walked around the bed and left. Some might argue that the lion was not hungry after eating a warthog. I discovered on the follow up that there were three lions (one male and two

171

lionesses). A small warthog would not satisfy the appetite of three lions.

I went back to Chobe camp to collect the two clients and by 10 o'clock we started tracking. Five hours later we found the lions stretched out fast asleep in the shade of a big tree. We manoeuvred until we could see the male clearly enough for a shot. The distance was about twenty yards. The lion died where he was sleeping and the two females ran off. I have often read that the lioness will attack the hunter when the male is shot but this has never been my experience. The only time I had a lioness come towards me or try to charge was when she was accompanied by small cubs.

Not all of our tracking was successful. On one occasion we were out early in the morning, having driven out of the Saile camp on the edge of the Chobe Swamp, heading into the mopane belts and scrubs. I stopped to listen for lion. Sure enough we heard roaring quite close and headed in the direction of the sound on foot. I climbed a couple of mopane trees but could not see any lion. Eventually we cut spoor which was heading in an easterly direction. We followed these tracks all day through the heat but that lion kept going. I kept thinking the lion would lie up, especially when we came to the sort of cover that lion favoured, but he kept up his pace. At 5 o'clock in the afternoon I decided to quit and head back. As it was cooling down, it was unlikely that the lion would be sleeping. It was possible that the lion had not lain up because he had seen us when we started after him. On the other hand he may have decided to change his territory. In Botswana lion and leopard walked vast distances. Twenty miles was not uncommon. We had a weary return to our vehicle. We ended the last few miles stumbling in the dark and eventually arrived at 8 o'clock.

Shortly after I began hunting in Botswana, I started thinking about building permanent camps in our concession areas. Every safari left from Kasane in a hunting vehicle transporting the clients and a couple of trackers. The truck followed with all the hunting gear such as tents, beds, bedding, provisions, refrigerator, tables, salt for treating the trophy skins and the camp staff. The staff included a cook and his assistant, the waiters and a skinner. The cook's assistant helped clean the dishes, heated the water for showers and baths, collected firewood for the cook and made the evening fire in front of the mess tent where the clients and professional hunters enjoyed their sundowners. Besides waiting at tables, the waiters also made the beds and cleaned the tents every day. The skinner took care of caping the trophies and cleaning the skulls. They had to be experts in this respect, otherwise the taxidermists would not be able to turn out mounts or rugs to the satisfaction of the client who very much wanted to show off his trophies back home.

We generally used the same camping sites for hunting, but soon discovered that the Africans in Botswana were not as capable in setting up camp as the East African natives had been. For one thing, they always mixed up the tent poles, so putting up camp in the dark became a tedious affair. Through mishandling and lack of experience, many poles were broken while erecting or dismantling the tents.

After consulting my fellow director, John Lawrence, we decided to build permanent camps. This was a great success and saved a lot of headaches and grief, and also reduced the use of the truck and consumption of petrol. Later we bought tractors with trailers to haul provisions and petrol to the camps. At the beginning of the season the tractors were used to mow the long grass on our hunting roads. This prevented grass seeds from clogging up the vehicle radiators. We also used a disc harrow towed by the tractor to improve our roads.

We made new tracks which opened new areas throughout the hunting concessions. Previously, we had gone across country through the bush, finding our way as best we could. Needless to say, the vehicles took a beating. The tyres were pierced by short pieces of wood and thorns. It was not unusual to have several flats a day and sometimes the tyre was totally ruined.

Later on I built an airstrip at Kwando in order to fly clients in and out of the area. This eliminated the long drive from Kasane (our headquarters), which took two days of rough going through soft sand and bumpy tracks. It was not easy to build the airstrip because we had to dig out some big lead wood trees (*combretum imberbe*). This is a hard wood tree and we had to dig and chop out the trunk and the entire root system. Then we had to level off the ground, so I loaded a grader onto the back of my four wheel drive Bedford truck and brought the grader from Kasane. My son, Cecil, helped with this bit of construction.

Tony Henley, a well-known professional hunter then working for Hunters Africa, was the first to bring clients into the camp. It was a big safari with two other well-known professional hunters and their clients. Shortly after starting the hunt, Tony and his clients (I think there were two) came across a large pride of lions and among them was a big maned male. One of the clients shot and wounded the big male and in the subsequent follow up, the lion charged. Tony's shot was not fatal and the lion sprang up and mauled him. Tony told me afterwards that he put his arms up to keep the beast off his neck and head. He remembered the awful smell of the animal's breath and the client standing by ready to shoot. He shouted to him to shoot the lion in the head as soon as it was raised. It seemed like an eternity before a shot went off and the beast collapsed on top of him. The client managed to shoot it in the head. All the camps had radio communication with the head office in Kasane. They arranged for a plane to fly Tony to the hospital in Bulawayo. Had there been no airstrip, the alternative would have been a rough two day ride which might have killed him.

Pat Carr Hartley and his wife Heather joined us. Pat became the manager and Heather the secretary of the company. We were lucky to have them. They performed their duties extremely well through the following years and were still holding the posts when I left in 1981. Pat Carr Hartley's father was well-known in East Africa where he captured wild game for zoos.

Soon after Pat and Heather joined the company, we were fortunate to get the services of Jim Cardwell and his wife Liz. Jim owned a Cessna aeroplane which was of valuable assistance in the field. When necessary he brought in spare motors and urgently needed supplies and ferried clients back and forth. By this time most of our camps had airstrips.

Hunting in Botswana differed from East Africa in many ways. For one thing, hunting in the swamps was a new experience, although I had done a little in the central Tanzania lake regions (west of Lake Victoria on the border of Ruanda Urundi on the Kagera River). I always got a thrill when I saw a male sitatunga walking slowly through the swamp with his spiralling horns showing over the reeds. They are truly impressive and always looked bigger when seen this way. I built numerous platforms in trees overlooking the swamp so that my clients could watch for sitatunga. I sometimes built ladders out of mopane poles and used the boat to haul them along the channel to a suitable site on the edge of a burn. The ladder was held up with a couple of stays or poles rather like a step ladder. This elevated the client twelve or fifteen feet and worked well in places where there were no trees along the channel.

The biggest sitatunga any of my clients shot in the Chobe swamps was taken by Louis Pearce. It measured thirty-one and three eighths inches which ranked high in Rowland Ward's Record Book. He shot it from a high platform on the edge of the swamp late one evening. It got dark before we were able to retrieve the trophy so we had to come back the next morning to look for it. In order to get to where the animal was shot, we swam across two deep channels. I did not fancy doing this because of the danger of crocodile, and we had seen a couple of big ones in the area. We found the sitatunga close to where it had been shot. The next biggest head, shot by Craig Leerberg, measured thirty-one and a quarter. He used a .257 Roberts because it had a flat trajectory and, with a Nosler bullet, was ideal for the occasion. Sometimes it was necessary to take a long shot and I found it difficult to accurately gauge the distance when looking across burnt patches of reeds.

I often waded out to the islands in the swamp and enjoyed finding islands that no other hunter had been able to reach. These places had not been disturbed by man and it was not unusual to see shy animals walking around at any time of the day. There was also an element of danger in wading through the reeds, often waist deep in the water with the reeds sometimes six to nine feet over my head. These reed patches were full of hippo paths which we used to get through to the islands. A path made by hippos was easy to recognise because a hippo cannot cross its legs so the back leg stepped in line with the front, with the result that a tramway effect was left on the ground. The left and right legs wore the ground away and grass grew in between. To my knowledge no other animal made such a track. To get over a channel which was very deep, I enlisted the aid of the crew and manhandled a small, light boat through the reed patches.

Once while I was wading through the reeds, I disturbed a hippo. I heard it coming but could not see it because of the reeds. I also heard my client and two trackers splashing off out of the way. I had my .470 double ready to shoot. The hippo burst into sight at close range but it turned and crashed off through the reeds when it saw me. Much to my relief, I did not have to shoot it, because hippo were protected in Botswana.

There were some giant crocodiles in the area. Seventeen foot monsters were seen basking on the banks along the channels. Wading always made me uneasy, especially when a client wounded a sitatunga and we had to follow it in the reed beds.

On another occasion, we waded to an island and came ashore as I heard an animal close by. All I saw were the short reeds shaking. A big male leopard jumped up into the fork of a nearby tree. It peered down at us for a couple of seconds and then jumped down and disappeared into the reeds. We found that it had killed a red lechwe. I often saw signs of both leopard and lion on the islands.

It was not unusual to see mamba and cobra here. The biggest mamba I have seen in the swamps was about fourteen feet. I have on occasion shot nine to eleven foot mambas. One time, while standing on an anthill looking at kudu, I heard a rustling of dry leaves. At first it sounded like the noise a breeze would make on dry leaves, but then I realised there was no wind. I glanced down and saw an enormous mamba making its way towards my anthill. It obviously had a home there. I jumped backwards off the anthill and landed on top of my client, but we soon picked ourselves up and made a hasty retreat. Only when we were a safe distance away did I tell him about the mamba. He had not seen it because the anthill had obscured his view.

Another time I was again standing on a small anthill on an island looking at lechwe through my binoculars, when I heard a rustling in the grass. I glanced down, saw a big cobra heading for my perch, and beat a hasty retreat. In many years of walking and running through the bush, I have had my share of close shaves with dangerous snakes, including cobras and mambas between my feet. Fortunately, I did not tread on them because I would have been bitten. My reflexes were always quick when evasive action was demanded. Snakes fear man as much as man fears snakes, and most snakes fortunately try to escape. I have had Egyptian cobras strike at me twice but I managed to jump back in time. I have had puffadders close to my feet when I have been tracking. I remember walking quickly along a track trying to catch up with a bull elephant. My sight was on the elephant which was receding fast when I felt my foot kick something soft and looked down to see a big puff adder going away as fast as it could. Fortunately, I had not stepped on it. I always wore boots that covered my ankles and thick stockings that protruded above the edges. This helped guard against puffadders but was no protection from mambas and cobras because the big snakes struck higher. From a high platform overlooking a sitatunga burn, I once spotted two cobras mating. I have been told that they can be aggressive at this time.

Jack Bousfield, who was known for the thousands of crocodiles he shot on Lake Rukwa in Tanganyika, introduced me to Bobby Wilmot. Bobby was a well-known crocodile hunter in Botswana. A couple of months afterwards I heard that Bobby Wilmot had died after he was bitten by a mamba on an island in the Okavango Swamps. He was able to get back to camp to inject himself with anti-venom serum, but too much time had elapsed from the time he was bitten and he died shortly afterwards.

At the beginning of the winter cold snap, I saw broad tracks in the soft sand on the swamp edge. These were made by pythons leaving the water in search of ant bear holes or pig holes to spend the winter in a warm place. The two coldest months are June and July. The nights are always cold but the days can be sunny and warm. I once saw two pythons sunning themselves outside a hole. One snake was very large, probably fifteen feet plus, with a body as thick as my thigh and the other was much smaller at seven to nine feet. They were probably a male and female, the female being the larger snake.

My first Botswana safari was with a couple from Boston. We did a short fly camp trip down to the Mababe flats. Fly camping meant taking the minimum camping equipment: folding camp beds, mosquito nets and one canvas sail in case we needed shelter from the midday sun. We used one vehicle with a trailer to carry extras such as petrol and water. The staff consisted of a cook and two trackers.

We arrived in the evening when it was already dark. As we approached our camp site, we were amazed to see a mass of mice moving across the track. It was the only time that I saw this. Shortly after arriving at camp, our beds were set up. The clients, Karl and Chili Landegger, sat on folding camp chairs and Chili appeared nervous. She obviously did not enjoy seeing the rodents all around. We were sitting around the fire having our soup and Chili had the soup plate resting in her lap. There was only a gas lamp providing light. Suddenly Chili let out a scream as something landed in her soup with a plop. She flung the plate of soup into the air and it landed all over Karl. A big grasshopper, attracted by the gas lamp, had landed in her bowl and she thought it was a mouse. I put a mosquito net over her bed and had to tuck it in, assuring her that the mice would not join her in bed.

I witnessed another mass migration, this time of frogs leaving the swamps for the hinterland. They used the tracks leading away from the water and the motion they made when hopping gave the impression that the road was moving up and down. It was quite a sight.

177

FOURTEEN

HUNTING IN BOTSWANA

A few years after I moved to Botswana, Hunters Africa purchased two valuable concession areas (previously owned by Botswana Hunters and then Ker & Downey Safaris). This came about through the invaluable help of a good friend and fellow professional hunter, Mike Rowbotham, with whom I had previously worked on joint safaris in Kenya. One area, called Nunga, was south of our Bore Hole 2 concession. Its southern boundary was a few miles south of Jarwe. It was a large area of about 150 x 90 miles. The second area, called Chobe, included part of the Savuti River (the overflow of the Linyanti Swamp). The southern boundary was the Chobe National Park and on the north-eastern side lay the Linyanti Swamp. This concession joined our Kwando concession in the north and was very good with large herds of buffalo, many lions and a good selection of other game.

With the addition of these new areas, Hunters Africa became the safari company with the best concessions in Botswana. However, this meant there were three new directors in addition to John Lawrence and myself. I did not relish this situation because Hunters Africa was now top heavy with directors and I felt the future looked bleak. I mentioned this to John, but he took no heed of my warning. Later I was proved right.

On a fly camp trip to Jarwe, we spent the first night near a waterhole hoping to find a big tusker. The next morning, while we were packing the vehicle, a very attractive mouse with a tuft on its tail appeared out of a cardboard box and disappeared into the back of the loaded vehicle. We were not going to unload the car to evict the mouse and so we took it with us. We duly arrived at Jarwe camp which was on a beautiful site with a wonderful grove of teak trees for shade.

When we unloaded the vehicle, the mouse appeared. It jumped onto the ground, hopped up a big teak tree and quickly disappeared in the overhead foliage. We forgot all about it. That night we were sitting around the camp fire having our drinks with the usual gas lamp burning. There was a squeak and the mouse tumbled out of the tree onto the ground. Instantly a pearl spotted owl swooped down to catch it but missed. The mouse wasted no time in getting out of sight, lucky to escape with its life.

On another occasion I camped with a party of Mexicans at Jarwe. This time we established a full camp. The company had sunk a borehole nearby which yielded excellent drinking water. We were hunting elephant when a cold snap arrived with driving rain. Early that morning we went out in the rain and found four elephant bulls, standing perfectly still and looking utterly miserable. Eventually, we turned back to camp because we realised that hunting would not be pleasurable nor successful.

When we got back, the clients played cards under the verandah of the mess tent. After they had started, there was a loud plop and a very large frozen boomslang landed on the ground right next to them. They took one horrified look and quickly scattered. The snake moved sluggishly away. The cold and wet in the tree tops rendered it unable to maintain its hold on the branches.

I was hunting with a Spanish client in the teak forest not far from Jarwe and we were on the trail of a big herd of fourteen bull elephant. They were spread out while feeding and we had to manoeuvre around to keep the wind in our favour until I finally spotted the largest bull, carrying seventy pound tusks. When we got about thirty yards away, I told my client to shoot it in the shoulder (earlier in camp I had drawn a diagram on a piece of paper explaining where to place the shot). We were so close that I was confident he would make a good shot. As the bullet hit, the bull took off. The others bunched around him and made off in a cloud of dust. I was unable to get a shot at him because he was obscured by the others. The bull had been hit too far back and would probably travel a long way.

Throughout my years of hunting I noticed that some clients forgot all they had been told about where to aim. They were overawed by the size of the animals and they tended to aim at the centre of the body and disregard previous advice on shot placement. The result was either a gut shot or a split tusk.

After the elephants disappeared through the trees, we followed the trail in the soft sand and an hour later came to the place where the herd had split into two groups. One lot veered left and the others carried straight on. We looked for blood but saw none which confirmed my suspicion of a gut shot. The digested food and the thick skin combined to plug the bullet hole and bleeding was minimal.

We decided to follow the group on our left and twenty minutes later we heard them just ahead. They were obviously standing still, nervously listening. We too were standing still and I tested the wind with a sock filled with wood ash. The wind was in our favour. Suddenly the elephant stampeded towards us, and I told my client and two trackers to hide behind a tree. I saw, out of the corner of my eye, the two trackers take off. The small herd of five or six bulls burst into view. They were all bunched up and not charging but fleeing in panic as elephant do when they are frightened. I stepped out into full view, yelled and waved my rifle. They promptly swerved away and went crashing off.

We waited about ten minutes for the two trackers to return. We then called them and eventually they came back very sheepishly. Wilson had blood streaming from his nose and I asked him what happened. Samson, the Bushman tracker, howled with laughter. When I could get some explanation, Samson recounted with tears streaming from his eyes, that he and Wilson were running away expecting the elephants to arrive on their heels any second. Wilson was looking back over his shoulder for the elephant and ran slap into a tree. Samson thought it was the funniest thing he had seen for a long time. So much for his sense of humour.

Before I built the Kwando camp, we needed a bridge over the Silinda Spillway. This was a watercourse which flowed from the Okavango Swamps into the Linyanti (Chobe) Swamp whenever the Okavango flooded. This did not take place every year, but for two seasons it did happen. In order to utilise the Kwando concession to the north, we had to build the bridge. The Kwando was between the Okavango and Linyanti Swamps, with the Silinda Spillway as the southern boundary and the Caprivi strip the northern boundary. The Silinda flowed west to east. The country was flat with almost no difference in elevation between the two swamps. The Okavango was a little higher so that the water flowed very slowly. In the years when the Linyanti came down in high flood, water flowed back up the Silinda Spillway into the Okavango Swamps. This demonstrated that the levels between the two swamps was minimal.

This concession had very few access roads. The main track was made by Tsetse Control (a Government Department) from Maun and it bisected the concession area. About thirty miles north of the Silinda, it forked – one fork going west to Seronga and the other north-east to the Caprivi strip and Kwando River. I chose a building site half a mile upstream on the Silinda where the track crossed the watercourse. Flooding usually occurred between May and November, so construction could only be carried out between November and May when no water flowed.

The building material consisted of mopane trees (*colophospermum mopane*) which grew in profusion and, as the trees were mostly straight, they were ideal for our purposes. In due course, I drove up with a crew in the Bedford truck and my Land Cruiser. Most of the track consisted of soft sand which made it heavy going for both vehicles. Both were equipped with four wheel drive and we did not bog down.

We used a power saw to cut the trees down and axes to trim the branches. As the bridge was one hundred yards long, we made a series of piers, six feet apart, and bridged with heavy poles. Each pier consisted of many poles laid crosswise until the desired height was obtained. The poles were kept in place by sturdy uprights. The whole area was devoid of rocks or stones which, if available, would also have made suitable piers. Mopane is a very heavy wood which does not float. If it were otherwise, the whole structure would have floated away when the water course flowed. When the bridge was halfway completed, Bill Morkel took over from me because I had to attend a game conference in San Antonio, U.S.A. Shortly afterwards, he had an accident while sawing a tree which flipped sideways and broke his arm. He had a painful ride to the hospital. On my return I completed the bridge and the final touches had to be done when the Silinda flooded. We had the satisfaction of being able to drive the loaded Bedford truck over the bridge and on to the Kwando camp.

On one of my trips to the Kwando camp site, I took my Land Rover and Peter Kibble, my son-in-law, kept me company. When we got into soft sand, the heavy going was too much for the Land Rover and the vehicle overheated. After frequent stops, we found that the radiator had no cowling around the fan. I had recently purchased the vehicle to use as a back up to my Land Cruiser and this was the first time I had used it. After many hours we arrived at the Savuti River. Enormous dead acacia trees lined the river bed. These obviously grew when the watercourse was dry but when the river started to flow again, the water killed the trees. This showed that the dry period was fifteen to twenty years long, which accounted for the size of the trees. We spent the next day making a radiator cowling using a discarded forty gallon drum which we found on the river bank. After this we had no more overheating problems.

Ten days later we returned to the Savuti River to find a partly submerged Land Rover on the other side, with a white man kneeling in prayer nearby. I waded across to meet the man and all he could say was, "Thank God you have come. I thought I was going to die here!" He was a German travelling from Victoria Falls to Windhoek via Maun. He had come from Windhoek via Johannesburg and for his return journey he decided to take a shorter route via the Savuti, and had been stranded for five days. When he arrived at the Savuti, he drove into the water without knowing the proper crossing point and ended up in a hippo hole. What he should have done was first to try the crossing on foot to find the shallowest part of the river. My Land Rover forded the river with no trouble and I attached a tow rope to the back of his vehicle and pulled it out backwards.

He had made a bed out of branches in the rear of the vehicle, above the floor in the back which was under water. He was terrified by the lion and elephant that came around every night. He was out of food when we arrived and had given up all hope. We drained all the oil in the engine and gearbox because water had seeped in. Fortunately, I had enough spare oil and he made it back to Victoria Falls and then home via Johannesburg. This was a painful experience for him.

During the first season we hunted in the Kwando concession, two professional hunters from Hunters Africa found two very big tuskers for their clients. One elephant was a ninety pounder and the other eighty plus. In the area between the bridge and Kwando camp, I managed to get my client a seventy pounder, although the previous day I had seen a bull that was eighty plus but we were unable to catch up with him because he had heard our vehicle and taken off. We tried tracking him but lost the tracks when he joined a big herd of cows. A few days later I noticed vultures circling in the sky which usually indicated a kill. When I investigated this, I came across several African hunters cutting the tusks out. The elephant had tusks of about 115 pounds each side. It was the largest elephant that I had seen shot in Botswana. The hunter had a licence to shoot an elephant, but I was nevertheless disappointed that I had not been able to hunt it for my client.

I am sure the presence of bull elephant with exceptionally heavy ivory in the Kwando area was the result of their being driven out of Southern Angola by the civil war raging there. The Caprivi strip, separating the two areas, was only about twenty miles wide and inhabited by a few Bushmen families. The elephant had only a short distance to travel.

183

In previous years, the safari companies had sole hunting rights. This worked very well because we did not over hunt the concession areas and consequently there was always good hunting for our clients. The Game Department allotted quotas for every type of huntable trophy and we did not hunt the species which were protected. The time came when the Botswana Government allowed its citizens to enter our concessions and they came in droves. Many came from the bigger towns to the south, such as Francistown and Gaborone. The Government had recently constructed a new tarred road to the Zambezi River and it was only a few hours drive. Hunters were now able to travel up for the weekend whereas before this road was built, the sand track made travelling slow and it took seventeen hours to travel from Kasane to Francistown. Now the same trip took only five hours. Many hunters purchased four wheel drive Toyota Land Cruisers or Land Rovers and high powered rifles with the proceeds from their sale of ivory.

Sometimes two or three vehicles, overloaded with black hunters armed with newly acquired rifles, came into our concession area. They camped on our best game waterholes and systematically hunted in all directions. Citizens paid very little in licence fees whereas our clients paid a lot. They took out licences for several animals such as buffalo, elephant, kudu, eland, zebra, wildebeest, tsessebe, impala and lion and overnight they made big money from the sale of elephant ivory as well as from zebra and lion hides. Antelope and buffalo meat was cut into strips, dried out and sold in various villages. The entire enterprise became a profitable commercial business for the majority of these hunters.

Hunting pressure became so great in our concession areas that within a few years it became difficult for professional hunters to get good trophies for their clients. We discovered many citizens hunting illegally. Some had elephant licences for other areas, but they would shoot their elephant in our concessions and put it down to the area for which their licence was valid. They also shot protected species and took only the meat after throwing the head and skin into the bush. Most of these citizen hunters had no regard for the law and flouted it at will. The Game Department was understaffed and seemed to lack the will to stop the wrongdoers. The last year I hunted in Botswana, I found it extremely difficult to find a legal bull elephant. The legal weight was only eleven kilograms (twenty-four pounds) per tusk. Before the locals were allowed into our concessions, we could usually get our clients elephant bulls carrying ivory of fifty to sixty pounds a side. Numerous elephants were wounded by inexperienced hunters, many of whom had never shot an elephant before and were afraid to approach too close for a

Sitatunga boat used in the swamps

Rondavel in Saile Camp

*Polling my vehicle across the Savuti
River on a ferry*

Chobe and Zambezi River in flood, Botswana 1969

The bridge I built over the Silinda Spillway, Botswana

Record kudu shot in Botswana by Mariano Salgado

Mariano Salgado with his lion

Record sitatunga shot by Louis Pearce III in Botswana

My tracker, Samson, with a zebra

killing shot. What invariably happened is best left to the imagination.

This brings to mind one incident which involved the hunting of a buffalo. The District Commissioner had recently received a brand new Land Rover from the Government. Independence Day was a couple of days off and the Commissioner asked a local hunter to shoot a buffalo so that there would be meat for the celebrations. His driver took the hunter and a few 'hangers on' out in the Land Rover.

In due course, they came across a buffalo herd which stampeded at the noise of the car. There was a bit of 'tally ho' and the hunter managed to bring down one buffalo, shooting from the back of the vehicle. When the buffalo went down, the driver brought the vehicle to a halt. The hunter was congratulated by his fellow men and he jumped down from the vehicle. He walked up to the fallen buffalo and as he got up to it, the buffalo leaped to its feet and went for the hunter. He hightailed it back to the Land Rover and when the buffalo almost had him, he managed to spring into the back of the Land Rover. The buffalo hit the side of the vehicle with tremendous force and almost knocked itself out. It soon recovered, shaking its head and promptly attacked the vehicle again. The hunter managed to kill it while standing in the back of the vehicle. The hunt ended with the buffalo carcass being brought back for the celebrations in a badly dented new Land Rover.

I was also involved with this same hunter in another buffalo incident. I was en route to a concession near Kachikau in the Chobe Swamp in the company of John Lawrence and two clients, Vince Andrus and Bob Model. Two trucks and two hunting cars were loaded with our camping gear and crew. Among the crew was a buffalo hunter, who had been employed to clear a new track to our camp because the usual approaches were impassable due to the arrival of an exceptional amount of water from the flooding Zambezi River. Because most of Botswana is flat with very little difference in terrain, the water in an area can flow in two different directions. It will normally flow west to east but when the Zambezi comes down in flood, part of it will flow in the opposite direction. The waters back up into the Chobe Swamp and flood the surrounding country for many miles.

We needed to make a detour so the crews were busy cutting a new track through the bush. The vehicles moved forward as the new track was cleared. We heard the crew talking while chopping away when there was a sudden hush and the next thing they all ran back. John Lawrence got out of his car and said, "Where do you think you are going - get back to work." One of the crew said they could not go back because a buffalo had chased them and had one of their number treed.

John, our two clients and I got our rifles, loaded up and went forward to investigate. We found the treed African who shouted to us that the buffalo was close by in a bush. We advanced cautiously and as we got within twenty yards of the bush, there was a snort. Out came a buffalo bull in full charge. John and his client both fired and dropped the buffalo. When we examined it afterwards, we found that it had been wounded a day earlier by local hunters. The treed African was nicknamed 'Buffalo Bill'.

After a few years of hunting buffalo in Botswana, I realised that their temperament differed from the East African buffalo. The northern buffalo were much more aggressive. In Kenya and Tanzania, a wounded buffalo ran off and usually stopped in thick bush, long grass, reeds or even in bamboo. When I got up close during a follow up, a full charge was the usual result. These charges typically ended with the beast being brought down at close range, but many a hunter in East Africa was not able to stop a charge and ended up either dead or badly injured. In Botswana, the bush was more open and as a result buffalo hunting was not nearly as dangerous. I had noted very few charges in the follow up of wounded animals. In Kwando my vehicle was charged two or three times at close quarters by old cantankerous bulls, but they were not obviously wounded. I just happened to drive by when they were resting and in all cases I managed to speed up and out distance the beasts, thus saving the vehicle from being bashed.

Some hunters say that male lions won't tackle an old bull buffalo and prefer calves and cows. On three occasions, I came across buffalo bulls that were tackled by lion. In the Kwando area I was driving along an elephant path, hoping to find a waterhole. The vehicle rounded a bush and I saw the dead body of a big buffalo bull lying on the path. The animal had been killed a few minutes earlier by two male lions. There was not much evidence of a battle and it seemed to have been killed easily. There were teeth marks around the throat, nose and hindquarters. Somehow the lions bowled it over and one went for the throat and held steadfastly until it died. The lions heard my vehicle and ran off. I knew they would not be far from their kill.

My client wanted to shoot a lion, so we built a blind close by. We sat up that evening but the lions did not return before dark. We made a fly camp nearby and returned to the blind on foot as it was getting light. We crept up unobserved but, as we got to the entrance of the blind, a jackal which was skulking around the bait, saw us. It was standing to our left and I had not noticed it. It started yapping a warning cry which they do when they see a human. The lions were on the buffalo carcass and started to slink off as I looked through the holes in the blind. They took heed of the jackal's warning.

In the hope that the lions would return, we sat in the blind for hours. The sun came up and it got very warm. Eventually, at around 10 o'clock, I stood up slowly and looked around through my binoculars. I was still screened by the tall bushes of the blind and was out of sight of any lion eyeing the kill. I peered through small gaps in the bush to observe anything beyond.

Sure enough, there was one lion, lying in long grass about 150 yards away. All I could see was the top of his head. I felt sure he would eventually come to the kill. After a while he got up, walked a short distance towards us and then lay down watching. After another forty-five minutes, he walked up to the kill and started feeding. My client fired his .375 H & H. The lion ran only a short distance and dropped.

It was not unusual to see really large buffalo herds, sometimes well over 1,000 animals in a single herd. One day while driving from the Kwando to Savuti, a distance of about fifty miles, I saw three big herds totalling about 3,000 animals in all. The best head I saw taken in Botswana had a forty-nine inch spread. John Martens, my client, shot it out of a very large herd. This head is recorded in Rowland Ward's Record Book. In the Savuti, I collected three other good heads: a forty-eight inch spread with a Spanish client and two that went forty-seven inches each.

I had some very successful lion and kudu hunts along the Savuti. Most of the lion we tracked but not all our efforts were successful. Sometimes the lions kept walking and we never caught up with them. I have, on occasion, seen lion spoor along a road for twenty miles before they left the track. If a lion knew he was being followed, he usually circled around, returned downwind and lay down. This enabled him to catch the scent of the hunters following his spoor. I have known it to happen many times.

Once we followed a big male lion downstream from the Savuti for a good ten miles and as it showed no sign of wanting to lie up, we had to turn back. The Savuti at that time had begun to dry up and consisted of a series of isolated deep pools. It was nearly dark and we were wearily walking back. We were not far from the vehicle, when we came across a lone hippo lying in a pool. We skirted the edge of the water and were not paying much attention to the hippo, when it suddenly submerged, surfaced close by and then charged us. It became apparent that the hippo had evil intentions because it came out of the water with a rush. I told my client, Lord MacPherson, to run and he and the trackers took off. I turned round to face the hippo with my rifle at the ready. When it realised I was not going to run, it suddenly had second thoughts and swerved away, crashing off into the bush.

187

In Botswana, I found hippo in big pans as much as seventy miles from the nearest permanent water. During the rainy season some hippo left the rivers and swamp areas and wandered overland from one waterhole to another. They travelled at night and when they found a really big waterhole situated in thick bush with no humans to disturb them, they stayed put for a month or two, venturing out only at night to feed mainly on grass and young reed shoots.

Another interesting thing about hippo was the speed at which they ran along the bottom of the swamp channels. Many times I was standing on the high platform in the sitatunga hunting boat and I could see the bottom of the channel below because the water was so clear. A hippo, disturbed by the noise of the outboard motor, would take off and I saw the spurts of sand as its feet touched the bottom, propelling it forward. The boat travelled at five to seven miles an hour and hippo could keep ahead quite easily. For such a large and clumsy looking animal, its speed and power in water was amazing. Hippo often attacked boats and killed many African fishermen every year. Our sitatunga boats were bitten a couple of times but fortunately no serious damage was done.

I found that if I was suitably armed, it was better to stand my ground and face a dangerous animal than to run. In many instances, I faced up to buffalo, lion and elephant and had them back off. This did not work with wounded animals because, more often than not, they came all the way. Most dangerous game tended to chase the person who was running away. A charging lion often went after a fleeing tracker while ignoring the armed hunter and passing within yards of him. This happened to John Lawrence and his party. When they got close, a wounded lion saw them and charged. John fired but failed to stop it. He tried to reload but his magazine rifle jammed. The charging lion went right past him and his client and ran after the tracker who was fleeing. The lion jumped on top of him and the tracker fell to the ground. The cat seized the man by the arm when he tried to fend it off. The client then shot and killed the lion. The tracker was flown to a hospital in Rhodesia where he was fortunate to have an experienced surgeon visiting from Cape Town, who set the shattered bones and saved his arm. The tracker recovered completely. John was using a magazine rifle and managed to get off only one shot. Had he been using a heavy double barrelled rifle, he would have been able to get off two shots, which would most likely have stopped the lion. I have stopped charging animals on many occasions with the second shot.

I had an experience with a cow elephant which proved that standing up to a dangerous animal paid dividends. I was driving very slowly through some really thick mopane scrub bush. Two Mexican clients were in the cab sitting next to me and two trackers, Samson and Wilson, were in the back. Samson hammered on the roof of the cab and leaned over and shouted in my ear that an elephant was charging. We had spotted the herd about 300 yards away. They were feeding and did not appear to be concerned about us, even though they must have heard the vehicle. Elephant depend mostly on scent and hearing because their eyesight is only good at short range. They start to see some movement at fifty yards.

One cow left the herd and came at us. I saw her over the top of the mopane, coming fast. I yelled to Samson to get my .470 out and be quick. All the rifles were in the gun rack behind the cab and I realised that Samson could not get my rifle out in time. Meanwhile the elephant was very close, and still coming. I made a quick decision to charge her with the vehicle. I slammed the vehicle into first gear and turned towards her with the engine roaring. We met head on with the cow skidding to a halt not more than a few yards from the front of the vehicle. I kept going. Just when it looked like the vehicle would hit her, she lost her nerve and spun around and started to head back to the herd with the vehicle chasing right behind. After two hundred yards I stopped. She immediately turned and charged again so I had to repeat our performance and chased her into the herd before I finally turned back. It was only when the chase was progressing well that Samson managed to get my rifle. My clients and the two trackers were absolutely petrified. It was some time before they were able to talk normally.

On a few occasions while walking through thick bush, I came upon an old bull buffalo lying down and did not see him until I was very close. He immediately got up and faced me. Fortunately, on all these occasions I had my heavy rifle. The buffalo kept shaking his head and sometimes snorted. I stood perfectly still facing him. Eventually the buffalo turned away and took off. Had I run, he would have given chase. Generally when Africans have been killed by lone buffalo bulls, it was because they had taken to their heels.

I disliked wild dogs because they moved into an area in packs and as soon as this happened, the small to medium size game animals moved out. On many occasions I saw a good variety of animals for a few days, then one day I travelled the same area and saw very, very few animals. Two or three days later I came across a pack of wild dogs and knew the reason why the game had abandoned the area. There was nothing, including humans, that game animals feared more than wild dogs. The situation became worse when the wild dogs had a breeding burrow in the area. While the pups were small, the adults hunted regularly with the result that game was scarce for ten or fifteen miles around the area. Only when the pups were big enough to join the pack and they moved away to other areas, did the game return. Wild dogs existed throughout Africa. I have come across packs from the moorlands of Mount Kenya down through the bamboo belt, forests, bush areas, savanna and semi-desert areas right down to the sea. Occasionally disease, such as distemper, decimated the packs but the wild dog has survived for centuries.

I became aware of the fear wild animals had of dogs when I was working for the Kenya Game Department. Around Mount Kenya and the Aberdares, where I had to control the buffalo that lived in the thick bush adjoining the farmers' cultivations, it became necessary to use dogs when following buffalo into cover. Within a day or two the whole area around was devoid of buffalo.

Conservationists say that wild dogs break large herds of antelope into splinter groups thus preventing inbreeding. They also kill the weaker animals. However most of the animals I have seen pulled down by wild dogs, have been healthy. The conservationists' theories apply perhaps to the days when Africa had vast herds of game, which today no longer exist. In some instances the wild dogs have eradicated an entire species in certain areas. One area is the riverine bush on the edge of the Linyanti and Chobe Swamp, from Saile camp to the Chobe camp and the Savuti River. When I first started doing safaris in the area, there were many Chobe bushbuck and it was always a pleasure to see them. When the wild dog became protected, the number of packs increased and very soon the Chobe bushbuck disappeared from the riverine bush. They were continually harassed and killed by the wild dogs. One day my wife was sitting near a camp fire in the Chobe camp when she heard a slight noise and looked up to see a female bushbuck trotting into the bush beyond the camp. There were three wild dogs giving chase. They did not give up when they saw my wife, but merely circled around her.

Wild dogs are also very bold. I witnessed them harassing a lioness on a kill and driving her off. I have seen them go for a hyena, ripping its rear end and chasing it for a considerable distance. They are not clean killers but will bring an animal down and tear chunks of flesh off its rear end before it is even dead. To me they are repulsive and destructive.

FIFTEEN

RANDOM THOUGHTS

Throughout my hunting career, I was always experimenting and trying to improve my hunting methods. Don Bousfield and I tried different types of shooting sticks for the clients to rest their rifles on, hoping that steadier shooting would result in greater accuracy. This was a great success for long distance shots and I have used them continuously. In time, more professional hunters started to use them as well. Sometimes I stood alongside the client and put out my arm to hold the sticks steady. Getting so close to the rifle when it was fired eventually affected my hearing with the result that I am slightly deaf but this could also be attributed to the many thousand rounds that I have fired over the years. The sticks were used mainly for standing shots and worked wonders for clients who could not hold a rifle steady when shooting offhand.

I also experimented with camouflage nets when stalking animals where there was little cover. The nets were light and large enough to cover myself and a client immediately behind me. I cut small holes in the net so that we could see the game. We made sure it covered our legs but were high enough from the ground so as not to snag on the low growing thorn bush or other ground cover. I found the direct approach worked best at a very slow pace. Whenever the animals looked towards us, I stopped and waited until they lost interest and settled down to feed.

Stalking under the nets was successful most of the time but there were a few animals that could not be fooled. It worked best with gemsbok, roan, kudu and buffalo, but sable, zebra and springbok were not deceived. The most gullible were the gemsbok, roan and buffalo, probably because they were highly curious animals who tried to identify this odd looking apparition. Once, while making steady progress towards an antelope, the client tapped me on the shoulder and whispered that there was an animal

191

growling at us. I lifted the net slightly to see what animal it was and there, following us a couple of yards away, was a lion-tailed mongoose with its head turned towards us. It was trying to peer up into our net while at the same time growling at what it thought was a new type of enemy invading its territory.

In Botswana I became aware of the light reflected by the rifle barrels and binoculars as well as from highly polished motor vehicles and windscreens. The sun in Botswana is very bright, more so than in Kenya and Tanzania.

While I was stalking gemsbok on the 'haemorrhoids' plains, I found the animals suddenly took flight for no apparent reason. I knew they could not have seen us because we were screened by bush and still a good distance away with the wind in our favour. I puzzled over this until one day I climbed a mopane tree to look over the grassy plains. Through my binoculars I spotted two gemsbok about a mile away and while I was watching them, they suddenly lay down in the grass and all I could see were their horns sticking up.

My two clients, a father and son, each wanted a gemsbok so we decided to approach them on foot. I carried the shooting sticks and they carried their rifles. The approach was easy because the animals were lying down and the grass was tall enough to hide us. I headed in the direction of the horns, hoping that the animals would stay down. If they got up, we would easily be visible. We got to within eighty yards before I stopped and looked through my binoculars again. The length of the horns looked good so we advanced cautiously, trying to get within forty yards. We moved a few steps at a time without making too much noise. Luckily, the wind was blowing across our front, which tended to soften any noise we made.

When we got to the place from which the clients would shoot, I put the sticks up, got the father into position and whispered to him to wait until the gemsbok got to their feet. After about fifteen minutes, one got up and started to feed. It had not seen us and I whispered to the client to shoot. He dropped it with one shot. At the sound of the shot the others jumped up and ran a few yards before they stopped to look back. The son got into position, also using the sticks, and managed to drop his gemsbok with an equally good shot.

I told my clients to stay with the gemsbok while I walked back for the vehicle. When I reached the Land Rover, I stopped and looked back to where we had shot the gemsbok and saw a couple of sharp flashes, almost like flashes from a mirror. I looked through my binoculars to get a better view. Both father and son had their rifles on their shoulders and they were walking around the gemsbok. Every now and again their rifle barrels reflected the sun. I now knew what had previously put the gemsbok to flight. From that time, whenever the sun was bright, I made my clients carry their rifles in a cover right up to the moment we were in position to shoot.

During the hunting season we kept permanent crews in the various camps. The professional hunter moved from one camp to another with his client and personal staff, which usually consisted of two trackers, a cook and a skinner. On one trip we arrived at Saile camp to find the permanent staff in quite a state of disarray. They had not slept because lions had come into the camp at night and smelt out any meat hanging in the trees nearby. They had lost some hindquarters from the previous hunting party. These lions even raided the biltong strung up outside their tents and campfires were no deterrent. I listened but did not take their stories very seriously.

At the time the dining room and mess buildings plus the *rondavels* (circular rooms) for the clients and the professional hunter had been completed. The staff quarters were still to be built so they slept in a big tent which was securely pegged down. The entrance flap was usually tied down with a big thorn bush branch propped up against it as further re-inforcement. The staff slept next to the kitchen which was behind the mess and the *rondavels*. There was a belt of thick palms separating the front and back of the camp with a pathway of about thirty-five yards connecting the two. The camp had the benefit of good shade trees, evergreen figs and palms which separated the main buildings in front from the staff quarters at the back and gave the camp an attractive look.

I went to bed in one of the *rondavels* and tried to fall asleep in spite of the conversation coming from staff sleeping quarters. One of the trackers was a great story teller and he was holding forth in a loud voice while the listeners laughed every now and again at something amusing. I remember thinking to myself that most Africans found it difficult to talk quietly but eventually I fell asleep.

A few hours later I was awakened by a lot of loud excited voices coming from the staff quarters. I lay in bed listening and heard something step over the dried leaves on the ground outside my window. When it stopped, I quietly got out of bed and opened the window with one hand while holding a flashlight in the other. I switched the flashlight on and saw a big male lion standing a few yards away, looking back towards the kitchen.

In his mouth he had the hind leg of a zebra. He had raided it from the skinning shed which was behind the Africans' tent. They had also heard him as he trotted past their tent and by now all were awake and talking excitedly.

As soon as the light shone on the lion, it turned and went off with the zebra meat in its mouth. It was joined by another lion and both disappeared into the palms. I went back to sleep and before long was awakened again by a lion grunting and hyenas jabbering and whooping. The hyenas were ganging up on the lions and trying to rob them of the meat. A short while later, I heard a lion chasing a hyena past the front door of the rondavel. The lion must have been very close because the hyena sounded frightened. Eventually all was quiet again. The lions and hyenas had eaten all they wanted and walked off.

We did not hunt the lions because my client did not want one and we left after a couple of days. The next party went after the two males and shot one of them. The other one moved away and there was no more trouble for a while.

A month later some young lions, attracted by the smell of meat in the trophy shed, started to come around Saile camp. The staff were still sleeping in the large tent because their quarters were under construction. My eldest son, Cecil, and Michael, my nephew, were in the camp helping with the construction. The staff were jittery with the lions regularly visiting the camp at night. Cecil and Michael decided to exploit this and went hunting for a springhare on the nearby airstrip one night. They chased a springhare using the vehicle and dazzled it with the headlights. When it stopped, not knowing which way to go, one of the boys jumped out and threw a sack over it. They manhandled it into the sack and brought it back to camp.

Everybody was sound asleep when they arrived back in camp. The two walked up to the big tent as quietly as they could and eased up the canvas side enough to release the springhare inside. Then they waited to see what would happen. For a few minutes nothing happened until the springhare happened to hop onto one of the sleeping men. Apparently he woke up, put his hand out, felt soft fur and yelled that there was a lion in the tent. With that, pandemonium reigned. The tent exploded as the various occupants lifted up the sides in desperation and scattered in all directions, followed shortly by the springhare hopping off to freedom. One person had a flashlight and happened to see the hare take off. He called the others back and explained what they were running away from. They then saw Michael and Cecil standing nearby, enjoying the show. Most Africans have a good sense of humour and they saw the funny side of it.

A couple of years later, when Michael became a successful professional

Crocodile shot by my German client

My trackers, Samson & Wilson, with a red lechwe

Lion shot by George Cowden after much tracking

Earl B. Mitchell Jr. with his fine roan antelope

With my nephew, Mike Bartlett, in Botswana

With the lion shot by Mr Salgado, Sr.

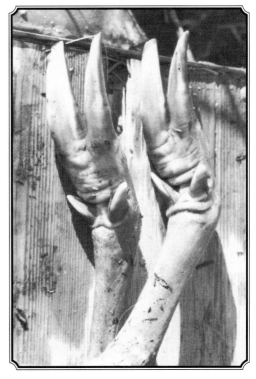

Sitatunga feet adapted to walking in the swamps

A happy client with his lion in Botswana

Sable shot by Dr. Olivetti

hunter, we often did joint safaris. On one occasion, he moved out of James camp (another of our camps on the edge of the Linyanti Swamp) and I moved in the same evening with my client.

We arrived at dusk and, after unloading our vehicle, I wanted a shower. The shower was open at the top with a water bucket suspended a little higher than head level. The walls were constructed from reeds cut in the nearby swamp and the entrance was also open. I left my flashlight outside on a chair. As I showered I heard a hiss, which was repeated when I moved. The first thing that came to mind was a snake. I leapt for the entrance expecting to be bitten but made it safely. I picked up my flashlight and cautiously went back to investigate. In the corner was an enormous tortoise with BK 20 (the registration number of my vehicle) painted on its shell. Michael had played one of his pranks on me.

The new concessions shortened the distance to Kwando camp considerably. We now went over the Savuti River and followed the edge of the Linyanti Swamp to James and Kwando camps. We no longer used the bridge that I had built over the Silinda. (It was eventually destroyed by a bush fire that swept up the Silinda in the dry season.) Near the Savuti crossing towards the main swamp, I remember seeing, on two occasions, a hippo with very long tusks that curved round like a hoop.

Another time I used the same *rondavel* at Saile camp that I used when the lion stole the zebra leg. One night I heard a lot of splashing at the edge of the swamp in front of my hut. I heard an animal bleating and then silence. Something had been caught. Next morning I walked to the swamp edge and found the carcass of a female lechwe which had been killed by a leopard. The leopard had eaten quite a lot and then abandoned the carcass. It had also attacked some towels hanging up on the clothes-line nearby. These had been pulled down and ripped to shreds. After this I noticed leopard tracks around the camp on a few occasions, but for reasons that I cannot remember, it was never hunted or shot.

Not many leopards were ever shot in our concession, primarily because there were not many to begin with. And those that were there did not take readily to bait. During the course of numerous safaris, it was more common to accidentally come across a leopard, especially in the swamps and on the islands.

I was only really successful with baiting on one occasion and that was in the Kwando area in the Linyanti Swamps. I was up a tree trying to spot game. The swamp had flooded and there was an open strip of water between where I was and an island on the other side. A female warthog, accompanied by her young family, was walking along the edge of the water.

195

While I was watching, she suddenly turned, looked back towards some thick cove, and immediately they went trotting off. Shortly afterwards a leopard stepped out and followed.

The leopard was a large male and, as my Canadian client wanted to shoot one, we went off to shoot a male warthog, the leopard's favourite meal, for bait. We made a drag in the area, tied the hog in a tree and built a blind nearby. We visited the bait the next day and found that a leopard had fed on it. That afternoon at 4 o'clock, we crept into the blind and waited. One hour later the leopard arrived and started feeding. My client, John Martens, shot it. John had to apply to the Canadian Wildlife Department for a permit to import the skin into Canada. Before he came on the hunt, John had asked the Canadian Game Department about importing a leopard if he managed to shoot one. He was told by an officer, John Heppes, to apply on his return if a permit was needed and he would make the necessary arrangements. I knew a John Heppes in Kenya. We were at school together in Nairobi and later we hunted elephant together while I was with the Game Department. I asked John Martens to inquire if this was the same John Heppes. Sure enough I heard from John Heppes who had emigrated to Canada from Uganda where he had been a game warden. The saying, 'it's a small world' is often true.

There were some very large crocodiles in the swamps. I spotted one sunning itself on the bank of the channel. It was so large that at first glance I thought it was a hippo lying down, but then it moved off the bank and as it slid into the water, I saw its enormous size. A few of my clients shot huge swamp crocodiles and the most exciting crocodile hunt occurred when I was with a German client. We spotted a crocodile on a ledge halfway up a bank, but it slid into the water when it saw us. Crocodile was on the client's list so we decided to return the next day to the bank above and catch the crocodile sunning itself.

When the sun was well up and it was warm enough for the crocodile to come out, we approached the edge of the bank without making a noise. There was a tree growing on the bank overlooking the shelf and we edged around it to get a look at the crocodile. Sure enough, there it was a few yards away. I signalled to my client to shoot. Before we went out, I explained where to place the shot. To anchor a crocodile, it was necessary to shoot it in the neck and break its vertebrae, or to hit behind the eye in the brain. A crocodile shot like this did not move. With a heart shot, the crocodile leapt into the water and went a good distance before dying, which meant that it was not usually recovered until a day or two later when it floated to the surface bloated with stomach gases. By then the skin was spoilt and worthless.

To continue with my story, the client slowly raised his rifle and aimed but the crocodile must have spotted the end of the rifle as it was eased forward, for it suddenly spun around and started to slide off the bank towards the water. The German fired but the crocodile disappeared. The water in the creek was not flowing and I watched the progress of the crocodile as it went through the still water. There was a series of bubbles coming up as it crossed to the other side, where it turned and followed the far bank and stopped under a partly submerged dead tree. Bubbles kept coming up, along with some dead reeds. Then nothing more appeared. I suspected a lung or heart shot hence the bubbles leaking from the lungs. It was obviously dead in the bottom of the channel and so I decided to return to camp for a small boat. We cut two long poles and attached a gaff to one end with thin wire. We wanted to gaff the crocodile once we located it and bring it to the surface.

We reached the place where we had last seen the bubbles rising and prodded the bottom with a pole. The channel was almost twelve feet deep in this spot and most of the pole disappeared into the water. Eventually Wilson said he felt the crocodile at the end of the pole. We hooked it with the gaff and hauled it slowly to the surface. As we got the body close to the boat, the gaff broke away from the pole, and the crocodile and my gaff sank to the bottom. We tried everything but were unable to hook the crocodile again and I did not have another gaff. We even tried to use some heavy gauge wire and bent it into the shape of a hook but it just straightened out.

For a while we sat in the boat debating what to do next. My client said that he was not going to leave the crocodile behind and that he would dive down and get it. I told him that it was madness to even think about such a thing but he was determined. I would never dream of diving in myself because I did not fancy the murky water. He stripped to his underpants. We had the poles down in the water and could still feel the body of the crocodile underneath. The German eased himself into the water, took a deep breath and disappeared following the poles down. He returned to the surface holding one leg of the crocodile. The two trackers held the leg and pulled the body up until each had the crocodile by a leg. We poled the boat back to the opposite bank and pulled the crocodile out. The crocodile was not the biggest I have seen but it was big enough to take a man - twelve feet from nose to tail.

197

Early one morning, accompanied by an American client and my two trackers, I left the James camp (on the edge of the Linyanti Swamp). One of the trophies the client wanted was a lion and periodically I stopped the vehicle to listen for lion calling. Eventually we got lucky. I had just stopped when I heard a lion close by but the call seemed to come from the direction of the swamp. I hoped that it was not coming from one of the islands because they were inaccessible. There was a possibility that it might be somewhere along the edge of the swamp and I decided to investigate. Taking our rifles and accompanied by one tracker, we headed in the direction of the calling.

After a few minutes we came to the edge of open ground where a fire had recently burnt off the grass and new succulent green shoots had popped up from the charred remains. Such places attracted game and consequently predators hunted there. On the opposite side of the open area I saw the tall reeds of the swamp. I stopped to look through my binoculars and immediately saw a well-maned lion walking about three hundred yards away. The lion disappeared behind a hillock without seeing us. We quickly crossed the open ground, hoping to get close to the hillock and then wait for the lion to reappear. When we were halfway across, the lion suddenly appeared and we were caught right out in the open. I crouched down and signalled to those behind to do likewise. The lion saw this and looked intently at us but we kept absolutely still.

After what seemed ages, when in fact it was probably about three minutes, the lion started walking in our direction. He did not know what he had seen and was merely coming closer to investigate. We were now about 150 yards away and there was a depression between us and the lion. As the lion went out of sight into the depression, I hurriedly got the client into a prone position and used our two jackets to make a rest for the rifle. I knew the lion would reappear about forty yards away. After a long wait he did just that right in front of us, first showing the top of the mane and then the head. He stopped to have a good look but he was unable to make out what we were. He came closer until the top half of his body was visible. He stopped again and I wondered whether he would come much closer. It was close enough for a shot so I said, "Shoot! Aim for the chest!" The lion dropped to the ground when the bullet hit him. We approached, ready in case he got up, but he never moved. We circled around until we were standing about fifteen yards to his rear. I picked up some clods of earth and threw them to see if there was any reaction but he was quite dead.

While on the subject of approaching a dangerous animal that has been shot, I have made it a practice always to approach only from the rear and never from the front. If the animal came to life and decided to charge, it had to get up and turn around. This gave an extra second or two advantage to the hunter who had to act quickly and fire at least another shot.

This lion had a short, thick sandy coloured mane. The body was small, about 325 pounds in weight. The leading edges of the mane had been shaved by the continuous passage through the swamp reeds and its pads were cracked from exposure to water. It was a typical swamp lion, different from the ones that lived in the hinterland. Most of those lions followed the large buffalo herds and relied on their weight and strength to tackle the large bovines. These cats, especially the males, often weighed over 400 pounds.

Besides tracking and baiting, I learnt through many years of lion hunting, that it was productive to listen for roaring during the night and the early mornings. When lions called it was possible to ascertain the direction in which the animal was moving and how far away it was. The distance over which the voice carried depended on the surrounding vegetation and hills. Over water, the sound carried a long way especially on calm nights. Once, while on safari in the western lake districts of Tanzania, I clearly heard the loud roar of a lion from across the other side of a lake which was about ten miles distant in Rwanda.

In the morning, when I worked out the direction of the last call, I took a compass bearing and drove until I thought we were close to the area where the spoor could be located. I proceeded slowly while the trackers looked for tracks. Most of northern Botswana was woodland and it was easy to see tracks in the soft sand. On one such occasion, we were in the Silinda area between the Linyanti and Okavango Swamps, heading in the direction of a lion which had been calling early in the morning. We found the tracks without much difficulty. I stopped and we followed them on foot. With me was a Mexican client, Mariano Salgado, who had hunted with me before. We followed the tracks for about six miles and I heard the lion calling twice just ahead. He was still moving. Eventually, in the heat of the midday sun, we came on him lying in the shade. We manoeuvred fairly close and had to wait until the cat got up before a shot was possible. After a few minutes, the lion did just that and my client shot a trophy with a very fine mane.

I am convinced lions can throw their voices like a ventriloquist, especially when calling softly to other members of the pride. The sound the use is a low moaning noise. This was noticeable on one occasion when we had lion feeding on a kill. The client and I made a cautious approach to our blind. When we got into position, I looked through the screen to see the cats we had heard a few minutes earlier. Then the sound, which was a very low moan, came again from the next ridge. Using my binoculars, I looked to towards the ridge but could not see the caller. I happened to look down and, only yards away, I saw the lion raise its head and again make the sound. It still sounded as if it was coming from a long way off. This was the only time I actually saw a lion calling in this way.

Botswana was home to some very large sable. I admired these noble looking animals, as well as the kudu. Most overseas hunters wanted to hunt both these animals. The biggest heads that my clients shot were forty-seven and a half inches and forty-seven inches for sable and fifty-five inches for kudu.

Three years after Hunters Africa acquired the new concessions, the company had problems with some of the directors. It was just as I had feared. Two directors left and we lost the Kwando concession as a result of the split. A third was later killed in an aircraft accident. By 1979, hunting by the local citizens had put so much pressure on the game population that there was a total absence of shootable elephant and a scarcity of many other species. I thought about leaving Botswana and, along with John Lawrence, I sold my shares. I moved to South Africa but returned for the next two hunting seasons. Eventually, I left at the end of 1981.

While I hunted in Botswana, my wife and I lived on the banks of the Okavango Swamps. The Okavango River formed the international boundary between South West Africa (the country had not yet become independent) and Angola. This river had many crocodile and while we were there, quite a few Africans were taken by crocodiles. I shot two crocodiles that attacked my dogs. Fortunately on both occasions the dogs escaped with minor injuries. The Africans who were taken were never seen again. One African was standing knee deep in the shallows of the river bathing when a crocodile came from behind and took him by the leg. His body was never recovered. Another victim was taken on the river below our house when she went to fetch water from the river at dusk. A big crocodile came out of the reeds, again from behind, and carried her off into the main stream. A week later her daughter was taken at the same spot.

One of the Africans who worked for me told me that his son, aged twelve, had gone to the river's edge for water. He was filling a plastic container when it was wrenched out of his hands by a big crocodile. The young man ran up the bank and looked back to see the crocodile holding the container in its mouth. He owed his life to the crocodile's mistake ... and the container.

My wife and I visited my son, Richard, and his wife, Wendy, at Katima Mulilo in the Eastern Caprivi where they lived on the banks of the Zambezi River. This is the international boundary between the Caprivi and Zambia. One afternoon we went out in Richard's boat and stopped on an island for refreshments. The river was in full flood and a lot of debris was floating down. My wife had taken my binoculars and was idly looking at the river which, at this point, was about three quarters of a mile wide. She saw the biggest crocodile she had ever seen. I took the binoculars and looked at the crocodile, which was floating on the surface, being carried along by the current. The river was flowing at about three miles an hour. The crocodile must have been at least fifteen feet from nose to tail. I could see the top portion of its body. There was something sticking out of its mouth but I was not sure what it was so Richard and I got into the boat, started the motor and eased over. When we got close, I used the binoculars again and realised that it was a human leg. The rest of the body was attached to the leg but we could not see it clearly because it was beneath the crocodile. The crocodile went under the water and did not reappear.

After a while we headed back upstream to Katima, where we found a huge crowd of highly agitated Africans on the Zambian side of the river. They had gathered there after the crocodile had taken its victim and they were still looking for the unfortunate person.

On another occasion a crocodile took the Katima Postmaster while he was sitting on a tree trunk with his legs hanging in the water. A woman and her two children were standing waist deep in the water nearby. The woman was standing with her legs apart and apparently she felt the crocodile go between her legs. It then latched onto the leg of the postmaster and dragged him into the water. He yelled for help but the rest of the party were paralysed by fear and did not go to his aid. The crocodile carried him off. My son Brian was in the search party which went out the next day and they eventually found the body wedged against a dead tree downstream from where he was taken. The crocodile had not eaten him but its teeth marks were evident on his leg.

While we were living on the banks of the Okavango River, we had an incident with a large mamba snake. My wife and I were sleeping in a tent because it was cooler there than in our caravan during the summer. The caravan was used for storing some of our valuables and foodstuffs. At about midnight there was a lot of lightning and thunder and it looked as if it was going to rain. My wife suggested that we move some provisions lying outside into the caravan. I carried the flashlight and followed her into the doorway. As I stepped inside, I heard something rattle the crockery on the table to my left. I swung the light around and saw parts of a large snake disappearing into the bunk. I said, "Snake! Get out." We shut all the windows and the door and retired to bed.

The next day we made a cautious search and removed everything that was not permanently installed but we could not find the snake. We kept the caravan locked up and periodically looked through the windows to see if the snake would show itself. We knew it was still inside. At dusk I looked in the window and saw the head and neck of the snake, which I now recognised as a mamba, appear from behind the refrigerator and called Jock. The reptile came out slowly and wound around the inside of the caravan until its whole body was exposed. It must have been nine or ten feet long. Eventually it coiled itself at the bottom of a far bunk. By this time it was getting dark and I fetched a 12 gauge shotgun and a flashlight for Jock to hold. We opened the caravan door and I went in first. I whispered to Jock to shine the light on the head of the snake but instead she put the light on its coiled up body. I thought I could make out the head, lined up the shotgun and fired but missed the snake. It reared up and started up the side of the caravan. Both of us rushed out and closed the door. The next day we checked for the snake but discovered it had escaped during the night through the big hole I had blown in the bottom of the caravan. To this day I do not know why I missed it. My only excuse was that the light was bad and range too close so the pellets were still compacted. While we were away, the snake was killed by one of the workers in camp.

I had one unusual experience with a flat tyre while staying in this camp. We had returned from a South African holiday in a Land Cruiser equipped with heavy duty tyres. We had travelled many thousands miles to South Africa and back without any flat tyres until we got to our turn-off, a few hundred yards from home. I changed the flat tyre at our entrance. When I repaired it, I found that an unfired cartridge from a military rifle had pierced it. Only the base of the cartridge was showing. Why it did not detonate, I do not know.

In 1982 I hunted on some big South African game ranches: two ranches near Kimberley owned by De Beers Diamond Mining Company, another in Zululand mainly for nyala and the fourth ranch on the Limpopo River. The hunting was enjoyable but I found the distances between areas was too great. I moved to South West Africa to work for a Portuguese who wanted to start a hunting company there with the idea of moving into Angola once their civil war ended. Unfortunately the company never got off the ground.

I was still keen to return to hunting so I looked further south. Most of the hunting in South West Africa was confined to game ranches, where the game hunted was mostly antelope. We moved to a ranch on the Waterberg near Otjiwarongo. It was owned by a wealthy Swiss businessman, and it had a variety of game animals, mainly kudu, oryx, eland, two types of zebra, impala, wildebeest, hartebeest, giraffe, ostrich and waterbuck. What interested me most was the leopard and the brown hyena living on the Waterberg Plateau. I decided to leave after a year because the ranch was managed by a young German and we did not get on at all.

My next move was to a bigger ranch about eighty miles east of Windhoek. This also had a good variety of game which was enclosed by a ten feet high fence with many strands of wire placed close together to prevent the game from entering or exiting. The only animals that had no problem in getting in and out were warthog and antbear, both of which could burrow underneath. Cheetah then used these holes. The ranch employed people to periodically inspect the fence line and close the holes. The most common antelope on this ranch was gemsbok or oryx. They roamed in huge herds and were very tame because very little shooting was done from vehicles. It was not unusual to see them standing watching a motor vehicle drive by which made them much easier to hunt than in Botswana.

After a couple of years, Jock and I moved to Knysna in the Cape where my daughter, Elizabeth, and her husband, Peter, had two properties. They had an active business in Namibia (previously South West Africa) and only went to the Cape for holidays. Jock and I once again came to live in South Africa. The area was part of the 'Garden Route', a most delightful location. I still did the occasional hunting trip down south to keep my eye in but nothing like I had done in the past.

I can look back on an exciting and fulfiling life, knowing that I have seen African wildlife at its best. It will never be the same again! I met well-known characters, such as Philip Percival, Jack Lucy, J.A. Hunter, George and Joy Adamson, Pat Ayre, Robert Ruark and many other famous people. As a professional hunter, I have guided nationals from most countries of the world. There is no better way to meet and share other people's points of view. It has been a valuable experience for me and through it I have made many friends among my hunting companions.

MAHARAWAL LAKSHMAN SINGH,

UDAI BILAS
DUNGARPUR,

Ho 708 /Ps/

Dated 25th October, 1977.

Dear Fred Bartlett,

On reaching Jaipur I have great
pleasure in writing to thank you
cordially for the manner you conducted
my safari. Your consideration in
putting me to the least possible
inconvenience while going after Elephant
has evoked my grateful appreciation.
Your skill and experience as a hunter
has made a lasting impression on my
mind and more than anything else the
Rifle that you lent me was a beauty.
I could not have hoped for a better
weapon for my use.

The arrangements at Camp left
nothing to be desired and the food
served was good and to my taste.

With my renewed thanks for all
the consideration and kindness you
showed me.

Yours sincerely,

Lakshman Singh

Fred Batlett Esq.,
C/O Hunters Africa(Botswana)Ltd.,
    P.O.Box-11 Kasane,
    Via Victoria Falls,
    BOTSWANA-AFRICA.

Good buffalo shot in Botswana

Elephant swimming across a river

Stalking game using a net

Spotting game in the Waterberg, S.W.A.

Up a tree scouting for game

Looking for gemsbok in Botswana